RUS

at your F

ork·

Other titles in this series

RUSSIAN

at your Fingertips

compiled by

LEXUS

with

Jekaterina Young, Chris Stephenson,
Christopher Barnes and Galya Aplin

London

First published 1990
by Routledge
11 New Fetter Lane, London EC4P 4EE

© Routledge Ltd 1990

Set in Baskerville by SB Datagraphics, Colchester, Essex
Printed in England by Cox & Wyman Ltd, Reading

British Library Cataloguing in Publication Data
Applied For

ISBN 0-415-02930-9

Contents

RUSSIAN PRONUNCIATION

Because you are likely to want to speak most the Russian given in this book rather than just understand its meaning, an indication of the pronunciation has been given in square brackets. If you pronounce this as though it were English, the result will be clearly comprehensible to a Russian.

Some comments on the pronunciation system used:

a	as in 'cat', 'mat'
ah	as in 'father'
oo	like the 'oo' in 'book', 'took'
ōo	like the 'oo' in 'soon', 'groom'
ı	like the 'y' in 'my', 'fly'
zh	like the 's' in 'leisure' or 'pleasure'
kh	like the 'ch' in the Scottish pronunciation of 'loch'
g	always as in 'get'
ya	as in 'yap'
ye	as in 'yet'
yi	as in 'Yiddish'
yo	as in 'yon'
yōo	as in 'youth'

Where the print for a letter (or several letters) is in bold type this means that this part of the word should be stressed. It is very important to get the stress right when speaking Russian.

English-Russian
A

a: four roubles a bottle четыре рубля за бутылку [*chiteer-ye roob-lya za boo-teel-kōō*]; *see page 108*

about: about 25 около 25 [*okul-uh*]; about 6 o'clock около 6 часов [*okul-uh shestee cha-soff*]; is the manager about? начальник здесь? [*nachahl-nik zdyiss*]; I was just about to leave я собирался уходить [*ya sabi-rahlsa ōō-khadeet*]; how about a drink? может, выпьем? [*mozhit vee-pyem*]

above над [*nad*]

abroad (*live*) за границей [*za gra-neetsay*]; (*go*) за границу [*za gra-neetsōō*]

abscess нарыв [*nareef*]

absolutely: it's absolutely perfect это просто замечательно [*ettuh prost-uh za-myichah-tyil-nuh*]; you're absolutely right вы совершенно правы [*vee sa-vyir-shenuh prahvee*]; absolutely! конечно! [*ka-nyesh-nuh*]

absorbent cotton вата [*vahta*]

accelerator акселератор [*ak-syilyirah-tur*]

accept принимать/принять [*prinimaht/prin-yaht*]

accident авария [*avahri-ya*]; (*road accident*) несчастный случай [*nyiss-chahstnee slōōchı*]; there's been an accident здесь произошёл несчастный случай [*zdyiss pra-izashol nyiss-chahstnee slōōchı*]; sorry, it was an accident извините, я это сделал нечаянно [*izvineet-ye ya ettuh zdyelal nyichı-yannuh*]

accommodation(s) номер [*no-myer*]

accurate точный [*tochnee*]

ache: I have an ache here у меня болит здесь [*ōō minya baleet zdyiss*]; it aches это болит [*ettuh baleet*]

across: across the street через дорогу [*che-ryiz da-rogōō*]

actor актёр [*ak-tyor*]

actress актриса [*aktreessa*]

adapter (*elec*) переходник [*pyiri-khodnik*]

address адрес [*ah-dryess*]; what's your address? Ваш адрес, пожалуйста? [*vash ah-dryess pa-zhahlsta*]

address book адресная книга [*ah-dryesna-ya k-neega*]

admission: how much is admission? сколько стоит билет? [*skol-kuh sto-yit bi-lyet*]

adore: I adore ... (*this food etc*) я обожаю ... [*ya abazha-yōō*]

adult взрослый [*vzro-slee*]

advance: I'll pay in advance я заплачу вперёд [*ya zaplachōō fpyi-ryot*]

advertisement реклама [*ryi-klahma*]

advise: what would you advise? что вы мне посоветуете? [*shto vee mnye pa-sa-vyetoo-yet-ye*]

aeroplane самолёт [*sama-lyot*]

affluent богатый [*bagahtee*]

Afghanistan Афганистан [*afganistan*]

afraid: I'm afraid of heights я боюсь высоты [*ya ba-yōōss vi-satee*]; don't be afraid не бойтесь [*nye boy-tyiss*]; I'm not afraid я не боюсь [*ya nye ba-yōōss*]; I'm afraid I can't help you извините, но помочь вам не могу [*izvinee-tye no pamoch vam nye magōō*]; I'm afraid so я очень жалею [*ya ochin zha-lye-yōō*]; I'm afraid not боюсь, что нет [*ba-yōōss shto nyet*]

after после [*poss-lye*]; after 9 o'clock после 9 часов [*poss-lye dyi-vyatee cha-soff*]; after you! прошу вас! [*prashōō vass*]

afternoon: in the afternoon днём [*dnyom*]; good afternoon добрый день [*dobree dyin*]; this afternoon сегодня днём [*syivo-dnya dnyom*]

aftershave одеколон для бритья [*a-dyi-kalon dlya bree-tya*]

afterwards потом [*patom*]

again снова [*snova*]

against против [*protif*]

age возраст [*vozrast*]; under age несовершеннолетний [*nyi-sa-vyir-shina-lyetnee*]; not at my age! в моём возрасте!

[*vma-yom vozrast-ye*]; it takes ages это длится вечность [*ettuh dleetsa vyechnust*]; I haven't been here for ages я так давно не был здесь [*ya tak davno nye beel zdyiss*]

agency агентство [*a-gyentst-vuh*]

aggressive агрессивный [*a-grye-seevnee*]

ago: a year/week ago год/неделю назад [*god/nyi-dyel-yōō nazat*]; it wasn't long ago это было недавно [*ettuh beeluh nyidahv-nuh*]

agony: it's agony одни мучения [*adnee moocheni-ya*]

agree: do you agree? вы согласны? [*vee saglah-snee*]; I agree (*man*) согласен [*saglah-syen*]; (*woman*) согласна [*saglah-sna*]; I don't agree (*man*) я не согласен [*ya nye saglah-syen*]; (*woman*) я не согласна [*ya nye saglah-sna*]; it doesn't agree with me мне это вредно [*mnye ettuh vryed-nuh*]

AIDS СПИД [*spid*]

air воздух [*voz-dookh*]; by air самолётом [*sama-lyotum*]

air-bed (*camping*) надувной матрац [*nadoov-noy matrats*]

air-conditioning кондиционирование воздуха [*kanditsion-eerwani-ye voz-dookha*]

air hostess стюардесса [*styōō-ar-dyessa*]

airmail: by airmail авиа почтой [*ahvi-ya pochtoy*]

airmail envelope конверт авиа [*kan-vyert ahvi-ya*]

airplane самолёт [*sama-lyot*]

airport аэропорт [*a-erraport*]

airport bus автобус в аэропорт [*avto-booss va-erraport*]

airsick: I get airsick мне обычно плохо в самолёте [*mnye abeech-nuh plokh-uh fsama-lyo-tye*]

airsickness воздушная болезнь [*vaz-dōōshna-ya ba-lyezn*]

à la carte на заказ [*na zakahss*]

alarm тревога [*tryivoga*]

alarm clock будильник [*boodeel-nik*]

Albania Албания [*al-bahniya*]

alcohol алкоголь (*m*) [*alkagol*]

alcoholic: is it alcoholic? это содержит алкоголь? [*ettuh sa-dyerzhit alkagol*]

alive живой [*zhivoy*]; is he still alive? он жив? [*on zhif*]

all: all the hotels все гостиницы [*fsye gastee-nitsee*]; all my friends все мои друзья [*fsye ma-yee droo-zya*]; all my

money все мои деньги [*fsye ma-yee dyengee*]; all of it всё [*fsyo*]; all of them все они [*fsye anee*]; all right ладно [*lahd-nuh*]; I'm all right у меня всё в порядке [*ōō minya fsyo fpa-ryaht-kye*]; that's all это всё [*ettuh fsyo*]; it's all changed теперь всё по-другому [*tyi-pyer fsyo pa droo-gomōō*]; thank you - not at all спасибо - не за что [*spa-see-buh - nye za shto*]

allergic: I'm allergic to ... у меня аллергия на ... [*ōō minya a-lyer-gee-ya na*]

allergy аллергия [*a-lyer-gee-ya*]

all-inclusive: an all-inclusive price цена, которая включает все услуги [*tsina katora-ya fklyoocha-yit fsye oo-slōōgee*]

allow разрешать/разрешить [*raz-ryishaht/raz-ryisheet*]; is it allowed? это разрешается? [*ettuh raz-ryisha-yitsa*]; I'm not allowed to eat salt мне нельзя есть соль [*mnye nyil-zya yist sol*]

all-risks (*insurance*) страхование на все случаи [*strakha-vahni-ye na fsye slōōcha-yee*]

almost почти [*pachtee*]

alone один [*adeen*]; are you alone? (*man*) вы один? [*vee adeen*]; (*woman*) вы одна? [*vee adna*]; leave me alone оставьте меня в покое [*astahv-tye minya fpako-ye*]

already уже [*oozh-e*]

also также [*takzh-e*]

alteration (*to plan etc*) изменение [*izmi-nyeni-ye*]

alternative: is there an alternative? разве есть выбор? [*rahz-vye yest veebur*]; we have no alternative выбора нет [*veebura nyet*]

alternator альтернатор [*al-tyir-nahtur*]

although хотя [*kha-tya*]

altogether вместе [*fmye-stye*]; what does that come to altogether? сколько всё это стоит? [*skol-kuh fsyo ettuh sto-yit*]

always всегда [*fsyigda*]

a.m.: at 8 a.m. в 8 часов утра [*v-vo-syim cha-soff ootra*]

amazing удивительный [*oodivee-tyelnee*]; it's amazing! это изумительно [*ettuh izoomeetyilnuh*]

ambassador посол [*pa-sol*]

ambulance скорая помощь [*skora-ya pomoshch*]; get an ambulance вызовите скорую помощь [*veeza-vee-tye skorōō-yōō pomoshch*]

America Америка [a-myerika]

American (man) американец [a-myiri-kahn-yits]; (woman) американка [a-myirikanka]; (adjective) американский [a-myirikanskee]; the Americans американцы [a-myirikantsee]

among среди [sryidee]

amp: a 13 amp fuse 13-й амперный предохранитель [treenad-sati-am-pyernee pryida-khranee-tyil]

an(a)esthetic наркоз [narkos]

ancestor предок [pryeduk]

anchor якорь [yakur]

anchovies анчоус [ancho-ōōss]

ancient древний [dryevnee]; (art) античный [anteechnee]

and и [ee]

angina стенокардия [styina-kardee-ya]

angry сердитый [syir-deetee]; I'm very angry about it это очень сердит меня [ettuh ochin syerdeet minya]

animal животное [zhivot-nuh-ye]

ankle лодыжка [ladeeshka]

anniversary годовщина [gadafsh-cheena]; it's our wedding anniversary today сегодня годовщина нашей свадьбы [syivo-dnya gadafsh-cheena nashay svahd-bee]

annoy: he's annoying me он раздражает меня [on razdrazha-yit minya]; it's so annoying так досадно [tak da-sahd-nuh]

anorak куртка [koortka]

another (different) другой [droogoy]; (extra) ещё [yish-cho]; can we have another room? дайте нам, пожалуйста, другой номер [dī-tye nam pa-zhahlsta droogoy no-myir]; another bottle, please ещё бутылку, пожалуйста [yish-cho booteel-kōō pa-zhahlsta]

answer: there was no answer ответа не было [at-vyeta nye-beeluh]; what was his answer? что он ответил? [shto on at-vyetil]

ant: ants муравьи [mooravee]

antibiotics антибиотики [anti-bee-otikee]

anticlimax спад [spaht]

antifreeze антифриз [anti-freess]

antihistamine антигистамин [anti-gistameen]

antique: is it an antique? это антикварная вещь? [ettuh antikvahrna-ya vyeshch]

antique shop антикварный магазин [antikvahrnee magazeen]

antisocial: don't be antisocial не будьте так недружелюбны [nye bōōd-tye tak nyi-droozhe-lyōobnee]

any: have you got any rolls/milk? у вас есть булочки/молоко? [ōō vass yist bōōluchkee/malako]; I haven't got any у меня нет [ōō minya nyet]

anybody кто-нибудь [kto-nibōōt]; can anybody help? может кто-нибудь помочь? [mozhit kto-nibōōt pamoch]; there wasn't anybody there там никого не было [tam nee-kavo nye-beeluh]

anything что-нибудь [shto-nibōōt]; I don't want anything мне ничего не нужно [mnye nee-chivo nye nōōzh-nuh]; don't you have anything else? разве у вас ничего другого нет? [rahz-vye ōō vass nee-chivo droogo-vuh nyet]

apart from кроме [kro-mye]

apartment квартира [kvarteera]

aperitif аперитив [a-pyiriteef]

apology извинение [izvi-nyeni-ye]; please accept my apologies пожалуйста, извините меня [pa-zhahlsta izvinee-tye minya]

appalling ужасный [ōōzhah-snee]

appear: it would appear that ... кажется, что ... [kah-zhitsa shto]

appendicitis аппендицит [a-pyindi-tseet]

appetite аппетит [a-pyiteet]; I've lost my appetite мне не хочется есть [mnye nye khochitsa yist]

apple яблоко [yabluk-uh]

apple pie яблочный пирог [yabluchnee pirok]

application form бланк заявления [blank za-yavlyeni-ya]

appointment (business) встреча [fstryecha]; (doctor) приём [pree-yom]; I'd like to make an appointment (business) я хочу условиться о встрече [ya khachōō oo-slovitsa a fstryech-e]; (doctor) я хочу записаться на приём [ya khachōō za-pissahtsa na pree-yom]

appreciate: thank you, I appreciate it (man) я вам очень признателен [ya vam ochin priznah-tyil-yin]; (woman) я вам очень признательна [ya vam ochin priznah-tyilna]

approve: she doesn't approve она не одобряет этого [ana nye ada-brya-yit ettuvuh]

apricot абрикос [*abrikoss*]

April апрель (*m*) [*a-pryel*]

aqualung акваланг [*ahkvalang*]

arch(a)eology археология [*arkhia-logi-ya*]

Arctic Circle Полярный круг [*palyarnee krook*]

are *see page 116*

area: I don't know the area мне незнакома эта местность [*mnye nyi-znakoma etta myest-nust*]

area code телефонный код [*tyili-fonnee kot*]

arm рука [*rooka*]

Armenia Армения [*ar-myeni-ya*]

arms race гонка вооружения [*gonka va-aroozheni-ya*]

around *see about*

arrangement: will you make the arrangements? вы примете меры? [*vee pree-myi-tye myeree*]

arrest арест [*a-ryest*]; he's been arrested его арестовали [*yivo a-ryista-vahlee*]

arrival приезд [*pree-yezd*]

arrive: when do we arrive in Moscow? в котором часу мы будем в Москве? [*fkatorom cha-soo mee boo-dyem vmask-vye*]; has my parcel arrived yet? моя посылка уже здесь? [*maya paseelka oozh-e zdyiss*]; let me know as soon as they arrive пожалуйста, дайте мне знать, как только они приедут [*pa-zhahlsta dɪ-tye mnye znaht kak tol-kuh anee pree-yedoot*]; we only arrived yesterday мы только вчера приехали [*mee tol-kuh fchira pree-yekhalee*]

art искусство [*iskoost-vuh*]

art gallery картинная галерея [*karteena-ya ga-lyi-ryeya*]

arthritis артрит [*artreet*]

artificial искусственный [*iskoost-vyenee*]

artist художник [*khoo-dozhnik*]

as: as fast as you can как можно скорее [*kak mozh-nuh ska-rye-ye*]; as much as you can сколько можете [*skol-kuh mozhit-ye*]; as you like как хотите [*kak khateet-ye*]; as it's getting late так как уже поздно [*tak kak oozh-e pozd-nuh*]

ashore: to go ashore сходить на берег [*skhadeet na bye-ryik*]

ashtray пепельница [*pye-pyilnitsa*]

aside from кроме [*kro-mye*]

ask спрашивать/спросить [*sprashivat/spra-seet*]; that's not what I asked for это

совсем не то, что я хотел [*ettuh sav-syem nye to shto ya kha-tyel*]; could you ask him to phone me back? попросите его, пожалуйста, перезвонить [*papra-see-tye yivo pa-zhahlsta pyiri-zvaneet*]

asleep: he's still asleep он всё ещё спит [*on fsyo yish-cho speet*]

asparagus спаржа [*sparzha*]

aspirin аспирин [*as-pyireen*]

assault: she's been assaulted на неё напали [*na nyi-yo napahlee*]; indecent assault изнасилование [*izna-seeluvani-ye*]

assistant (*helper*) помощник [*pamoshnik*]; (*in shop*) (*man*) продавец [*prada-vyets*]; (*woman*) продавщица [*pradaf-cheetsa*]

assume: I assume that ... я предполагаю, что ... [*ya pryid-palaga-yoo shto*]

asthma астма [*astma*]

astonishing удивительный [*oodivee-tyilnee*]

at: at the café в кафе [*fkaff-e*]; at the hotel в гостинице [*vgasteenits-e*]; at 8 o'clock в 8 часов [*v-vo-syim cha-soff*]; see you at dinner встретимся за ужином [*fstrye-timsa za oozhin-um*]

Atlantic Атлантический океан [*atlanteechiskee a-ke-an*]

atmosphere атмосфера [*atma-sfyera*]

attractive привлекательный [*pri-vlyi-kah-tyilnee*]; you're very attractive вы очень привлекательны [*vee ochin pri-vlyi-kah-tyilnee*]

aubergine баклажан [*baklazhan*]

auction аукцион [*a-ooksyon*]

audience публика [*pooblika*]

August август [*ahvgoost*]

aunt: my aunt моя тётя [*ma-ya tyo-tya*]

au pair (*girl*) няня [*nya-nya*]

Australia Австралия [*av-strahliya*]

Australian (*man*) австралиец [*avstra-lee-yits*]; (*woman*) австралиика [*avstra-leeka*]; (*adjective*) австралийский [*avstra-leeskee*]; the Australians австралийцы [*avstra-leetsee*]

Austria Австрия [*av-stria*]

authorities начальство [*na-chahlst-vuh*]

automatic автоматический [*avta-mateechiskee*]

automobile машина [*masheena*]

autumn осень (*f*) [*o-syin*]; in the autumn осенью [*o-syin-yoo*]

available: when will it be available? когда это будет готово? [*kagda ettuh bōo-dyit gatovuh*]; **when will he be available?** когда с ним можно будет поговорить? [*kagda sneem mozh-nuh bōo-dyet pa-gavareet*]

avenue проспект [*pra-spyekt*]

average: the average Russian обычный русский человек [*abeechnee rooskee chila-vyek*]; **an above average hotel** хорошая гостиница [*kharosha-ya gastee-nitsa*]; **a below average hotel** посредственная гостиница [*pa-sryedst-vyina-ya gastee-nitsa*]; **the food was only average** еда была сносной [*yida beela sno-snoy*]; **on average** в среднем [*fsryed-nyem*]

awake: is she awake? она проснулась? [*ana pra-snōolass*]

away: is it far away? это далеко? [*ettuh da-lyiko*]; **go away!** уходите прочь! [*ookhadeet-ye proch*]

awful ужасный [*ōozhah-snee*]

axle ось (*f*) [*oss*]

Azerbaijan Азербайджан [*azirbyjan*]

B

baby ребёнок [*ryi-byonuk*]

baby-carrier переносная кроватка [*pyiri-nossnah-ya kravatka*]

baby-sitter приходящая няня [*pree-kha-dyashcha-ya nya-nya*]; **can you get us a baby-sitter?** найдите нам, пожалуйста, няню [*nidee-tye nam pa-zhahlsta nya-nyoo*]

bachelor холостяк [*khala-styak*]

back: I've got a bad back у меня болит спина [*ōo minya baleet speena*]; **at the back** сзади [*zahdee*]; **in the back of the car** на заднем сидении [*na za-dnyem si-dyeni-ee*]; **I'll be right back** я сейчас вернусь [*ya si-chass vyir-nōoss*]; **when do you want it back?** когда вернуть вам это? [*kagda vyirnōot vam ettuh*]; **can I have my money back?** пожалуйста, верните мне деньги [*pa-zhahlsta vyir-nee-tye mnye dyen-gee*]; **come back!** вернитесь! [*vyir-nee-tyiss*]; **I go back home tomorrow** я возвращаюсь домой завтра [*ya vazvra-shah-yooss damoy zaftra*]; **we'll be back next year** мы приедем на следующий год [*mee pree-ye-dyem na slyedoo-yooshchee got*]; **when is the last bus back?** когда отходит последний автобус? [*kagda at-khodit pa-slyednee avto-booss*]

backache: I have a backache у меня болит поясница [*ōo minya baleet pa-yasneetsa*]

back door чёрный ход [*chornee khot*]

backgammon триктрак [*trik-trak*]

backpack рюкзак [*ryook-zak*]

back seat заднее сиденье [*zad-nye-ye si-dye-nye*]

back street закоулок [*zaka-ōoluk*]

bacon бекон [*byikon*]; **bacon and eggs** яичница с беконом [*ya-eechnitsa zbyi-konum*]

bad плохой [*plakhoy*]; **this meat's bad** мясо тухлое [*mya-suh tōokh-luh-ye*]; **I've got a bad headache** у меня ужасно болит голова [*ōo minya ōozhah-snuh baleet galava*]; **it's not bad** неплохо [*nyi-plokhuh*]; **too bad!** ничего не поделаешь! [*nee-chivo nye pa-dyela-yish*]

badly: he's been badly injured он был тяжело ранен [*on beel tyazhilo ra-nyen*]

bag (*suitcase*) чемодан [*chimadan*]; (*carrier bag etc*) сумка [*soomka*]

baggage багаж [*bagahsh*]

baggage allowance максимальный вес багажа [*maksi-mahlnee vyess bagazha*]

baggage checkroom камера хранения [*ka-myira khra-nyeniya*]

bakery булочная [*bōoluchna-ya*]

balalaika балалайка [*balalika*]

balcony балкон [*balkon*]; **a room with a balcony** комната с балконом [*komnata zbalkon-um*]; **on the balcony** на балконе [*na balkon-ye*]

bald лысый [*leesee*]

ball мяч [*myach*]

ballet балет [*ba-lyet*]

ball-point pen шариковая ручка [*sharikava-ya rōochka*]

Baltic: Baltic Sea Балтийское море [*bal-teeskuh-ye mor-ye*]; **the Baltic States** Прибалтика [*pree-baltika*]

banana банан [*banan*]

band (*music*) оркестр [*ar-kyestr*]; (*pop*) группа [*grōopa*]

bandage бинт [*bint*]; could you change the bandage? пожалуйста, наложите новую повязку [*pa-zhahlsta nalazhee-tye novoo-yoo pa-vyaskoo*]

bandaid лейкопластырь (*m*) [*lyayka-plasteer*]

bank банк [*bank*]; when does the bank open? когда открывается банк? [*kagda atkriva-yitsa bank*]

bank account счёт в банке [*s-chot vbank-ye*]

bar бар [*bar*]; let's meet in the bar давайте встретимся в баре [*davi-tye fstryetimsa vbar-ye*]; a bar of chocolate плитка шоколада [*pleetka shakalada*]

barbecue барбекю [*barb-e-kyoo*]

barber (*shop*) парикмахерская [*parikmakh-yirska-ya*]

bargain: it's a real bargain это очень дёшево [*ettuh ochin dyo-shivuh*]

barmaid официантка в баре [*afitsi-antka vbar-ye*]

barman бармен [*bar-myen*]

barrette заколка [*zakolka*]

bartender бармен [*bar-myen*]

basic: the hotel is rather basic это очень скромная гостиница [*ettuh ochin skromna-ya gastee-nitsa*]; will you teach me some basic phrases? научите меня, пожалуйста, нескольким простым фразам [*na-oochee-tye minya pa-zhahlsta nyeskol-kim prasteem frahzam*]

basket корзина [*karzeena*]

bath ванна [*vanna*]; can I take a bath? можно искупаться? [*mozh-nuh iss-koopatsa*]; could you give me a bath towel? дайте мне, пожалуйста, банное полотенце [*di-tye mnye pa-zhahlsta bannuh-ye pala-tyents-e*]

bathing купание [*koopahni-ye*]

bathing costume купальник [*koopalnik*]

bathrobe купальный халат [*koopalnee khalaht*]

bathroom ванная [*vanna-ya*]; a room with a private bathroom номер с ванной [*no-myir zvannoy*]; can I use your bathroom? где туалет? [*gdye too-al-yet*]

battery батарейка [*bata-ryayka*]; the battery's flat батарейка села [*bata-ryayka syela*]

bay залив [*zaleef*]

be быть [*beet*]; be reasonable будьте благоразумны [*bood-tye blaga-razoom-nee*]; don't be lazy не ленитесь [*nye lyinee-tyiss*]]; where have you been? где

вы были? [*gdye vee beelee*]; I've never been to Moscow в Москве я не бывал [*vmask-vye ya nye bivahl*]; see page 116

beach пляж [*plyazh*]; on the beach на пляже [*na plyazh-e*]; I'm going to the beach я иду на пляж [*ya idoo na plyazh*]

beach mat пляжная подстилка [*plyazhna-ya pad-steelka*]

beach towel купальное полотенце [*koo-pahlnuh-ye pala-tyents-e*]

beach umbrella пляжный зонт [*plyazh-nee zont*]

beads бусы [*boossee*]

beans бобы [*babee*]

beard борода [*barada*]

beautiful прекрасный [*pryikrah-snee*]; (*meal, holiday*) великолепный [*vyilika-lyepnee*]; thank you, that's beautiful большое спасибо, это замечательно [*bal-sho-ye spa-see-buh ettuh za-myichah-tyil-nuh*]

beauty salon косметический кабинет [*kaz-myiteechiskee kabi-nyet*]

because потому что [*pata-moo-shtuh*]; because of the weather из-за погоды [*iz za pagodee*]

bed кровать (*f*) [*kravat*]; single bed односпальная кровать [*adna-spalna-ya kravat*]; double bed двуспальная кровать [*dvoo-spalna-ya kravat*]; you haven't made my bed вы не постелили мою постель [*vee nye pa-styilee-lee ma-yoo pa-styel*]; he's still in bed он всё ещё спит [*on fsyo yish-cho speet*]; I'm going to bed я ложусь спать [*ya lazhooss spaht*]

bed and breakfast ночлег и завтрак [*nach-lyek ee zaftrak*]

bed linen постельное бельё [*pa-styel-nuh-ye byi-lyo*]

bedroom спальня [*spal-nya*]

bee пчела [*pchila*]

beef говядина [*ga-vyadina*]

beer пиво [*peevuh*]; two beers, please две кружки пива, пожалуйста [*dvye kroozh-kee peeva pa-zhahlsta*]

before: before breakfast перед завтраком [*pye-ryid zaftrak-um*]; before I leave до отъезда [*da at-yezda*]; I haven't been here before я здесь раньше не бывал [*ya zdyiss rahn-she nye bivahl*]

begin: when does it begin? когда начинается? [*kagda nachina-yitsa*]

beginner начинающий [*nachina-yoosh-chee*]; I'm just a beginner я начинающий [*ya nachina-yoosh-chee*]

beginning: at the beginning сначала [*snachahluh*]

behavio(u)r поведение [*pa-vyi-dyeni-ye*]

behind за [*za*]; the driver behind me водитель, едущий за мной [*vadee-tyil yedōōsh-chee zamnoy*]

beige бежевый [*bye-zhevee*]

Belgium Бельгия [*byelgi-ya*]

believe верить [*vyereet*]; I don't believe you я не верю вам [*ya nye vye-ryōō vam*]; I believe you я верю вам [*ya vye-ryōō vam*]

bell колокол [*kolukul*]

belong: that belongs to me это моё [*ettuh ma-yo*]; who does this belong to? чьё это? [*chyo ettuh*]

belongings: all my belongings все мои вещи [*fsye ma-yee vyesh-chee*]

below: below the knee ниже колена [*neezh-e ka-lyena*]

belt (*clothing*) пояс [*po-yass*]

bend (*in road*) изгиб [*iz-geep*]

berries ягоды [*yagudee*]

berth место [*myest-uh*]

beside: beside the church у церкви [*ōō tserkvee*]; sit beside me садитесь рядом [*sadee-tyiss ryadum*]

besides: besides that кроме того [*kro-mye tavo*]

best лучший [*lōōchee*]; the best hotel in town самая лучшая гостиница в городе [*sahma-ya lōōcha-ya gastee-nitsa vgorud-ye*]; that's the best meal I've ever had это самый вкусный обед, который я когда-либо отведал [*ettuh sahmee fkōō-snee a-byet katoree ya kagda leebuh at-vyedal*]

bet: I bet you 10 roubles спорим на 10 рублей [*sporeem na dye-syat roob-lyay*]

better лучше [*lōōch-e*]; that's better! так лучше! [*tak lōōch-e*]; are you feeling better? вы чувствуете себя лучше? [*vee chōōst-voo-yitye si-bya lōōch-e*]; I'm feeling a lot better мне намного лучше [*mnye nam-noguh lōōch-e*]; I'd better be going мне пора идти [*mnye para eed-tee*]

between между [*myezh-dōō*]

beyond за [*za*]; beyond the mountains за горами [*za garah-mee*]

bicycle велосипед [*vyi-lyassi-pyet*]; can we rent bicycles here? у вас есть велосипеды напрокат? [*ōō vass yist vyi-lyassi-pyedee naprakaht*]

big большой [*bal-shoy*]; that's too big слишком большой [*sleesh-kum bal-shoy*]; it's not big enough недостаточно большой [*nyedasta-tuchnuh bal-shoy*]

bigger больше [*bolsh-e*]

bike велосипед [*vyi-lyassi-pyet*]

bikini бикини [*bikeenee*]

bill счёт [*s-chot*]; could I have the bill, please? я хочу рассчитаться [*ya khachōō rass-chitahtsa*]

billfold бумажник [*boomahzh-nik*]

billiards бильярд [*bi-lyart*]

birch tree берёза [*byi-ryoza*]

bird птица [*pteetsa*]

biro (*tm*) шариковая ручка [*sharikava-ya rōōchka*]

birthday день рождения [*dyin razh-dyeni-ya*]; it's my birthday сегодня мой день рождения [*syivo-dnya moy dyin razh-dyeni-ya*]; when is your birthday? когда ваш день рождения? [*kagda vash dyin razh-dyeni-ya*]; happy birthday! с днём рождения! [*zdnyom razh-dyeni-ya*]

biscuit печенье [*pyichen-ye*]

bit: just a little bit for me я возьму только маленький кусок [*ya vazmōō tol-kuh mah-lyenkee koo-sok*]; a big bit большой кусок [*bal-shoy koo-sok*]; a bit of that cake кусок того торта [*koo-sok tavo torta*]; it's a bit too much for me это слишком много для меня [*ettuh sleesh-kum mnoguh dlya minya*]; it's a bit cold today холодновато сегодня [*khalad-navah-tuh syivo-dnya*]

bite укус [*oo-kōōss*]; I've been bitten меня что-то укусило [*minya shto-tuh oo-kōō-see-luh*]; do you have something for bites? у вас есть что-то от укусов? [*ōō vass yist shto-tuh at oo-kōō-suff*]

bitter (*taste*) горький [*gorkee*]

black чёрный [*chornee*]; black and white film (*for camera*) чёрно-белая плёнка [*chorn-uh byela-ya plyonka*]

blackout: he's had a blackout он потерял сознание [*on pa-tyi-ryal saznahni-ye*]

Black Sea Чёрное море [*chornuh-ye mor-ye*]

bladder мочевой пузырь [*machivoy poozeer*]

blanket одеяло [*a-dyiyah-luh*]; I'd like another blanket дайте мне, пожалуйста, ещё одно одеяло [*da-tye mnye pa-zhahlsta yish-cho adno a-dyiyah-luh*]

bleach (*for toilet etc*) хлорка [*khlorka*]

bleed истекать кровью [*iss-tyikaht kro-vyōō*]; **he's bleeding** он истекает кровью [*on iss-tyika-yit kro-vyōō*]

bless you! (*after sneeze*) будьте здоровы! [*bōōd-tye zdarovee*]

blind слепой [*slyipoy*]

blinds жалюзи [*zha-lyōōzee*]

blind spot (*driving*) слепое пятно [*slyipo-ye pyatno*]

blister волдырь (*m*) [*valdeer*]

blizzard вьюга [*vyōōga*]

blocked (*road*) закрыт [*zakreet*]; **the drain's blocked** труба засорилась [*trooba za-sareelass*]

block of flats многоквартирный дом [*mnaga-kvarteernee dom*]

blond (*adjective*) белокурый [*byila-kōōree*]

blonde блондинка [*blandeenka*]

blood кровь (*f*) [*krof*]; **his blood group is . . .** у него . . . группа крови [*ōō nyivo . . . grōōpa krovee*]; **I have high blood pressure** у меня высокое давление [*ōō minya vee-sokuh-ye dav-lyeni-ye*]

bloody Mary коктейль из водки и томатного сока [*kak-tyayl iz votkee ee tamahtnuh-vuh soka*]

blouse блузка [*blōōzka*]

blue синий [*seenee*]

blusher (*cosmetic*) румяна [*roo-myana*]

board: **full board** комната с полным пансионом [*komnata spolnim pan-syonum*]; **halfboard** комната с завтраком и ужином [*komnata z-zaftrakum ee ōōzhinum*]

boarding house пансион [*pan-syon*]

boarding pass посадочный талон [*pa-saduchnee talon*]

boat лодка [*lotka*]

body тело [*tyeluh*]

boil (*on body*) фурункул [*foor-oonkool*]; **to boil the water** кипятить воду [*ki-pyateet vodōō*]

boiled egg (*soft*) яйцо всмятку [*yitso fsmyat-kōō*]; (*hard*) яйцо вкрутую [*yitso vkrootōō-yōō*]

boiling hot (*weather*) жара [*zhara*]; (*food*) горячий [*ga-ryachee*]

bomb (*noun*) бомба [*bomba*]

bone кость (*f*) [*kost*]

bonnet (*of car*) капот [*kapot*]

book книга [*k-neega*]; **I'd like to book a table for two** я хочу заказать стол на двоих [*ya khachōō zakazat stol na dva-yeekh*]

bookshop, bookstore книжный магазин [*k-neezhnee magazeen*]

boot (*on foot*) сапог [*sapok*]; (*of car*) багажник [*bagahzh-nik*]

booze выпивка [*veepifka*]; **I had too much booze** я выпил слишком много [*ya veepil sleesh-kum mnoguh*]

border (*of country*) граница [*graneetsa*]

bored: **I'm bored** мне скучно [*mnye skōōsh-nuh*]

boring скучный [*skōōsh-nee*]

born: **I was born in April** (*man*) я родился в апреле [*ya radeel-sa va-pryel-ye*]; **I was born in London** (*woman*) я родилась в Лондоне [*ya radee-lass vlon-dun-ye*]

borrow: **may I borrow . . . ?** можно взять взаймы . . . ? [*mozh-nuh vzyat vzimee*]

boss босс [*boss*]

both оба [*oba*]; (*two feminine nouns*) обе [*ob-ye*]; **I'll take both of them** я возьму оба [*ya vazmōō oba*]; **we'll both come** мы придём вдвоём [*mee pree-dyom vdva-yom*]

bother: **sorry to bother you** извините за беспокойство [*izvinee-tye za byi-spakoyst-vuh*]; **it's no bother** ничего [*nee-chivo*]; **it's such a bother** чёрт возьми! [*chort vaz-mee*]

bottle бутылка [*booteelka*]; **a bottle of wine** бутылка вина [*booteelka vina*]; **another bottle, please** ещё одну бутылку, пожалуйста [*yish-cho adnōō bootee-kōō pa-zhahlsta*]

bottle-opener открывалка [*atkreevalka*]

bottom дно [*dno*]; **at the bottom of the hill** у подножия горы [*ōō pad-nozhi-ya garee*]

bottom gear первая скорость [*pyerva-ya skorust*]

bouncer (*at club*) вышибала [*vishee-bahla*]

bowels кишечник [*kishech-nik*]

bowling игра в шары [*eegra fsharee*]

box коробка [*karopka*]

box office театральная касса [*tee-atralna-ya kassa*]

boy мальчик [*mahl-chik*]

boyfriend: **my boyfriend** мой друг [*moy drōōk*]

bra бюстгальтер [*byoost-gahl-tyir*]

bracelet браслет [*bra-slyet*]

brake fluid тормозная жидкость [*tarmazna-ya zheedkust*]

brake lining тормозная накладка [*tarmazna-ya naklatka*]

brakes тормоза [*tarmaza*]; there's something wrong with the brakes с тормозами что-то неладно [*starmazahmee shto-tuh nyi-ladnuh*]; can you check the brakes? можете проверить тормоза? [*mozhit-ye pra-vyereet tarmaza*]; I had to brake suddenly я должен был внезапно затормозить [*ya dolzhen beel vnye-zapnuh zatarma-zeet*]

brandy коньяк [*ka-nyak*]

brave храбрый [*khrahbree*]

bread хлеб [*khlyep*]; could we have some bread and butter? дайте нам, пожалуйста, хлеба с маслом [*dı-tye nam pa-zhahlsta khlyeba smaslum*]; some more bread, please ещё хлеба, пожалуйста [*yish-cho khlyeba pa-zhahlsta*]; white bread белый хлеб [*byelee khlyep*]; brown bread чёрный хлеб [*chornee khlyep*]; wholemeal bread хлеб из непросеянной муки [*khlyep iz nyipra-sye-yannoy mookee*]; rye bread ржаной хлеб [*rzhanoy khlyep*]

break ломать/сломать [*lamaht/slamaht*]; I think I've broken my ankle мне кажется, что я сломал ногу [*mnye kahzhit-sa shto ya slamahl nogoo*]; it keeps breaking это всё время ломается [*ettuh fsyo vrye-mya lamah-yitsa*]

breakdown: I've had a breakdown у меня сломалась машина [*oo minya slamahlass masheena*]; nervous breakdown нервное расстройство [*nyervnuh-ye rastroyst-vuh*]

breakfast завтрак [*zaftrak*]

break in: somebody's broken in кто-то нас ограбил [*kto-tuh nas a-grahbil*]

breast грудь (*f*) [*groot*]

breast-feed кормить грудью [*karmeet groo-dyoo*]

breath дыхание [*dikhahni-ye*]; to be out of breath запыхаться [*za-pikhahtsa*]

breathe дышать [*dishaht*]; I can't breathe мне трудно дышать [*mnye trood-nuh dishaht*]

breathtaking поразительный [*parazeetyilnee*]

breeze ветерок [*vyi-tyirok*]

breezy прохладно [*prakhlahd-nuh*]

bride невеста [*nyi-vyesta*]

bridegroom жених [*zheneekh*]

bridge (*over river*) мост [*mosst*]

brief (*stay, visit*) короткий [*karotkee*]

briefcase портфель (*m*) [*part-fyel*]

bright (*colour*) яркий [*yarkee*]; bright red ярко-красный [*yarka-krah-snee*]

brilliant (*idea, colour*) блестящий [*blyistyahsh-chee*]

bring приносить/принести [*preenasseet/pree-nyistee*]; could you bring it to my hotel? пожалуйста, принесите это в мою гостиницу [*pa-zhahlsta pree-nyisee-tye ettuh vma-yoo gastee-nitsoo*]; I'll bring it back я верну вам это [*ya vyir-noo vam ettuh*]; can I bring my girlfriend too? можно прийти с подругой? [*mozh-nuh preetee spa-droogoy*]

Britain Великобритания [*vyilika-britani-ya*]

British британский [*britanskee*]; the British британцы [*britantsee*]

brochure брошюра [*brashoora*]; do you have any brochures on ...? у вас есть брошюра о ...? [*oo vass yist brashoora a*]

broke: I'm broke у меня ни копейки денег [*oo minya nee ka-pyaykee dye-nyek*]

broken сломанный [*slomannee*]; you've broken it вы сломали это [*vee slamahlee ettuh*]; it's broken это сломалось [*ettuh slamahluss*]; broken nose сломанный нос [*slomannee noss*]

brooch брошь (*f*) [*brosh*]

brother: my brother мой брат [*moy braht*]

brother-in-law: my brother-in-law мой шурин [*moy shoorin*]

brown коричневый [*kareech-nyiwee*]; I don't go brown я не загораю [*ya nye zagara-yoo*]

browse: may I just browse around? я только хочу посмотреть [*ya tol-kuh khachoo pasma-tryet*]

bruise (*noun*) ушиб [*oosheep*]

brunette брюнетка [*bryoo-nyetka*]

brush (*noun*) щётка [*shchotka*]

bubble bath пенящееся средство для ванны [*pye-nyash-che-yessa sryedst-vuh dlya vannee*]

bucket ведро [*vyidro*]

buffet буфет [*boo-fyet*]

bug (*insect*) букашка [*bookashka*]; she's caught a bug она чем-то заразилась [*ana chem-tuh za-razeelass*]; (*microphone*) потайной микрофон [*patınoy meekrafon*]; is this room bugged? в этой комнате потайной микрофон? [*vettoy komnat-ye patınoy meekrafon*]

building здание [*zdahni-ye*]

bulb (*elec*) лампочка [*lampuchka*]; a new bulb новая лампочка [*nova-ya lampuchka*]

Bulgaria Болгария [*bal-gahri-ya*]

bull бык [*beek*]

bump: I bumped my head я ушиб голову [*ya oosheep golavoo*]

bumper бампер [*bam-pyer*]

bumpy (*road, flight*) ухабистый [*oo-khahbistee*]

bunch of flowers букет цветов [*boo-kyet tsvitoff*]

bungalow одноэтажный дом [*adna-ettahzhnee dom*]

bunion шишка на большом пальце ноги [*sheeshka na bal-shom palts-e nagee*]

bunk койка [*koyka*]; bunk beds двухэтажные койки [*dvookh-etahzhni-ye koykee*]

buoy буй [*boo-ee*]

burglar вор [*vor*]

burn: do you have an ointment for burns? у вас есть мазь от ожогов? [*oo vass yist mass at azhoguff*]

burnt: this meat is burnt это мясо подгорело [*ettuh mya-suh padga-ryeluh*]; my arms are so burnt у меня обгорели руки [*oo minya abga-ryelee rookee*]

burst: a pipe has burst труба лопнула [*trooba lopnoola*]

bus автобус [*avto-booss*]; is this the bus for Leningrad? этот автобус едет в Ленинград? [*ettut avto-booss ye-dyit vlyinin-graht*]; when's the next bus? когда отходит следующий автобус? [*kagda at-khodit slyedoo-yoosh-chee avto-booss*]

bus driver водитель автобуса [*vadee-tyil avto-boossa*]

business дело [*dyeluh*]; I'm here on business я в командировке [*ya fkaman-diroff-kye*]; it's a pleasure to do business with you очень приятно с вами работать [*ochin pree-yahtnuh svahmee rabotat*]

bus station автобусная станция [*avto-boossna-ya stantsi-ya*]

bus stop остановка автобуса [*astanofka avto-boossa*]; will you tell me which bus stop I get off at? можете мне сказать, где мне сойти? [*mozhit-ye mnye skazaht gdye mnye sitee*]

bust (*of body*) грудь (*f*) [*groot*]; (*measurement*) размер окружности груди [*raz-myer akroozh-nustee groodee*]

bus tour экскурсия автобусом [*eks-koorsi-ya avto-boossum*]

busy (*street*) людный [*lyoodnee*]; (*restaurant*) шумный [*shoomnee*]; I'm busy this evening вечером я занят [*vyecherum ya zah-nyat*]; the line's busy (*telec*) линия занята [*leeni-ya za-nyata*]

but но [*no*]; not ... but ... не... а ... [*nye ... a ...*]

butcher (*shop*) мясной магазин [*mya-snoy magazeen*]

butter масло [*mah-sluh*]

butterfly бабочка [*bahbuchka*]

button пуговица [*pooguvitsa*]

buy: I'll buy it я возьму это [*ya vazmoo ettuh*]; where can I buy ...? где продаётся ...? [*gdye prada-yotsa*]

by: by train/car/boat поездом [*po-yezdum*]/машиной [*masheenoy*]/пароходом [*para-khodum*]; who's it written by? кто автор? [*kto ahvtur*]; the picture's by Repin картина написана Репиным [*karteena napee-sana rye-pinum*]; I came by myself (*man*) я пришёл один [*ya preeshol adeen*]; (*woman*) я пришла одна [*ya preeshla adna*]; a seat by the window место у окна [*myest-uh oo akna*]; by the sea у моря [*oo mor-ya*]; can you do it by Wednesday? можете это сделать до среды? [*mozhit-ye ettuh zdyelat da-sryidee*]

bye-bye до свидания [*da svidani-ya*]

Byelorussia Белоруссия [*byila-roossi-ya*]

bypass (*road*) объезд [*ab-yest*]

C

cab (*taxi*) такси [*taksee*]

cabbage капуста [*ka-poosta*]

cabin (*boat*) каюта [*ka-yoota*]

cable (*elec*) кабель (*m*) [*kah-byel*]

cablecar канатная дорога [*kanahtna-ya da-roga*]

café кафе [*kaff-e*]

caffeine кофеин [*kaffe-een*]

cake торт [*tort*]; a piece of cake кусок
торта [*koo-sok torta*]

calculator калькулятор [*kalkoo-lyahtur*]

calendar календарь (*m*) [*ka-lyindar*]

call: what is this called? как это
называется? [*kak ettuh nazivah-yetsa*];
call the manager! позовите
администратора! [*pazavee-tye adminis-
trah-tuhra*]; I'd like to make a call to
England мне нужно позвонить в
Англию [*mnye noōzh-nuh pa-zvaneet vang-
glee-yoo*]; I'll call back later (*come back*) я
зайду позже [*ya zidoō pozh-e*]; (*phone
back*) я позвоню ещё раз [*ya pazva-nyoō
yish-cho rass*]; I'm expecting a call from
London я жду звонок из Лондона [*ya
zhdoō zvanok iz londuna*]; would you give
me a call at 7.30? пожалуйста,
разбудите меня в 7.30 [*pa-zhahlsta raz-
boodeet-ye minya fpalaveen-ye vass-movuh*];
the outing/meeting has been called off
поездка отменена/собрание отменено
[*pa-yezdka at-myin-yina/sabrahni-ye at-myin-
yino*]

call box телефон-автомат [*tyilifon
avtamaht*]

calm спокойный [*spakoynee*]; calm down!
успокойтесь! [*oō-spakoy-tyiss*]

Calor gas (*tm*) баллонный газ [*balonee
gahss*]

calories калории [*kalori-yee*]

camera фотоаппарат [*foto-aparaht*]

camp: is there somewhere we can camp?
где можно разбить лагерь? [*gdye mozh-
nuh razbeet lah-gyir*]; can we camp here?
здесь можно разбить лагерь? [*zdyiss
mozhnuh razbeet lah-gyir*]

campbed раскладушка [*rass-kladoōshka*]

camping жить в палатках [*zheet fpalaht-
kakh*]

campsite кемпинг [*kyemping*]

can (*tin*) банка [*banka*]

can: can I ...? можно мне ...? [*mozhnuh
mnye*]; can you ...? вы можете ...? [*vee
mozhit-ye*]; can he ...? он может ...? [*on
mozhit*]; can we ...? нам можно ...?
[*nam mozhnuh*]; can they ...? они могут
...? [*anee mogoōt*]; I can't ... мне
нельзя ... [*mnye nyil-zya*]; he can't ...
ему нельзя... [*yimoō nyil-zya*]; can I
keep it? вы это мне можете дать? [*vee
ettuh mnye mozhit-ye daht*]; if I can если
возможно [*yeslee vaz-mozhnuh*]; that

can't be right это, должно быть,
ошибка [*ettuh dalzhno beet a-sheepka*]

Canada Канада [*kanada*]

Canadian (*man*) канадец [*kanah-dyits*];
(*woman*) канадка [*kanaht-ka*]; (*adjective*)
канадский [*kanahd-skee*]; the Canadians
канадцы [*kanahd-tsee*]

cancel отменять/отменить [*at-myi-
nyaht/at-myineet*]; can I cancel my reservation? я хочу отменить заказ на
место [*ya khachoō at-myineet zakahss na
myestuh*]; can we cancel dinner for
tonight? мы хотим отменить
сегодняшний ужин [*mee khateem at-
myineet syivod-nyash-nee oōzhin*]; I can-
celled it я это отменил [*ya ettuh at-
myineel*]

cancellation отмена [*at-myena*]

candies конфеты [*kan-fyetee*]; a piece of
candy конфета [*kan-fyeta*]

candle свеча [*svyicha*]

can-opener консервный нож [*kanservnee
nosh*]

cap (*headwear*) шапка [*shapka*]; bathing cap
купальная шапочка [*koopalna-ya
shapuchka*]

capital city столица [*staleetsa*]

capitalism капитализм [*kapitaleezm*]

capitalist (*noun*) капиталист [*kapitaleest*];
(*adjective*) капиталистический [*kapitali-
steechiskee*]

capital letter прописная буква
[*prapissna-ya boōkva*]

capsize: the boat capsized лодка
опрокинулась [*lotka aprakee-noolass*]

captain (*of ship*) капитан [*kapitan*]

car машина [*masheena*], автомобиль (*m*)
[*avta-mabeel*]

carafe графин [*grafeen*]

carat: is it 9/14 carat gold? это золото
9/14 каратов? [*ettuh zolut-uh dyi-
vyatee/chitirnad-tsatee karah-tuff*]

caravan автофургон [*avta-foorgon*]

carbonated газированный [*gazir-ovanee*]

carburet(t)or карбюратор [*kar-
byoorahtur*]

card: do you have a (*business*) card? у вас
есть визитная карточка? [*oō vas yist
vizeetna-ya kartuchka*]

cardboard box картонная коробка
[*kartona-ya karopka*]

cardigan кофта [*kofta*]

cards карты [*kartee*]; do you play cards? вы играете в карты? [*vee eegrah-yit-ye fkartee*]

care: goodbye, take care до свидания. Будьте осторожны! [*da svidani-ya boodtye asta-rozhnee*]; will you take care of this bag for me? вы присмотрите за моей сумкой? [*vee pree-smotreet-ye za ma-yay soomkoy*]; care of . . . для передачи . . . [*dlya pyiri-dachee*]

careful: be careful осторожно [*asta-rozhnuh*]

careless: that was careless of you это было легкомысленно с вашей стороны [*ettuh beel-uh lyikhka-meesslyinuh zvashay staranee*]; careless driving неосторожная езда [*nyi-asta-rozhna-ya yizda*]

car ferry паром [*parom*]

car hire бюро автомобильного проката [*byooro avta-mabeelnuh-vuh prakahta*]

car key ключ от машины [*klyooch at masheenee*]

carnation гвоздика [*gvazdeeka*]

carnival карнавал [*karnavahl*]

car park стоянка [*sta-yanka*]

carpet ковёр [*ka-vyor*]

car rental бюро автомобильного проката [*byooro avta-mabeelnuh-vuh prakahta*]

carrot морковь (*f*) [*markoff*]

carry нести/носить [*nyistee/nasseet*]; could you carry this suitcase up for me? понесите, пожалуйста, этот чемодан наверх [*pa-nyissee-tye pa-zhahlsta ettut chimadan na-vyerkh*]

carry-all дорожная сумка [*darozhna-ya soomka*]

carry-cot переносная кроватка [*pyiri-nassnah-ya kravaht-ka*]

car-sick: I get car-sick меня укачивает в машине [*minya oo-kahchiva-yit vmasheen-ye*]

carton картонка [*kartonka*]; a carton of milk пакет молока [*pa-kyet malaka*]

carving резьба [*ryizba*]

carwash мойка машин [*moyka masheen*]

case (*suitcase*) чемодан [*chimadan*]; in any case во всяком случае [*va fsyahkum sloocha-ye*]; in that case в таком случае [*ftakom sloocha-ye*]; it's a special case это исключительный случай [*ettuh issklyoo-chee-tyilnee sloo-chi*]; in case he comes back на случай, если он

вернётся [*na sloo-chi yeslee on vyirnyotsa*]; I'll take two just in case я возьму, на всякий случай, два [*ya vazmoo na fsyahkee sloo-chi dva*]

cash наличные [*naleechni-ye*]; I don't have any cash у меня нет денег [*oo minya nyet dye-nyek*]; I'll pay cash я заплачу наличными [*ya zaplachoo naleech-nimee*]; will you cash a cheque/check for me? я хочу получить деньги по чеку [*ya khachoo pa-loocheet dyen-gee pa chekoo*]

cashdesk касса [*kassa*]

cash register касса [*kassa*]

casino казино [*kazeeno*]

Caspian Sea Каспийское море [*ka-speeskuh-ye mor-ye*]

cassette кассета [*ka-syeta*]

cassette player, cassette recorder кассетный магнитофон [*ka-syetnee magnitafon*]

castle замок [*zahmuk*]

casual: casual clothes повседневная одежда [*pa-fsyi-dnyevna-ya a-dyezhda*]

cat кошка [*koshka*]

catamaran катамаран [*katamaran*]

catastrophe катастрофа [*kata-strofa*]

catch: where do we catch the bus? откуда отходит автобус? [*at-kooda at-khodit avto-booss*]; he's caught some strange illness он заразился какой-то странной болезнью [*on zarazeel-sa kakoy-tuh strannoy ba-lyez-nyoo*]

catching: is it catching? это заразительно? [*ettuh zarazee-tyilnuh*]

cathedral собор [*sabor*]

Catholic (*adjective*) католический [*kata-leechiskee*]

Caucasus Кавказ [*kavkaz*]

cauliflower цветная капуста [*tsvitna-ya kapoosta*]

cause причина [*pricheena*]

cave пещера [*pyish-chera*]

caviar икра [*ikra*]; black caviar чёрная икра [*chorna-ya ikra*]; red caviar кетовая икра [*kyetuva-ya ikra*]; soft caviar зернистая икра [*zyirneesta-ya ikra*]; pressed caviar паюсная икра [*pa-yoossna-ya ikra*]

ceiling потолок [*patalok*]

celebrations празднование [*prazdnuvani-ye*]

celery сельдерей [*syil-dyi-ryay*]

cellophane целлофан [*tsillafahn*]

cemetery кладбище [*klahd-bishch-e*]

center центр [*tsentr*]; *see also* centre

centigrade стоградусный [*sta-grahdooss-nee*]; 10° centigrade 10 градусов Цельсия [*dye-syat grah-doossuf tselssi-ya*]; *see page 121*

centimetre, centimeter сантиметр [*santi-myetr*]; *see page 120*

central центральный [*tsintrahl-nee*]; we'd prefer something more central мы хотим остановиться ближе к центру [*mee khateem astana-veetsa bleezh-e k-tsentroo*]

Central Asia Средняя Азия [*sryed-nya-ya ahzi-ya*]

central heating центральное отопление [*tsin-trahlnuh-ye ata-plyeni-ye*]

central station центральный вокзал [*tsin-trahlnee vagzal*]

centre центр [*tsentr*]; how do we get to the centre? как попасть в центр? [*kak papast ftsentr*]; in the centre (*of town*) в центре города [*ftsent-rye goruda*]

century столетие [*sta-lyeti-ye*]; in the 19th century в 19 веке [*vdyi-vyat-nahd-tsatum vye-kye*]

ceramics керамика [*kyiramika*]

certain определённый [*a-pryi-dyi-lyonee*]; are you certain? вы уверены? [*vee oo-vye-ryinee*]; I'm absolutely certain я совершенно уверен [*ya sa-vyir-shennuh oo-vye-ryin*]

certainly конечно [*ka-nyesh-nuh*]; certainly not ни в коем случае [*nee fkoy-em sloocha-ye*]

certificate удостоверение [*oodasta-vyiryeni-ye*]; birth certificate метрика [*myetrika*]

chain цепь [*tsep*]; (*around neck*) цепочка [*tsipochka*]

chair стул [*stool*]

chambermaid горничная [*gornichna-ya*]

champagne шампанское [*shampan-skuh-ye*]

chance: quite by chance совершенно случайно [*savyir-shennuh sloochi-nuh*]; no chance! ни малейшей надежды! [*nee ma-lyayshay na-dyezhdee*]

change: could you change this into roubles? можете обменять это на рубли? [*mozhit-ye abmi-nyaht ettuh na rooblee*]; I haven't got any change у меня нет мелочи [*oo minya nyet myeluchee*]; can you give me change for a 10 rouble note? можете разменять 10 рублей? [*mozhit-ye razmi-nyaht dye-syat roob-lyay*]; do we

have to change (*trains*)? нам нужно сделать пересадку? [*nam noozhnuh zdyelat pyiri-sahtkoo*]; for a change для разнообразия [*dlya razna-abrahzi-ya*]; you haven't changed the sheets вы не поменяли постельное бельё [*vee nye pami-nyahlee pastyel-noye byi-lyo*]; the place has changed so much здесь всё так изменилось [*zdiss fsyo tak iz-myineeluss*]; do you want to change places with me? вы хотите поменяться со мной местами? [*vee khateet-ye pami-nyahtsa samnoy myistahmee*]; can I change this for …? можно поменять это на …? [*mozhnuh pami-nyaht ettuh na*]

changeable (*weather*) неустойчивая погода [*nye-oostoy-chiva-ya pagoda*]

channel: the English Channel Ла-Манш [*la mansh*]

chaos хаос [*kha-oss*]

chap парень [*pah-ryen*]; the chap at reception этот малый в регистратуре [*ettut mahlee vregistra-too-rye*]

chapel часовня [*chassov-nya*]

charge: is there an extra charge? за это полагается дополнительная оплата? [*za ettuh palaga-yitsa dapalnee-tyilna-ya aplahta*]; what do you charge? сколько это стоит? [*skolkuh ettuh sto-yit*]; who's in charge here? кто заведует этим заведением? [*kto za-vyedoo-yet ettim zavi-dyeniyem*]

charming очаровательный [*acharavah-tyilnee*]

chart карта [*karta*]

charter flight чартерный рейс [*char-tyernee ryayss*]

chassis шасси [*shassee*]

cheap дешёвый [*dyi-shovee*]; do you have something cheaper? у вас есть что-то подешевле? [*oo vass yist shto-tuh pa-dyishev-lye*]

cheat: I've been cheated меня обманули [*minya ab-manoolee*]

check: will you check? можете проверить? [*mozhit-ye pra-vyereet*]; will you check the steering? проверьте, пожалуйста, рулевое управление [*pra-vyer-tye pa-zhahlsta roo-lyivo-ye oopravlyeni-ye*]; will you check the bill? проверьте, пожалуйста, счёт [*pra-vyer-tye pa-zhahlsta s-chot*]; I've checked it я проверил [*ya pra-vyeril*] check (*financial*) чек [*chek*]; will you take a check? можно заплатить чеком? [*mozh-nuh zaplateet chekum*]

check (*bill*) счёт [*s-chot*]; may I have the check please? я хочу заплатить [*ya khachoo zaplateet*]

checkbook чековая книжка [*chekuva-ya k-neezhka*]

checked (*shirt*) клетчатый [*klyet-chatee*]

checkers шашки [*shashkee*]

check-in (*luggage*) сдать багаж [*zdaht bagahsh*]

checkroom гардероб [*gar-dyirop*]

cheek (*on face*) щека [*shchika*]; what a cheek! какая наглость! [*kaka-ya nahglust*]

cheeky нахальный [*nakhalnee*]

cheerio (*bye-bye*) до свидания [*da svidani-ya*]

cheers (*toast*) за ваше здоровье [*za vash-e zdarov-ye*]; (*thank you*) спасибо [*spa-see-buh*]

cheer up не унывай! [*nye ooniva1*]

cheese сыр [*seer*]

cheesecake сладкая ватрушка [*slahtka-ya va-trooshka*]

chef повар [*povar*]

chemist (*shop*) аптека [*ap-tyeka*]

cheque чек [*chek*]; will you take a cheque? можно заплатить чеком? [*mozhnuh zaplateet chekum*]

cheque book чековая книжка [*chekuva-ya k-neezhka*]

cheque card банковская кредитная карточка [*bankuvska-ya kryideetna-ya kartuchka*]

cherry вишня [*veesh-nya*]

chess шахматы [*shakh-mahtee*]

chest (*body*) грудная клетка [*groodna-ya klyetka*]

chewing gum жвачка [*zhvachka*]

chicken цыплёнок [*tsi-plyonuk*]

chickenpox ветрянка [*vi-tryanka*]

child ребёнок [*ri-byonuk*]

child minder приходящая няня [*prikha-dyash-cha-ya nya-nya*]

child minding service присмотр за детьми [*preesmotr za dyitmee*]

children дети [*dyetee*]

children's playground детская площадка [*dyetska-ya plash-chatka*]

children's pool детский бассейн [*dyetskee ba-syayn*]

children's portion детская порция [*dyetska-ya portsi-ya*]

children's room детская комната [*dyetska-ya kom-nata*]

chilled (*wine*) охлаждённый [*akhlazh-dyonee*]; it's not properly chilled недостаточно холодно [*nye-dastahtuch-nuh kholudnuh*]

chilly холодный [*khalodnee*]

chimney дымоход [*dimakhot*]

chin подбородок [*pad-baroduk*]

china фарфор [*farfor*]

China Китай (*m*) [*kit1*]

chips жареный картофель [*zha-ryenee karto-fyil*]; potato chips хрустящий картофель [*khroo-styash-chee karto-fyil*]

chiropodist педикюрша [*pyidee-kyoorsha*]

chocolate шоколад [*shakalaht*]; a chocolate bar плитка шоколада [*pleetka shakalahda*]; a box of chocolates коробка шоколадных конфет [*karopka shakalahd-nikh kan-fyet*]; a hot chocolate какао [*kaka-oo*]

choke (*on car*) подсос [*pad-soss*]

choose: it's hard to choose трудно выбирать [*troodnuh veebirat*]; you choose for us выберите для нас [*vee-byeree-tye dlya nass*]

chop: a pork/lamb chop свиная/баранья отбивная котлета [*svina-ya/barahn-ya atbivna-ya kat-lyeta*]

Christian name имя [*ee-mya*]

Christmas рождество [*razh-dyistvo*]; merry Christmas счастливого рождества [*s-chast-leevuh-vuh razh-dyistva*]

church церковь (*f*) [*tserkuff*]; where is the Orthodox/Protestant/Catholic church? где православная/протестантская/католическая церковь? [*gdye prava-slahvna-ya/prati-stantska-ya/kataleechiska-ya tserkuff*]

cider сидр [*seedr*]

cigar сигара [*sigara*]

cigarette сигарета [*siga-ryeta*]; tipped cigarette сигарета с фильтром [*siga-ryeta sfiltrum*]; (*Russian cigarette*) папироса [*papirossa*]

cigarette lighter зажигалка [*zazhi-galka*]

cine-camera кино-камера [*kino ka-myira*]

cinema кино [*kino*]; I'd like to go to the cinema я хочу идти в кино [*ya khachoo eed-tee fkino*] circle круг [krōok]; (in theatre) ярус [yarooss]

citizen: I'm a British/American citizen я подданный Великобритании/Америки [ya pod-danee vyilika-britani-ee/a-myerikee]

city город [gorut]

city centre, city center центр города [tsentr goruda]

claim (noun: insurance) требование о выплате страховки [tryebuvani-ye a veeplat-ye strakhofkee]

claim form заявление [za-yav-lyeni-ye]

clarify выяснять/выяснить [vee-ya-snyat/ vee-ya-sneet]

classical классический [klasseechiskee]

clean (adjective) чистый [cheestee]; may I have some clean sheets? пожалуйста, принесите мне чистую простыню [pazhahlsta pri-nyi-seet-ye mnye cheestoo-yōo prasti-nyōo]; our room hasn't been cleaned today в нашем номере сегодня не убирали [vnashem nomyer-ye sivo-dnya nye ōobirahlee]; it's not clean это не чисто [ettuh nye cheestuh]; can you clean this for me? можете почистить это? [mozhit-ye pa-cheestit ettuh]

cleaning solution (for contact lenses) дезинфицирущий раствор для контактных линз [dyizin-fitseer-ōo-yōosh-chee rastvor dlya kantakt-nikh lins]

cleansing cream (cosmetic) очищающий крем [achisha-yoosh-chee kryem]

clear: it's not very clear это непонятно [ettuh nyipan-yahtnuh]; OK, that's clear ладно, понятно [lahdnuh pan-yahtnuh]

clever умный [ōom-nee]

cliff скала [skala]

climate климат [kleemat]

climb: it's a long climb to the top до вершины далеко [da vyirsheenee da-lyiko]

climber альпинист [alpineest]

climbing boots альпинистские ботинки [alpineest-ski-ye bateenkee]

clinic клиника [kleenika]

clip (ski) крепление [kryip-lyeni-ye]

cloakroom (for coats) гардероб [gar-dyirop]; (WC) уборная [ōoborna-ya]

clock часы [chassee]

close: is it close? это недалеко? [ettuh nyida-lyiko]; close to the hotel недалеко от гостиницы [nyida-lyiko at gastee-nitsee]; close by рядом [ryahdum]

close: when do you close? когда вы закрываете? [kagda vee zakriva-yit-ye]

closed закрыто [zakreet-uh]; they were closed там было закрыто [tam beel-uh zakreet-uh]

closet шкаф [shkaff]

cloth (material) ткань (f) [tkan]; (rag) тряпка [tryapka]

clothes одежда [a-dyezhda]

clothes line бельевая верёвка [byi-lyiva-ya vyi-ryofka]

clothes peg, clothespin прищепка для белья [preesh-chepka dlya byi-lya]

clouds облака [ablaka]; it's clouding over небо покрылось тучами [nyeb-uh pa-kreeluss tōochamee]

cloudy облачный [oblachnee]

club клуб [kloop]

clubhouse здание клуба [zdahni-ye klooba]

clumsy неуклюжий [nyi-oo-klyōozhee]

clutch (car) сцепление [stsip-lyeni-ye]; the clutch is slipping сцепление не держит [stsip-lyeni-ye nye dyer-zhit]

coach (long distance bus) междугородный автобус [myizhdoo-garodnee avto-booss]

coach party тургруппа [toor-groopa]

coach trip экскурсия автобусом [ekskōorsi-ya avto-boossum]

coast берег [bye-ryek]; at the coast на берегу моря [na byi-ryigōo mor-ya]

coastguard береговая охрана [byi-ryigava-ya akhrahna]

coat (overcoat etc) пальто [palto]; (jacket) пиджак [pidzhak]

coathanger вешалка [vyeshalka]

cobbled street улица мощённая булыжником [ōolitsa mash-chonna-ya boo-leezhnikum]

cobbler сапожник [sapozhnik]

cockroach таракан [tarakan]

cocktail коктейль (m) [kak-tyayl]

cocktail bar коктейль-бар [kak-tyayl-bar]

cocoa какао [kaka-ōo]

coconut кокос [kakoss]

code: what's the (dialling) code for ...? скажите мне, пожалуйста, телефонный код ... [skazheet-ye pa-zhahlsta tyilifonnee kot]

coffee кофе [koff-ye]; a white coffee, a coffee with milk кофе с молоком [koff-ye smalakom]; a black coffee чёрный кофе [chornee koff-ye]; two coffees, please две чашки кофе, пожалуйста [*dvye chashkee koff-ye pa-zhahlsta*]

coin монета [*ma-nyeta*]

Coke (*tm*) пепси-кола [*pyepsi-kola*]

cold (*adjective*) холодный [*khalodnee*]; I'm cold мне холодно [*mnye kholudnuh*]; I have a cold я простужен [*ya prastoozhen*]

cold cream кольдкрем [*kald-kryem*]

Cold War холодная война [*khalodna-ya vina*]

collapse: he's collapsed он потерял сознание [*on pa-tyi-ryahl saznani-ye*]

collar воротник [*varatneek*]

collar bone ключица [*klyoo-cheetsa*]

colleague: my colleague мой коллега [*moy ka-lyega*]; your colleague ваш коллега [*vash ka-lyega*]

collect: I've come to collect . . . я пришёл за . . . [*ya prishol za*]; I collect . . . (*stamps etc*) я собираю . . . [*ya sabeerah-yoo*]; I want to call New York collect я хочу позвонить в Нью Йорк за счёт вызываемого [*ya khachoo pa-zvaneet vnyoo-york zass-shot vizivah-yemuv-uh*]

collect call звонить за счёт вызываемого [*zvaneet zass-chot vizivah-yemuv-uh*]

collective farm колхоз [*kalkhoz*]

college колледж [*ka-lyedzh*]

collision столкновение [*stalkna-vyeni-ye*]

cologne одеколон [*a-dyikalon*]

colo(u)r цвет [*tsvyet*]; do you have any other colo(u)rs? в других цветах это тоже есть? [*vdroo-geekh tsvitakh ettuh tozh-e yist*]; colo(u)r film цветная плёнка [*tsvitna-ya plyonka*]

comb (*noun*) расчёска [*rass-choska*]

come приходить/прийти [*pree-khadeet/preetee*]; I come from London я из Лондона [*ya iz londuna*]; where do you come from? откуда вы? [*at-kooda vee*]; when are they coming? когда они придут? [*kagda anee preedoot*]; come here! идите сюда! [*eedeet-ye syooda*]; come with me идёмте со мной [*ee-dyom-tye samnoy*]; come back! вернись! [*vyirneess*]; I'll come back later я вернусь позже [*ya vyirnooss pozh-e*]; come in! войдите! [*videet-ye*]; he's coming on very well (*improving*) он делает успехи [*on dyela-yet oo-spyekhee*]; come on! давай скорей! [*davi ska-ryay*]; do you want to come out this evening? вы хотите куда-

нибудь пойти вечером? [*vee khateet-ye kooda-niboot ptiee vyecherum*]; these two pictures didn't come out эти две фотографии у меня не получились [*ettie dvye fata-grahfee-ee oo minya nye paloocheeless*]; the money hasn't come through yet деньги ещё не получены [*dyen-gee yish-cho nye pa-loochinee*]

comfortable удобный [*oodob-nee*]; it's not very comfortable здесь не очень удобно [*zdyiss nye ochin oodob-nuh*]

Common Market Общий рынок [*obshchee reenuk*]

communism коммунизм [*kamooneezm*]

communist (*noun*) коммунист [*kamooneest*]; (*adjective*) коммунистический [*kamooni-steechiskee*]

Communist Party Коммунистическая партия [*kamooni-steechiska-ya parti-ya*]

company (*firm*) фирма [*feerma*]

comparison: there's no comparison их нельзя сравнить [*ikh nyil-zya sravneet*]

compartment (*train*) купе [*koop-e*]

compass компас [*kompass*]

compensation возмещение [*vaz-myish-cheni-ye*]

complain жаловаться [*zhahluvat-sa*]; I want to complain about my room я недоволен своим номером [*ya nyidavolyen sva-yeem no-myerum*]

complaint жалоба [*zhahluba*]; I have a complaint я хочу жаловаться [*ya khachoo zhahluvat-sa*]

complete: the complete set полный комплект [*polnee kam-plyekt*]; it's a complete disaster это полная катастрофа [*ettuh polna-ya kata-strofa*]

completely совершенно [*sa-vyir-shenuh*]

complicated: it's very complicated очень сложно [*ochin slozh-nuh*]

compliment: my compliments to the chef передайте повару, что обед был отменным [*pyiri-di-tye povaroo shto a-byed beel at-myenim*]

comprehensive (*insurance*) полное страхование [*polnuh-ye strakha-vahni-ye*]

compulsory обязательный [*a-byazah-tyilnee*]

computer компьютер [*kam-pyoo-tyer*]

comrade товарищ [*tavarishch*]

concern: we are very concerned нас это очень беспокоит [*nass ettuh ochin byi-spakoy-it*]

concert концерт [*kantsert*]

concussion сотрясение мозга [sa-trya-seni-ye mozga]

condenser (in car) конденсатор [kan-dyin-sahtur]

condition: it's not in very good condition это не в особенно хорошем состоянии [ettuh nye vasso-byennuh kharoshem sa-sta-yahni-ee]

conditioner (for hair) укрепляющий состав для волос [ōō-kryip-lya-yoosh-chee sastaff dlya valoss]

condom презерватив [prizervateef]

conductor (on train) проводник [pravadneek]

conference конференция [kan-fyi-ryentsi-ya]

confirm: can you confirm the reservation? можете подтвердить бронь? [mozhit-ye pad-tverdeet bron]

confuse: it's very confusing всё это сбивает с толку [fsyo ettuh zbiva-yet stolkōō]

congratulations! поздравляю! [pazdrav-lyah-yōō]

conjunctivitis конъюнктивит [kan-yoonktiveet]

connection (in travelling) согласованность расписания [sagla-sovanust raspi-sahni-ya]

connoisseur знаток [znatok]

conscious (medically) в сознании [fsaznahni-ee]

consciousness: he's lost consciousness он потерял сознание [on pa-tyi-ryal saznahni-ye]

constipation запор [zapor]

consul консул [konsool]

consulate консульство [konsoolst-vuh]

contact: how can I contact ...? как можно связаться с ...? [kak mozhnuh svyazahtsa s]; I'm trying to contact ... я хочу связаться с ... [ya khachōō svyazahtsa s]

contact lenses контактные линзы [kantaktnee-ye linzee]

contraceptive (noun) противо-зачаточное средство [prateeva-zachahtuch-nuh-ye sryedst-vuh]

convenient удобный [ōōdob-nee]; that's not convenient меня это не устраивает [minya ettuh nye oostrah-eeva-yit]

cook: it's not properly cooked (is underdone) это не прожарено [ettuh nye prazha-ryenuh]; it's beautifully cooked замечательно приготовлено [za-myichah-tyil-nuh preegatov-lyinuh]; he's a good cook он хорошо готовит [on kharasho gatovit]

cooker духовка [dookhofka]

cookie печенье [pyichen-ye]

cool прохладный [prakhlahd-nee]

corduroy вельвет [vyil-vyet]

cork (in bottle) пробка [propka]

corkscrew штопор [shtopur]

corn (on foot) мозоль (f) [mazol]

corner: on the corner (of street) на углу [na ooglōō]; in the corner в углу [vooglōō]; a corner table столик в углу [stolik vooglōō]

cornflakes кукурузные хлопья [koo-koorōōz-nee-ye khlo-pya]

coronary (noun) коронарный тромбоз [kara-narnee tramboss]

correct (adjective) правильный [prah-vilnee]; please correct me if I make a mistake пожалуйста, скажите, если делаю ошибку [pa-zhahlsta skazheet-ye yeslee dyela-yōō a-sheepkōō]

corridor коридор [karidor]

corset корсет [kar-syet]

cosmetics косметика [kaz-myetika]

cosmonaut космонавт [kazma-naft]

Cossak казак [kazak]

cost: what does it cost? сколько стоит? [skol-kuh sto-yit]

cot (for baby) детская кроватка [dyetska-ya kravatka]; (camping) раскладушка [rass-kladōōshka]

cottage коттедж [ka-tyedzh]

cotton (fabric) хлопчатобумажная ткань [khlop-chata-boomazhna-ya tkan]

cotton wool вата [vahta]

couch кушетка [kooshetka]

couchette спальное место [spalnuh-ye myestuh]

cough кашель (m) [kah-shyil]

cough medicine средство от кашля [sryedst-vuh at kah-shlya]

cough tablets таблетки от кашля [ta-blyetkee at kah-shlya]

could: could you ...? можете ли вы ...? [mozhit-ye lee vee]; could I have ...? могу ли я попросить ...? [magōō lee ya pa-prasseet]; I couldn't ... я не мог ... [ya nye mog]

country (nation) страна [strana]; in the country (countryside) в деревне [vdyi-ryev-nye]

countryside деревня [*dyi-ryev-nya*]

couple (*man and woman*) пара [*pahra*]; a couple of... несколько... [*nye-skolkuh*]

courier курьер [*koo-ryer*]

course (*of meal*) блюдо [*blyōōduh*]; of course конечно [*ka-nyesh-nuh*]; of course not конечно нет [*ka-nyesh-nuh nyet*]

court (*law*) суд [*sōōt*]; (*tennis*) корт [*kort*]

courtesy bus (*airport to hotel etc*) бесплатный автобус [*byiss-platnee avto-booss*]

cousin: my cousin (*male*) мой кузен [*moy koo-zyen*]; (*female*) моя кузина [*ma-ya koozeena*]

cow корова [*karova*]

crab краб [*krap*]

cracked (*plate etc*) треснувший [*tryess-noovshee*]

cracker (*biscuit*) крекер [*krye-kyer*]

craftshop художественный салон [*khoo-dozhist-vyinnee salon*]

cramp судорога [*sōō-daruga*]

crankshaft коленчатый вал [*ka-lyenchatee vahl*]

crash: there's been a crash произошла авария [*pra-izashla avari-ya*]

crash course интенсивный курс [*intyinseevnee koorss*]

crash helmet защитный шлем [*zash-cheetnee shlyem*]

crawl (*swimming*) кроль (*m*) [*krol*]

crazy сумасшедший [*sōōma-shedshee*]

cream (*on milk*) сливки [*sleefkee*]; (*for face, in cake*) крем [*kryem*]

crèche детские ясли [*dyetski-ye yah-slee*]

credit card кредитная карточка [*kryideetna-ya kartuchka*]

crib (*cot*) детская кроватка [*dyetska-ya kravatka*]

Crimea Крым [*krim*]

crisis кризис [*kreeziss*]

crisps хрустящий картофель [*khroo-styash-chee karto-fyil*]

crockery посуда [*passōōda*]

crook: he's a crook он мошенник [*on mashennik*]

crossing (*by sea*) переправа [*pryiri-prahva*]

crossroads перекрёсток [*pyiri-kryostuk*]

crosswalk переход [*pyiri-khot*]

crowd толпа [*talpa*]

crowded (*streets, bars*) переполненный народом [*pyiri-po-lnyinnee narodum*]

crown (*on tooth*) коронка [*karonka*]

crucial: it's absolutely crucial это совершенно необходимо [*ettuh sa-vyir-shennuh nye-abkhadeem-uh*]

cruise (*by ship*) круиз [*kroo-eez*]

crutch (*of body*) промежность (*f*) [*pra-myezhnust*]

crutches костыли [*kastilee*]

cry (*shout*) кричать/закричать [*kreechaht/za-krichaht*]; (*weep*) плакать/заплакать [*plahkat/za-plahkat*]; don't cry не плачь [*nye plach*]

cucumber огурец [*agoo-ryets*]

cuisine кухня [*kookh-nya*]

cultural культурный [*kool-tōōrnee*]

cup чашка [*chashka*]; a cup of coffee чашка кофе [*chashka koff-ye*]

cupboard шкаф [*shkaff*]

cure: have you got something to cure it? у вас есть средство что это болезни? [*ōō vass yist sryedst-vuh at ettoy ba-lyeznee*]

curlers бигуди [*bigoodee*]

current (*elec*) ток [*tok*]; (*in water*) течение [*tyi-cheni-ye*]

curry кэрри [*kerree*]

curtains занавески [*zana-vyeskee*]

curve (*noun: in road*) изгиб [*izgeep*]

cushion подушка [*padōōshka*]

custom обычай [*abeechı*]

Customs таможня [*tamozh-nya*]

cut: I've cut myself я порезался [*ya pa-ryezalsa*]; could you cut a little off here? можете отрезать чуть-чуть отсюда? [*mozhit-ye at-ryezat chōōt chōōt at-syōōda*]; we were cut off (*telec*) нас разъединили [*nass raz-yidineelee*]; the engine keeps cutting out двигатель всё время глохнет [*dveega-tyil fsyo vrye-mya glokh-nyet*]

cutlery ножевые изделия [*nazhevee-ye iz-dyeli-ya*]

cutlet отбивная котлета [*at-bivna-ya kat-lyeta*]

cycle: can we cycle there? велосипедом туда можно? [*vyi-lassi-pyedum tooda mozhnuh*]

cyclist велосипедист [*vyi-lassi-pyideest*]

cylinder (*of car*) цилиндр [*tsi-lindr*]

cylinder-head gasket прокладка цилиндра [*pra-klatka tsi-lindra*]

cynical циничный [*tsineech-nee*]

cystitis цистит [*tsisteet*]

Czechoslovakia Чехословакия [*chikha-slavahki-ya*]

D

damage: you've damaged it вы это испортили [*vee ettuh iss-portilee*]; it's damaged это повреждено [*ettuh pavryizh-dyino*]; there's no damage никакого ущерба нет [*nee-kakov-uh ooshcherba nyet*]

damn! к чёрту! [*kchor-tōō*]

damp (*adjective*) сырой [*siroy*]

dance: a Russian dance русский народный танец [*rooskee narodnee tanyits*]; do you want to dance? хотите танцевать? [*khatee-tye tantsivat*]

dancer: he's a good dancer он хорошо танцует [*on khara-sho tantsōō-yet*]

dancing: we'd like to go dancing мы хотим пойти танцевать [*mee khateem pıtee tantsivat*]; traditional (*Russian*) dancing традиционные русские танцы [*traditsi-onni-ye rooskee-ye tantsee*]

dandruff перхоть (*f*) [*pyerkhut*]

dangerous опасный [*apah-snee*]

dare: I don't dare я не смею [*ya nye smye-yōō*]

dark (*adjective*) тёмный [*tyom-nee*]; dark blue тёмно-синий [*tyom-nuh seenee*]; when does it get dark? когда темнеет? [*kagda tyim-nye-yit*]; after dark после наступления темноты [*poss-lye nastooplyeni-ya tyim-natee*]

darling (*man*) дорогой [*daragoy*]; (*woman*) дорогая [*daraga-ya*]

dashboard приборный щиток [*preebornee shchitok*]

date: what's the date? какое сегодня число? [*kako-ye syivo-dnya chislo*]; on what date? какого числа? [*kako-vuh chisla*]; can we make a date? (*romantic, to business partner*) можем договориться о встрече? [*mozhem da-gavareetsa a fstryech-e*]

dates (*to eat*) финики [*feenikee*]

daughter: my daughter моя дочь [*ma-ya doch*]

daughter-in-law сноха [*snakha*]

dawn (*noun*) рассвет [*ras-svyet*]; at dawn на рассвете [*na ras-svyet-ye*]

day день (*m*) [*dyin*]; the day after послезавтра [*pa-slyi-zahftra*]; the day before накануне [*nakanōō-nye*]; every day каждый день [*kazhdee dyin*]; one day однажды [*adnahzh-dee*]; can we pay by the day? можно оплачивать по суткам? [*mozhnuh a-plahchivat pa sōōtkam*]; have a good day! всего хорошего! [*fsyi-vo kharoshe-vuh*]

daylight robbery (*extortionate prices*) грабёж среди бела дня [*gra-byozh sryidee byela dnya*]

day trip экскурсия [*ekskōōrsi-ya*]

dead мёртвый [*myortvee*]

deaf глухой [*glookhoy*]

deaf-aid слуховой аппарат [*slookha-voy apparaht*]

deal (*business*) сделка [*zdyelka*]; it's a deal (*man*) согласен [*saglah-syin*]; (*woman*) согласна [*saglah-sna*]; will you deal with it? вы займётесь этим? [*vee zımyo-tyiss ettim*]

dealer (*agent*) торговый агент [*targovee a-gyent*]

dear (*expensive*) дорогой [*daragoy*]; Dear Comrades уважаемые товарищи [*ōōvazha-yemi-ye tavahrish-chee*]; Dear Sir уважаемый господин [*ōōvazha-yemee gaspadeen*]; Dear Madam уважаемая госпожа [*ōōvazha-yema-ya gaspazha*]; Dear Vanya милый Ваня [*meelee va-nya*]

death смерть (*f*) [*smyert*]

decadent декадент [*dyika-dyent*]

December декабрь (*m*) [*dyikabr*]

decent: that's very decent of you очень мило с вашей стороны [*ochin meel-uh zva-shay staranee*]

decide решать/решить [*ryishaht/ryisheet*]; we haven't decided yet мы ещё не решили [*mee yish-cho nye ryishee-lee*]; you decide for us можете вы за нас решить [*mozhit-ye vee za nass ryisheet*]; it's all decided уже всё решено [*oozh-e fsyo ryishino*]

decision решение [*ryisheni-ye*]

deck (*on ship*) палуба [*pahlooba*]

deckchair шезлонг [*shez-long*]

declare: I have nothing to declare у меня ничего нет, подлежащего пошлине [*ōō minya nee-chivo nyet pad-lyizhahsh-chivuh poshlin-ye*]

decoration (*in room*) украшение [*ōōkra-sheni-ye*]

deduct вычитать/вычесть [*vichitaht/ veechest*]

deep глубокий [*gloobokee*]; is it deep here? здесь глубоко? [*zdyiss gloobako*]

deep-freeze морозильник [*marazeel-nik*]

definitely разумеется [*razoo-mye-yitsa*]; definitely not ни в коем случае [*nee fko-yem slōōcha-ye*]

degree (*university*) степень (*f*) [*stye-pyin*]; (*temperature*) градус [*grahdooss*]

dehydrated: she is dehydrated она страдает дегидрацией [*ana strada-yet dyi-gidrahtsi-yay*]

de-icer антиобледенитель (*m*) [*anti-a-blyi-dyinee-tyil*]

delay: our flight was delayed наш рейс опоздал [*nash ryayss apazdal*]

deliberately нарочно [*naroch-nuh*]

delicacy: a local delicacy местный деликатес [*myestnee dyilika-tyess*]

delicious вкусный [*fkōō-snee*]

deliver: will you deliver it? можете это доставить? [*mozhit-ye ettuh dastahvit*]

delivery: is there another mail delivery today? сегодня будут ещё разносить письма? [*syivo-dnya bōō-dōōt yish-cho razna-seet peesma*]

de luxe первоклассный [*pyirva-klassnee*]

denims джинсы [*jeenzee*]

Denmark Дания [*dahni-ya*]

dent: there's a dent in it здесь вмятина [*zdyiss vmyatina*]

dental floss вощёная нитка для чистки зубов [*vash-chona-ya neetka dlya cheestkee zooboff*]

dentist зубной врач [*zoobnoy vrach*]

dentures зубной протез [*zoobnoy pra-tyess*]

deny: he denies it он отрицает это [*on atrit-sa-yit ettuh*]

deodorant дезодоратор [*dyiz-adarahtur*]

department store универмаг [*ooni-vyirmak*]

departure отъезд [*at-yezd*]

departure lounge зал ожидания [*zahl azhidani-ya*]

depend: it depends это зависит [*ettuh zavee-sit*]; it depends on ... это зависит от ... [*ettuh zavee-sit at*]

deposit (*downpayment*) задаток [*zadahtuk*]

depressed подавленный [*padahv-lyinee*]

depth глубина [*gloobina*]

description описание [*apissahni-ye*]

deserted (*beach, area*) безлюдный [*byiz-lyōōdnee*]

dessert сладкое блюдо [*slatkuh-ye blyōōduh*]

destination место назначения [*myestuh naz-nacheni-ya*]

detergent моющее средство [*mo-yōōsh-e-ye sryedst-vuh*]

detour объезд [*ab-yezd*]

devalue проводить девальвацию [*pravadeet dyi-valvahtsi-yōō*]

develop: could you develop these films? можете проявить эти плёнки? [*mozhit-ye pra-yaveet ettee plyonkee*]

diabetic (*noun*) диабетик [*dee-a-byetik*]

diagram диаграмма [*dee-a-grama*]

dialect диалект [*dee-a-lyekt*]

dialling code (*for city*) телефонный код города [*tyili-fonnee kod goruda*]

diamond (*mineral*) алмаз [*almass*]; (*gem*) бриллиант [*brilliant*]

diaper пелёнка [*pyi-lyonka*]

diarrhoea понос [*panoss*]; do you have something to stop diarrhoea? у вас есть что-то от поноса? [*ōō vass yist shto-tuh at panossa*]

diary (*business etc*) записная книжка-календарь [*zapissna-ya k-neezhka ka-lyindahr*]; (*for personal experiences*) дневник [*dnyivneek*]

dictionary словарь (*m*) [*slavar*]; a Russian-English dictionary русско-английский словарь [*rooskuh ang-gleeskee slavar*]

didn't *see* not *and page 117*

die умирать/умереть [*ōōmirat/ōō-myi-ryet*]; I'm absolutely dying for a drink мне очень хочется пить [*mnye ochin khochitsa peet*]

diesel (*fuel*) дизельное топливо [*dee-zyilnuh-ye toplivuh*]

diet диета [*dee-ye-ta*]; I'm on a diet я на диете [*ya na dee-ye-tye*]

difference разница [*raznitsa*]; what's the difference between ...? какая разница между ...? [*kaka-ya* ra*znitsa* m*yezh-doo*]; I can't tell the difference я не вижу никакой разницы [*ya nye veezhoo nee-kakoy raznitsee*]; it doesn't make any difference всё равно [*fsyo ravno*]

different: they are different они отличаются друг от друга [*anee atlicha-yootsa drook at drooga*]; **they are very different** они совершенно разные [*anee sa-vyirshen-uh rahzni-ye*]; **it's different from this one** это совсем не то, что это [*ettuh sav-syem nye to shto ettuh*]; **may we have a different table?** нам хотелось бы сесть к другому столику [*nam kha-tyeluss bee syist k droo-gomoo stolikoo*]; **ah well, that's different** ну да, это совсем другое дело [*noo da ettuh sav-syem droogo-ye dyeluh*]

difficult трудный [*troodnee*]

difficulty затруднение [*zatrood-nyeni-ye*]; (*obstacle*) препятствие [*pryi-pyatstvi-ye*]; **without any difficulty** без труда [*byess trooda*]; **I'm having difficulties with ...** у меня проблемы с ... [*oo minya pra-blyemee s*]

digestion пищеварение [*peeshchiva-ryeni-ye*]

dining car вагон-ресторан [*vagon ryistaran*]

dining room столовая [*stalova-ya*]

dinner ужин [*oozhin*]

dinner jacket смокинг [*smokink*]

dinner party званый ужин [*zvahnee oozhin*]

dipped headlights ближний свет фар [*bleezhnee svyet far*]

dipstick указатель уровня [*ookazah-tyil ooruv-nya*]

direct (*adjective*) прямой [*pryamoy*]; **does this train go direct?** этот поезд идёт без пересадки [*ettut po-yezd ee-dyot byez pyiri-satkee*]

direction направление [*naprav-lyeni-ye*]; **in which direction is it?** в каком это направлении? [*fkakom ettuh naprav-lyeni-ee*]; **is it in this direction?** это в этом направлении? [*ettuh vettum naprav-lyeni-ee*]

directory: telephone directory телефонный справочник [*tyili-fonnee sprah-vuch-nik*]

directory enquiries справочная [*sprahvuchna-ya*]

dirt грязь (*f*) [*gryass*]

dirty (*hands, sheets, room*) грязный [*gryaznee*]; (*habit*) непристойный [*nyi-preestoy-nee*]

disabled инвалид [*invaleet*]

disagree: it disagrees with me (*food*) это плохо действует на мой желудок [*ettuh plokhuh dyayst-voo-yit na moy zhilooduk*]; **I disagree** (*man*) я несогласен [*ya nyi-saglah-syin*]; (*woman*) я несогласна [*ya nyi-saglah-sna*]

disappear исчезать/исчезнуть [*iss-chizaht/iss-cheznoot*]; **it's just disappeared** это пропало [*ettuh pra-pahluh*]

disappointed: I was disappointed меня это разочаровало [*minya ettuh raz-acharaval-uh*]

disappointing: we found the concert disappointing концерт нас разочаровал [*kantsert nass raz-acharavahl*]

disaster катастрофа [*kata-strofa*]

discharge (*pus*) выделение [*vee-dyi-lyeni-ye*]

disc jockey диск-джокей [*disk-jokay*]

disco дискотека [*diska-tyeka*]

disco dancing танцы в дискотеке [*tantsee fdiska-tyek-ye*]

discount (*noun*) скидка [*skeetka*]

disease болезнь (*f*) [*ba-lyezn*]

disgusting отвратительный [*atvratee-tyilnee*]

dish (*meal*) блюдо [*blyooduh*]; (*plate*) миска [*meeska*]

dishcloth кухонное полотенце [*kookhunuh-ye pala-tyents-e*]

dishwashing liquid жидкость для мытья посуды [*zheetkust dlya mi-tya pa-soodee*]

disinfectant (*noun*) дезинфицирующее средство [*dyiz-infitseeroo-yoosh-che-ye sryed-stvuh*]

dislocated shoulder вывихнутое плечо [*veevikh-nootuh-ye plyicho*]

dispensing chemist фармацевт [*farma-tseft*]

disposable nappies бумажные пелёнки [*boomazhni-ye pyi-lyonkee*]

dissident диссидент [*dissi-dyent*]

distance расстояние [*rasta-yani-ye*]; **what's the distance from ... to ...?** как далеко от ... до ...? [*kak da-lyiko at ... da ...*]; **in the distance** вдали [*vdalee*]

distilled water дистиллированная вода [*distilli-rovana-ya vada*]

distributor (*in car*) распределитель зажигания [*rass-pryi-dyilee-tyil za-zhigahni-ya*]

disturb: the disco is disturbing us нам мешает шум дискотеки [*nam myisha-yit shōōm diska-tyekee*]

diversion (*traffic*) объезд [*ab-yezd*]

diving board трамплин [*trampleen*]

divorced разведённый [*razvi-dyonee*]

dizzy: I feel dizzy у меня кружится голова [*ōō minya krōō-zhitsa galava*]; I get dizzy spells у меня время от времени кружится голова [*ōō minya vrye-mya at vrye-myinee krōō-zhitsa galava*]

do делать/сделать [*dyelat/zdyelat*]; what shall I do? что мне делать? [*shto mnye dyelat*]; what are you doing tonight? что вы делаете сегодня вечером? [*shto vee dyela-yit-ye syivo-dnya vyechirum*]; how do you do it? как это сделать? [*kak ettuh zdye-lat*]; will you do it for me? пожалуйста, сделайте это для меня [*pa-zhahlsta zdye-lı-tye ettuh dlya minya*]; who did it? кто это сделал? [*kto ettuh zdye-lal*]; the meat's not done мясо не прожарено [*mya-suh nye prazha-ryinuh*]; what do you do? кем вы работаете? [*kyem vee rabota-yitye*]; do you have ...? у вас есть ...? [*ōō vas yist*]

docks пристань (*f*) [*preestan*]

doctor врач [*vrach*]; he needs a doctor ему нужен врач [*yimōō nōōzhen vrach*]; can you call a doctor? вызовите, пожалуйста, врача [*veezavee-tye pa-zhalsta vracha*]

document документ [*dakōō-myent*]

dog собака [*sabahka*]

doll кукла [*kōōkla*]

dollar доллар [*dollar*]

donkey осёл [*a-syol*]

don't! перестань! [*pyiri-stan*]; see **not** *and page 117*

door дверь (*f*) [*dvyer*]; (*of car*) дверца [*dvyertsa*]

doorman швейцар [*shvay-tsar*]

dosage доза [*doza*]

double: double room двойной номер [*dvi-noy no-myir*]; double bed двуспальная кровать [*dvoo-spalna-ya kravat*]; double brandy двойной коньяк [*dvi-noy kan-yak*]; double "s" два "с" [*dva ess*]; it's all double Dutch to me мне это совершенно непонятно [*mnye ettuh sa-vyirshen-uh nyi-panyat-nuh*]

doubt: I doubt it я сомневаюсь [*ya sam-nyiva-yōōss*]

douche (*medical*) обливание [*ab-livahni-ye*]

doughnut пончик [*pon-chik*]

down: get down! спуститесь! [*spōō-stee-tyiss*]; he's not down yet (*is in room*) он всё ещё в своём номере [*on fsyo yish-cho fsva-yom no-myi-rye*]; further down the road дальше по этой дороге [*dalsh-e pa ettoy daro-gye*]; I paid 20% down я заплатил 20% наличными [*ya za-plateel dvad-sat pra-tsentuff na-leech-numee*]

downmarket (*restaurant, hotel*) второсортный [*vtara-sortnee*]

downstairs внизу [*vneezōō*]; (*go*) вниз [*vneess*]

dozen дюжина [*dyōōzhina*]; half a dozen полдюжины [*pal-dyōōzhinee*]

drain (*in sink, street*) канализация [*kana-leezahtsi-ya*]

draughts (*game*) шашки [*shash-kee*]

draughty: it's draughty here здесь сквозняк [*zdyiss skvaz-nyak*]

drawing pin кнопка [*k-nopka*]

dreadful ужасный [*ōōzhah-snee*]

dream (*noun*) сон [*son*]; it's like a bad dream это кошмар [*ettuh kash-mar*]

dress (*woman's*) платье [*plah-tye*]; I'll just get dressed я сейчас оденусь [*ya si-chass a-dyenōōss*]

dressing (*for wound*) перевязка [*pyiri-vyaska*]; (*for salad*) приправа [*pree-prava*]

dressing gown халат [*khalaht*]

drink (*verb*) пить/выпить [*peet/veepeet*]; can I get you a drink? вы хотите выпить что-нибудь? [*vee khateet-ye veepeet shto-nee-bōōt*]]; I don't drink я не пью [*ya nye pyōō*]; I must have something to drink мне нужно выпить что-нибудь [*mnye nōōzh-nuh veepeet shto-nee-bōōt*]; a long cool drink большой стакан холодного напитка [*bal-shoy stakan kha-lodnuv-uh na-peetka*]; may I have a drink of water? дайте мне, пожалуйста, стакан воды [*dı-tye mnye pa-zhahlsta stakan vadee*]; drink up! допейте! [*da-pyay-tye*]; I had too much to drink я выпил слишком много [*ya veepil sleesh-kum mnoguh*]

drinkable: is the water drinkable? это питьевая вода? [*ettuh pee-tyiva-ya vada*]

drive: we drove here мы приехали сюда на машине [*mee pree-yekhalee syōōda na masheen-ye*]; I'll drive you home я отвезу вас домой [*ya at-vyiz*$\overline{oo}$ *vas damoy*]; do you want to come for a drive with us? вы хотите поехать покататься с нами? [*vee khatee-tye pa-yekhat pakatahtsa snahmee*]; it's a very long drive это далеко ехать [*ettuh da-lyiko yekhat*]

driver водитель [*vadee-tyil*]

driver's license водительские права [*vadee-tyilski-ye prava*]

drive shaft трансмиссия [*transmissi-ya*]

driving licence водительские права [*vadee-tyilski-ye prava*]

drizzle: it's drizzling моросит [*mara-seet*]

drop: just a drop (*of drink*) чуть-чуть [*ch*$\overline{oo}$*t ch*$\overline{oo}$*t*]; I dropped it я уронил это [*ya* $\overline{oo}$*raneel ettuh*]; drop in some time заходите когда-нибудь [*za-khadeet-ye kagda nee-b*$\overline{oo}$*t*]

drown: he's drowning он тонет [*on to-nyit*]

drug (*medical*) лекарство [*lyi-karst-vuh*]; (*narcotic*) наркотик [*narkotik*]

drunk (*adjective*) пьяный [*pyanee*]

drunk driving вождение автомобиля в нетрезвом виде [*vazh-dyeni-ye avta-mabee-lya vnyi-tryezvum vee-dye*]

dry (*adjective*) сухой [*sookhoy*]

dry-clean: can I get these dry-cleaned? можно это подвергнуть химической чистке? [*mozhnuh ettuh pad-vyergn*$\overline{oo}$*t khimee-chiskoy cheest-kye*]

dry-cleaner химчистка [*khim-cheestka*]

duck утка [$\overline{oo}$*tka*]

due: when is the bus due? когда прибывает автобус? [*kagda pree-biva-yit avto-booss*]

dumb (*can't speak*) немой [*nyimoy*]; (*stupid*) глупый [*gl*$\overline{oo}$*pee*]

dummy (*for baby*) соска-пустышка [*soska poosteeshka*]

durex (*tm*) презерватив [*pryi-zirvateef*]

during в течение [*ftyicheni-ye*]

dust пыль (*f*) [*peel*]

dustbin мусорный ящик [*m*$\overline{oo}$*-sornee yash-chik*]

duty-free (*goods*) не подлежащий обложению таможенной пошлиной [*nye pad-lyizha-sh-chee abla-zheni-y*$\overline{oo}$ *tamo-zhenoy poshlinoy*]

dynamo динамо [*dee-nahmuh*]

dysentery дизентерия [*dizin-tyiree-ya*]

E

each: each of them каждый из них [*kazh-dee iz neekh*]; each time каждый раз [*kazh-dee rass*]; how much are they each? сколько стоит каждый? [*skol-kuh sto-yit kazh-dee*]; give us one each дайте нам по одному [*d*ι*-tye nam pa adna-m*$\overline{oo}$]; we know each other мы знакомы [*mee znakomee*]

ear ухо [$\overline{oo}$*kh-uh*]

earache: I have earache у меня болит ухо [$\overline{oo}$ *minya baleet* $\overline{oo}$*kh-uh*]

early ранний [*rahn-nee*]; early in the morning рано утром [*rahn-uh* $\overline{oo}$*trum*]; it's too early слишком рано [*sleesh-kum rahn-uh*]; a day earlier на день раньше [*na dyin rahnsh-e*]; half an hour earlier на полчаса раньше [*na palchassa rahnsh-e*]; I need an early night я должен лечь спать пораньше [*ya dolzhen lyech spaht pa-rahnsh-e*]

early riser: I'm an early riser я обычно рано встаю [*ya abeech-nuh rahn-uh fsta-y*$\overline{oo}$]

earring серьга [*syirga*]

earth (*soil*) земля [*zim-lya*]

earthenware глиняная посуда [*glee-nyana-ya pa-s*$\overline{oo}$*da*]

earwig уховёртка [$\overline{oo}$*kha-vyortka*]

east восток [*vastok*]; in the east на востоке [*na vastok-ye*]; to the east of ... к востоку от ... [*k-vastok*$\overline{oo}$ *at*]

Easter Пасха [*pah-skha*]

easy лёгкий [*lyokh-kee*]; easy with the cream! не так много сливок! [*nye tak mnoguh sleevuk*]

eat есть/съесть [*yist/syist*]; something to eat что-нибудь поесть [*shto-nib*$\overline{oo}$*t pa-yist*]; we've already eaten мы уже поели [*mee oozh-e pa-yelee*]

eau-de-Cologne одеколон [*a-dyikalon*]

eccentric чудаковатый [*ch*$\overline{oo}$*odaka-vahtee*]

edible съедобный [*syi-dobnee*]

efficient хорошо организованный [*khara-sho argani-zovannee*]

egg яйцо [*y*ι*tso*]

eggplant баклажан [*baklazhan*]

Eire Эйре [*e-rye*]

either: either ... or ... или ...или ... [*eelee*... *eelee*]; I don't like either of them мне ни одно не нравится [*mnye nee adno nye nrahvitsa*]; I don't like it either мне тоже не нравится [*mnye tozh-e nye nrahvitsa*]; either will do подойдёт и тот и другой [*padɪ-dyot ee tot ee droogoy*]

elastic (*noun*) резинка [*ryi-zeenka*]

elastic band резинка [*ryi-zeenka*]

Elastoplast (*tm*) лейкопластырь (*m*) [*lyayka-plasteer*]

elbow локоть (*m*) [*lokut*]

electric электрический [*e-lyektreechi-skee*]

electric blanket электро-одеяло [*e-lyektra-a-dyi-yahluh*]

electric cooker электрическая духовка [*e-lyek-treechiska-ya dōokhofka*]

electric fire электро-камин [*e-lyektra-kameen*]

electrician электромонтёр [*e-lyektra-mantyor*]

electricity электричество [*e-lyektreechistvuh*]

electric outlet розетка [*ra-zyetka*]

elegant элегантный [*e-lyigant-nee*]

elevator лифт [*leeft*]

else: something else что-то другое [*shto-tuh drōogo-ye*]; somewhere else где-нибудь в другом месте [*gdye-nibōot vdrōogom myest-ye*]; let's go somewhere else давайте пойдём куда-то в другое место [*davɪ-tye pɪ-dyom kōoda-tuh vdrōogo-ye myestuh*]; what else? что ещё? [*shto yish-cho*]; nothing else, thanks спасибо, ничего больше не хочу [*spa-see-buh neechivo bolsh-e nye khachōo*]

embarrassed: he's embarrassed он стесняется [*on styiss-nya-yitsa*]

embarrassing смущающий [*smoosh-cha-yoosh-chee*]

embassy посольство [*pa-solstvuh*]

emergency критическое положение [*kritee-chiskuh-ye palazheni-ye*]; this is an emergency это критический случай [*ettuh kritee-chiskee slōochɪ*]

emery paper наждачная бумага [*nazh-dachna-ya boomahga*]

emotional эмоциональный [*ematsianahl-nee*]

empty пустой [*pōostoy*]

end (*noun*) конец [*ka-nyets*]; at the end of the road в конце улицы [*vkants-e ōolitse*] when does it end? когда это кончается? [*kagda ettuh kancha-yitsa*]

energetic энергичный [*e-nyirgeech-nee*]

energy энергия [*e-nyergi-ya*]

engaged (*to be married*) обручённый [*abroo-chonnee*]; (*toilet*) занято [*zah-nyatuh*]

engagement ring обручальное кольцо [*abroo-chalnuh-ye kaltso*]

engine (*motor*) двигатель (*m*) [*dveega-tyil*]; (*railway*) локомотив [*laka-mateef*]

engine trouble проблемы с мотором [*pra-blyemee smatorum*]

England Англия [*an-gli-ya*]

English английский [*ang-gleeskee*]; (*language*) английский язык [*ang-gleeskee yazik*]; the English англичане [*ang-gleechahn-ye*]; I'm English (*man*) я англичанин [*ya ang-gleechah-nin*]; (*woman*) я англичанка [*ya ang-gleechahnka*]; do you speak English? вы говорите по-английски? [*vee gavareet-ye pa-ang-gleeskee*]

Englishman англичанин [*ang-gleechah-nin*]

Englishwoman англичанка [*ang-gleechahnka*]

enjoy: I enjoyed it very much мне очень понравилось [*mnye ochin pan-rahviluss*]; enjoy yourself! желаю приятно провести время [*zhelah-yōo pree-yahtnuh pra-vyistee vrye-mya*]

enjoyable приятный [*pree-yahtnee*]

enlargement (*of photo*) увеличение [*ōo-vyili-cheni-ye*]

enormous огромный [*agromnee*]

enough достаточно [*dastahtuch-nuh*]; there's not enough недостаточно [*nyi-dastahtuch-nuh*]; it's not big enough это недостаточно большой [*ettuh nyi-dastahtuch-nuh bal-shoy*]; thank you, that's enough спасибо, этого достаточно [*spa-see-buh ettuvuh dastahtuch-nuh*]

entertainment развлечение [*raz-vlyicheni-ye*]

enthusiastic восторженный [*vastor-zhennee*]

entrance (*noun*) вход [*fkhot*]

envelope конверт [*kan-vyert*]

epileptic эпилептик [*epi-lyeptik*]

equipment (*in apartment*) оборудование [*aba-rōoduvani-ye*]; (*for climbing etc*) снаряжение [*sna-ryazheni-ye*]

eraser резинка [*ryizeenka*]

erotic эротический [*era-teechiskee*]

error ошибка [*asheepka*]

escalator эскалатор [*eskalahtur*]

especially особенно [*a-so-byinnuh*]

espionage шпионаж [*shpee-anahsh*]

essential: it is essential that ... необходимо, чтобы ... [*nyi-abkhadeem-uh*]

Estonia Эстония [*estoni-ya*]

ethnic (*restaurant, clothes*) в народном стиле [*vnarodnum steel-ye*]

Europe Европа [*yivropa*]

European (*adjective*) европейский [*yivra-pyay-skee*]; (*man*) европеец [*yivra-pye-yits*]; (*woman*) европейка [*yivra-pyayka*]

even: even the English даже англичане [*dahzh-e ang-gleechahn-ye*]; even if ... даже если ... [*dahzh-e ye-slee*]

evening вечер [*vyechir*]; good evening добрый вечер [*dobree vyechir*]; this evening сегодня вечером [*syivo-dnya vyechirum*]; in the evening вечером [*vyechirum*]; evening meal ужин [*ōōzhin*]

evening dress (*for man*) фрак [*frak*]; (*for woman*) вечернее платье [*vyicher-nye-ye plah-tye*]

eventually в конце концов [*fkants-e kantsoff*]

ever: have you ever been to ...? вы когда-либо бывали в ...? [*vee kagda-leebuh bivahlee v*]; if you ever come to Britain если вы когда-либо будете в Великобритании [*ye-slee vee kagda-leebuh bōō-dyi-tye v-vyilika-britani-ee*]

every каждый [*kazh-dee*]; every day каждый день [*kazh-dee dyin*]

everyone все [*fsye*]

everything всё [*fsyo*]

everywhere всюду [*fsyōō-dōō*]

exactly! вот именно! [*vot ee-myinnuh*]

exam экзамен [*ekzah-myin*]

example пример [*pri-myer*]; for example например [*napri-myer*]

excellent отличный [*at-leechnee*]; excellent! отлично! [*at-leechnuh*]

except кроме [*kro-mye*]; except Sunday кроме воскресенья [*kro-mye vaskri-syen-ya*]

exception исключение [*iss-klyōōcheni-ye*]; as an exception в виде исключения [*v-vee-dye iss-klyōōcheni-ya*]

excess baggage перевес багажа [*pyiri-vyess bagazha*]

excessive чрезмерный [*chryiz-myernee*]; that's a bit excessive это уж слишком [*ettuh ōōzh sleesh-kum*]

exchange (*verb: money*) менять/поменять [*myi-nyaht/pa-myi-nyaht*]; in exchange в обмен [*vab-myen*]

exchange rate: what's the exchange rate? каков курс дня? [*kakoff kōōrss dnya*]

exchange student студент, приехавший по обмену [*stoo-dyent pree-yekhavshee pa ab-myenōō*]

exciting (*day, holiday, film*) увлекательный [*ōō-vlyikah-tyilnee*]

exclusive (*club, hotel*) с ограниченным доступом [*sagra-neechinnim dostōōpum*]

excursion экскурсия [*eks-kōōrsi-ya*]; is there an excursion to ...? есть ли у вас экскурсия в ...? [*yist lee ōō vass eks-kōōrsi-ya v*]

excuse me (*to get past*) извините! [*izvinee-tye*]; (*to get attention*) простите [*pra-stee-tye*]; (*pardon?*) что вы сказали? [*shto vee skazahlee*]; (*sorry*) виноват [*veenavaht*]

exhaust (*on car*) выхлопная труба [*vikhlapna-ya trōōba*]

exhausted (*tired*) измученный [*iz-mōōchinnee*]

exhibition выставка [*vee-stafka*]

exist: does it still exist? это ещё существует? [*ettuh yish-cho sōōsh-chist-vōō-yit*]

exit выход [*veekhot*]

expect: I expect so думаю, что да [*dōōma-yōō shto da*]; she's expecting она беременна [*ana byi-rye-myenna-ya*]

expensive дорогой [*daragoy*]

experience: it's an absolutely unforgettable experience это совершенно незабываемо [*ettuh sa-vyirshenn-uh nyi-zabiva-yimuh*]

experienced опытный [*opitnee*]

expert специалист [*spetsialeest*]

expire: my visa's expired моя виза просрочена [*ma-ya veeza pra-srochina*]

explain объяснять/объяснить [*ab-yass-nyaht/ ab-yassneet*]; would you explain that to me? можете мне это объяснить? [*mozhit-ye mnye ettuh ab-yassneet*]

explore исследовать [*is-slyeduvaht*]; I just want to go and explore я только хочу пойти и посмотреть [*ya tol-kuh khachōō ptee ee pa-sma-tryet*]

export (*verb*) вывозить [*vee-vazeet*]; (*noun*) вывоз [*veevuss*]

exposure meter экспонометр [*ekspano-myetr*]

express (*mail*) срочное отправление [*srochnuh-ye atprav-lyeni-ye*]; (*train*) экспресс [*ekspress*]

extra: can we have an extra chair? дайте нам, пожалуйста, ещё один стул [*dı-tye nam pa-zhahlsta yish-cho adeen stool*]; is that extra? (*in cost*) это за дополнительную оплату? [*ettuh za dapalnee-tyilnoo-yoo aplahtoo*]

extraordinarily необычайно [*nyi-abichnuh*]

extraordinary (*very strange*) очень странный [*ochin strannee*]

extremely крайне [*krı-nye*]

extrovert экстроверт [*ekstra-vyert*]

eye глаз [*glass*]; will you keep an eye on my bags for me? присмотрите, пожалуйста, за моим багажом [*preesmatree-tye pa-zhahlsta za ma-yeem bagazhom*]

eyebrow бровь (*f*) [*broff*]

eyebrow pencil карандаш для бровей [*karandash dlya bra-vyay*]

eye drops глазные капли [*glaznee-ye kahplee*]

eyeliner карандаш для подкрашивания глаз [*karandash dlya pad-krahshivani-ya glass*]

eye shadow тени для век [*tyenee dlya vyek*]

eye witness очевидец [*achivee-dyits*]

F

fabulous замечательный [*za-myichah-tyilnee*]

face лицо [*litso*]

face cloth (*flannel*) тряпочка для лица [*tryapuchka dlya litsa*]

face mask (*for diving*) маска [*maska*]

face pack (*cosmetic*) косметическая маска [*kaz-myiteechiska-ya maska*]

facing: facing the street выходящий на улицу [*vikha-dyash-chee na oolitsoo*]

fact факт [*fakt*]

factory завод [*zavot*]

Fahrenheit *see page 121*

faint: she's fainted она упала в обморок [*ana oopahla vobmuruk*]; I'm going to faint я упаду в обморок [*ya oopadoo vobmuruk*]

fair (*fun-fair*) ярмарка [*yarmarka*]; (*commercial*) выставка [*veestafka*]; it's not fair это несправедливо [*ettuh nyi-spravyidlee-vuh*]; OK, fair enough ладно, согласен [*lahdnuh saglah-syin*]

fake подделка [*pad-dyelka*]

fall: he's had a fall он упал [*on oopahl*]; he fell off his bike он упал с велосипеда [*on oopahl zvyilassi-pyeda*]; in the fall (*autumn*) осенью [*o-syin-yoo*]

false ложный [*lozhnee*]

false teeth вставные зубы [*fstavnee-ye zoobee*]

family семья [*syim-ya*]

family hotel частная гостиница [*chastna-ya gastee-nitsa*]

family name фамилия [*fameeli-ya*]

famished: I'm famished я умираю с голоду [*ya oomira-yoo zgoludoo*]

famous знаменитый [*zna-myineetee*]

fan (*mechanical*) вентилятор [*vyintilyahtur*]; (*hand held*) веер [*vye-yir*]; (*football etc*) болельщик [*ba-lyelsh-chik*]; (*film etc*) поклонник [*paklonnik*]

fan belt ремень вентилятора [*ryi-myen vyinti-lyahtura*]

fancy: he fancies you вы ему нравитесь [*vee yimoo nrahvi-tyiss*]

fancy dress party маскарад [*maskarat*]

fantastic фантастический [*fanta-steechiskee*]

far далеко [*da-lyiko*]; is it far? это далеко? [*ettuh da-lyiko*]; how far is it to ...? как далеко до ...? [*kak da-lyiko da*]; as far as I'm concerned что касается меня [*shto ka-sa-yitsa minya*]

fare стоимость проезда [*sto-yimust pra-yezda*]; what's the fare to ...? сколько стоит проезд в ...? [*skol-kuh sto-yit pra-yezd v*]

farewell party прощальная вечеринка [*prash-chalna-ya vyichirinka*]

farm ферма [*fyerma*]; (*collective farm*) колхоз [*kalkhoz*]; (*state farm*) совхоз [*savkhoz*]

farther дальше [*dalsh-e*]; farther than ... более отдалённый чем ... [*bo-lye-ye atda-lyonnee chem*]

fashion (*clothes*) мода [*moda*]

fashionable модный [*modnee*]

fast быстрый [*beestree*]; not so fast не так быстро [*nye tak beestruh*]

fastener (*on clothes*) застёжка [*za-styozhka*]

fat (*person*) толстый [*tolstee*]; (*on meat*) жир [*zhir*]

father: my father мой отец [*moy a-tyets*]

father-in-law (*father of husband*) свёкор [*svyokur*]; (*father of wife*) тесть [*tyest*]

fathom морская сажень [*marska-ya sazhen*]

fattening (*food*) сытный [*seetnee*]

faucet кран [*krahn*]

fault (*defect*) недостаток [*nyi-dastahtuk*]; it was my fault я виноват [*ya veenavaht*]; it's not my fault я не виноват [*ya nye veenavaht*]

faulty испорченный [*ispor-chennee*]

favo(u)rite любимый [*lyōō-beemee*]; that's my favo(u)rite это мой любимый [*ettuh moy lyōō-beemee*]

fawn (*colour*) желтовато-коричневый [*zhelta-vatuh kareech-nyivee*]

February февраль (*m*) [*fyivrahl*]

fed up: I'm fed up мне надоело [*mnye nada-yeluh*]; I'm fed up with excursions мне надоели экскурсии [*mnye nada-yelee eks-kōōrsi-ee*]

feeding bottle бутылочка [*boo-teeluchka*]

feel: I feel hot/cold мне жарко/холодно [*mnye zharkuh/kholud-nuh*]; I feel like a drink мне хочется пить [*mnye khochitsa peet*]; I don't feel like it мне не хочется [*mnye nye khochitsa*]; how are you feeling? как вы себя чувствуете? [*kak vee sibya chōōst-vōō-yit-ye*]; I'm feeling a lot better мне намного лучше [*mnye nam-noguh lōōch-e*]

felt-tip (*pen*) фламастер [*flamah-styir*]

fence забор [*zabor*]

fender (*of car*) крыло [*krilo*]

ferry паром [*parom*]; what time's the last ferry? когда отходит последний паром? [*kagda at-khodit pa-slyednee parom*]

festival фестиваль (*m*) [*fyistival*]

fetch: I'll go and fetch it я пойду и принесу это [*ya pɪdōō ee pree-nyi-sōō ettuh*]; will you come and fetch me? вы зайдёте за мной? [*vee zɪ-dyo-tye zamnoy*]

fever лихорадка [*leekha-ratka*]

feverish: I'm feeling feverish меня лихорадит [*minya leekha-radeet*]

few: only a few всего несколько [*fsyivo nye-skolkuh*]; a few minutes несколько минут [*nye-skolkuh minōōt*]; he's had a

good few (*to drink*) он выпил довольно много [*on veepeel davolnuh mnoguh*]

fiancé: my fiancé мой жених [*moy zheneekh*]

fiancée: my fiancée моя невеста [*ma-ya nyi-vyesta*]

fiasco: what a fiasco! полный провал! [*polnee pravahl*]

field поле [*po-lye*]

fifty-fifty разделённый пополам [*raz-dyi-lyonnee papalam*]

fig фига [*feega*]; figs инжир [*inzheer*]

fight (*noun*) драка [*draka*]

figure (*of person*) фигура [*figōōra*]; (*number*) цифра [*tseefra*]; I have to watch my figure я слежу за фигурой [*ya slyizhōō za figōōroy*]

fill наполнять/наполнить [*napal-nyat/na-polneet*]; fill her up please заливайте бак доверху [*zaleevɪ-tye bak do-vyirkhōō*]; will you help me fill out this form? помогите, пожалуйста, заполнить бланк? [*pama-gee-tye pa-zhahlsta za-polneet blank*]

filling (*in tooth*) пломба [*plomba*]; it's very filling (*food*) эта пища очень сытная [*etta peesh-cha ochin seetna-ya*]

filling station бензозаправочная станция [*byinza-zaprahvuchna-ya stantsi-ya*]

film (*in cinema*) кинофильм [*keena-feelm*]; (*for camera*) плёнка [*plyonka*]; do you have this type of film? у вас есть плёнка такой марки? [*ōō vass yist plyonka takoy markee*]; 16mm film 16-миллиметровая плёнка [*shist-nahd-tsati-milli-myetrova-ya plyonka*]; 35mm film 35мм плёнка [*trid-tsati-pyatee-milli-myetrova-ya plyonka*]

filter (*for camera, coffee*) фильтр [*filtr*]

filter-tipped с фильтром [*sfiltrum*]

filthy (*room etc*) грязный [*gryaznee*]

find находить/найти [*nakhadeet/ntee*]; I can't find it я не могу найти [*ya nye magōō ntee*]; if you find it если вы найдёте [*ye-slee vee n-dyo-tye*]; I've found a ... (*man*) я нашёл ... [*ya nashol*]; (*woman*) я нашла ... [*ya nashla*]

fine: it's fine weather хорошая погода [*kharosha-ya pagoda*]; a 30 rouble fine штраф в 30 рублей [*shtraf ftreed-tsat roob-lyay*]; how are you? - fine thanks как жизнь? - спасибо, хорошо [*kak zheezn - spa-see-buh khara-sho*]

finger палец [*pah-lyits*]

fingernail ноготь [*nogut*]

finish: I haven't finished я ещё не кончил [*ya yish-cho nye konchil*]; when I've finished когда я кончу [*kagda ya konchōō*]; when does it finish? когда кончается? [*kagda kancha-yitsa*]; finish off your drink допейте, пожалуйста [*da-pyay-tye pa-zhahlsta*]

Finland Финляндия [*fin-lyandi-ya*]

fire: fire! пожар! [*pazhar*]; may we light a fire here? здесь можно разложить костёр? [*zdyiss mozh-nuh razlazheet ka-styor*]; it's on fire горит [*gareet*]; it's not firing properly (*car*) зажигание не работает [*za-zhigahni-ye nye rabota-yet*]

fire alarm пожарная тревога [*pazharna-ya tryivoga*]

fire brigade/department пожарная команда [*pazharna-ya kamanda*]

fire escape пожарный выход [*pazharnee veekhut*]

fire extinguisher огнетушитель [*ag-nyitooshee-tyil*]

firm (*company*) фирма [*feerma*]

first первый [*pyervee*]; I was first (*man*) я был первым [*ya beel pyervum*]; (*woman*) я была первой [*ya bila pyervoy*]; at first сначала [*sna-chahla*]; the first time первый раз [*pyervee rass*]; for the first time впервые [*fpyirvee-ye*]

first aid скорая помощь [*skora-ya pomushch*]

first aid kit аптечка [*aptyechka*]

first class первый класс [*pyervee klass*]; a first class hotel первоклассная гостиница [*pyirva-klassna-ya gastee-nitsa*]

first name имя [*ee-mya*]

fish (*noun*) рыба [*reeba*]

fisherman рыбак [*ribak*]

fishing рыбная ловля [*reebna-ya lov-lya*]

fishing boat рыбачья лодка [*ribach-ya lotka*]

fishing net рыболовная сеть [*ribalovna-ya syet*]

fishing rod удочка [*ōōduchka*]

fishing tackle рыболовные снасти [*ribalov-nuh-ye snastee*]

fishing village рыбачий посёлок [*ribachee pa-syoluk*]

fit (*healthy*) здоровый [*zdarovee*]; I'm not very fit мне неважно [*mnye nyi-vazhnuh*]; he's a keep fit fanatic он заядлый физкультурник [*on za-yadlee fizkool-tōōrnik*]; it doesn't fit me это не сидит на

мне хорошо [*ettuh nye seedeet na mnye khara-sho*]

fix: can you fix it? можете починить? [*mozhit-ye pachineet*]; let's fix a time давайте договоримся когда встретимся [*davi-tye dagavareem-sa kagda fstryetim-sa*]; it's all fixed up всё готово [*fsyo gatovuh*]; I'm in a bit of a fix я попал в затруднительное положение [*ya papahl vza-troodnee-tyilnuh-ye palazheni-ye*]

fizzy газированный [*gazeer-ovannee*]

fizzy drink газированный напиток [*gazeer-ovannee na-peetuk*]

flabby вялый [*vyalee*]

flag флаг [*flak*]

flannel тряпочка для лица [*tryapuchka dlya litsa*]

flash (*for camera*) вспышка [*fspeeshka*]

flashlight фонарик [*fanarik*]

flashy (*clothes etc*) кричащий [*kreechash-chee*]

flat (*adjective*) гладкий [*glatkee*]; this beer is flat это пиво выдохлось [*ettuh peevuh veedukh-luss*]; a flat tyre/tire спущенная шина [*spōōsh-chenna-ya sheena*]; (*apartment*) квартира [*kvarteera*]

flatterer льстец [*l-styets*]

flatware (*cutlery*) столовые приборы [*stalovuh-ye priboree*]; (*crockery*) посуда [*pa-sōōda*]

flavo(u)r вкус [*fkōōss*]

flea блоха [*blakha*]

flea powder порошок от блох [*parashok at blokh*]

flexible гибкий [*geepkee*]

flies (*on trousers*) ширинка [*shireenka*]

flight полёт [*pa-lyot*]; flight number ... рейс номер ... [*ryayss no-myir*]

flippers ласты [*lahstee*]

flirt кокетничать [*ka-kyetnichat*]

float плавать [*plahvat*]; (*for fishing*) поплавок [*paplavok*]

flood наводнение [*navad-nyeni-ye*]

floor (*of room*) пол [*pol*]; on the floor на полу [*na palōō*]; on the second floor (*UK*) на третьем этаже [*na trye-tyem ettazh-e*]; (*US*) на втором этаже [*na ftarom ettazh-e*]

flop (*failure*) неудача [*nyi-oodacha*]

florist цветочная лавка [*tsvyitochna-ya lafka*]

flour мука [*mooka*]

flower цветок [*tsvyitok*]

flu грипп [*greep*]

fluent: he speaks fluent Russian он свободно говорит по-русски [*on svabodnuh gavareet pa-rooskee*]

fly (*verb*) летать/лететь [*lyitaht/lyi-tyet*]; **can we fly there?** мы можем лететь туда? [*mee mozhem lyi-tyet tooda*]

fly (*insect*) муха [*mōōkha*]

fly spray отрава для мух [*atrava dlya mōōkh*]

foggy: it's foggy туманно [*tooman-nuh*]

fog lights фары для тумана [*faree dlya toomana*]

folk dancing народные танцы [*narodnee-ye tantsee*]

folk music народная музыка [*narodna-ya mōōzika*]

follow следовать [*slyeduvat*]; **follow me** следуйте за мной [*slyedōō-i-tye zam-noy*]

fond: I'm quite fond of . . . мне нравится . . . [*mnye nrahvitsa*]

food еда [*yida*]; **the food's excellent** еда замечательная [*yida za-myicha-tyilna-ya*]

food poisoning пищевое отравление [*peesh-chivo-ye atrav-lyeni-ye*]

food store продовольственный магазин [*prada-volst-vyinnee magazeen*]

fool дурак [*doorak*]

foolish глупый [*glōōpee*]

foot нога [*naga*]; **on foot** пешком [*pyish-kom*]; *see page 120*

football футбол [*footbol*]

for: is that for me? это для меня? [*ettuh dlya minya*]; **what's this for?** для чего это? [*dlya chivo ettuh*]; **for two days** на два дня [*na dva dnya*]; **I've been here for a week** я пробыл здесь неделю [*ya prabeel zdyiss nyi-dye-lyōō*]; **a bus for . . .** автобус в . . . [*avto-booss v*]

forbidden запрещённый [*za-pryish-chonnee*]

forehead лоб [*lop*]

foreign иностранный [*ina-strannee*]

foreigner (*man*) иностранец [*ina-stran-yits*]; (*woman*) иностранка [*ina-stranka*]

foreign exchange (*money*) обмен иностранной валюты [*ab-myen ina-strannoy va-lyōōtee*]

forest лес [*lyess*]

forget забывать/забыть [*zabivat/zabeet*]; **I forget, I've forgotten** я забыл [*ya zabeel*]; **don't forget** не забудьте [*nye zabōōd-tye*]

fork (*for eating*) вилка [*veelka*]; (*in road*) развилка [*raz-veelka*]

form (*document*) бланк [*blank*]

formal (*dress*) вечерний [*vyichernee*]; (*person, language*) официальный [*afitsi-ahlnee*]

fortnight две недели [*dvye nyi-dyelee*]

fortunately к счастью [*k s-cha-styōō*]

forward: could you forward my mail? пожалуйста, перешлите мне мою почту [*pa-zhahlsta pyiri-shlee-tye mnye ma-yōō pochtōō*]

forwarding address адрес для пересылки [*ah-dryess dlya pyiri-seelkee*]

foundation cream дермокол [*dyirma-kol*]

fountain фонтан [*fantan*]

foyer (*of hotel, theatre*) фойе [*fo-ye*]

fracture (*noun*) перелом [*pyiri-lom*]

fractured skull трещина в черепе [*tryesh-cheena fche-ryi-pye*]

fragile хрупкий [*khrōōpkee*]

frame (*for picture*) рама [*rahma*]

France Франция [*frantsi-ya*]

fraud обман [*abmahn*]

free (*at liberty*) свободный [*svabodnee*]; (*costing nothing*) бесплатный [*byiss-platnee*]; **admission free** вход бесплатный [*fkhot byiss-platnee*]

freeze мёрзнуть/замёрзнуть [*myorznōōt/za-myorznōōt*]; **my hands are freezing** у меня руки замёрзли [*ōō minya rōōkee za-myorzlee*]

freezer морозилка [*mara-zeelka*]

freezing: freezing cold ледяной холод [*lyi-dyanoy kholut*]; **below freezing** ниже нуля [*neezh-e nool-ya*]

French французский [*frantsōōz-skee*]; **do you speak French?** вы говорите по-французски? [*vee gavareet-ye pa-frantsōōz-skee*]

French fries жареный картофель [*zha-ryinee karto-fyil*]

frequent частый [*chahstee*]

fresh (*weather, fruit*) свежий [*svyezhee*]; (*cheeky*) нахальный [*na-khalnee*]; **don't get fresh with me** перестаньте дерзить [*pyiri-stant-ye dyirzeet*]

fresh orange juice натуральный апельсиновый сок [*natoorahl-nee apyil-seenuvee sok*]

friction tape изоляционная лента [*eeza-lyatsi-onna-ya lyenta*]

Friday пятница [*pyatnitsa*]

fridge холодильник [*khala-deelnik*]

fried egg яичница [*ya-eechnitsa*]

fried rice жареный рис [*zha-ryinee reess*]
friend друг [*dr̄ook*]
friendly дружеский [*dr̄oozhiskee*]
frog лягушка [*lyaḡooshka*]
from: I'm from London я из Лондона [*ya iz londuna*]; from here to the sea отсюда до моря [*at-sȳooda da mor-ya*]; the next boat from ... следующий пароход из ... [*slyedoo-ȳoosh-chee parakhot iz*]; as from Tuesday со вторника [*sa ftornika*]
front передний [*pyi-ryednee*]; in front впереди [*fpyiri-dee*]; in front of us перед нами [*pye-ryid nahmee*]; at the front впереди [*fpyiri-dee*]
frost мороз [*maroz*]
frostbitten отмороженный [*at-marozhennee*]
frozen замёрзший [*za-myorz-shee*]; the river is frozen over река замёрзла [*ryika za-myorzla*]; I'm frozen stiff (*man*) я промёрз насквозь [*ya pra-myorz naskvoz*]; (*woman*) я промёрзла насквозь [*ya pra-myorzla naskvoz*]
frozen food замороженная пища [*za-marozhenna-ya peesh-cha*]
fruit фрукты [*frooktee*]
fruit juice фруктовый сок [*frooktovee sok*]
fruit salad фруктовый салат [*frooktovee salaht*]
frustrating: it's very frustrating очень досадно [*ochin da-sahdnuh*]
fry жарить [*zhareet*]; I can't eat anything fried мне нельзя есть ничего

жареного [*mnye nyil-zya yist nee-chivo zha-ryinuvuh*]
frying pan сковородка [*skavarotka*]
full полный [*polnee*]; it's full of ... в этом полно ... [*vettum polnuh*]; I'm full (*eating*) я сыт [*ya seet*]
full-board полный пансион [*polnee pan-si-on*]
full-bodied (*wine*) крепкий [*kryepkee*]
fun: it's fun это забавно [*ettuh zabavnuh*]; it was great fun there там было весело [*tam beeluh vye-syiluh*]; just for fun ради шутки [*radee sh̄ootkee*]
funeral похороны [*pokhurunee*]
funny (*strange*) странный [*strannee*]; (*amusing*) забавный [*zabavnee*]
fur мех [*myekh*]
fur hat меховая шапка [*myikhava-ya shapka*]
furniture мебель (*f*) [*mye-byil*]
further дальше [*dalsh-e*]; 2 kilometres further ещё два километра [*yish-cho dva kila-myetra*]; further down this road дальше по этой дороге [*dalsh-e pa ettoy darog-ye*]
fuse предохранитель (*m*) [*pryida-khranee-tyil*]; the lights have fused пробки перегорели [*propkee pyiri-ga-ryelee*]
fuse wire плавкий предохранитель [*plafkee pryida-khranee-tyil*]
future будущее [*b̄oodoosh-che-ye*]; in future в будущем [*vb̄oodoosh-chem*]

G

gale буря [*b̄oo-rya*]
gallon *see page 121*
gallstone жёлчный камень [*zholch-nee kah-myin*]
gamble играть на деньги [*eegraht na dyen-gee*]; I don't gamble я не играю на деньги [*ya nye eegrah-ȳoo na dyen-gee*]
game игра [*eegra*]
games room игротека [*eegra-tyeka*]
gammon ветчина [*vyitcheena*]
garage (*petrol*) бензозаправочная станция [*byinza-zaprahvuchna-ya stantsi-ya*]; (*repair*) техмастерская [*tyikh-mast-yirska-ya*]; (*for parking*) гараж [*garahsh*]
garbage мусор [*m̄oo-sur*]
garden сад [*sat*]

garlic чеснок [*chisnok*]
gas газ [*gahss*]
gas cylinder баллон [*balon*]
gasket прокладка [*praklatka*]
gasoline бензин [*byinzeen*]
gas pedal педаль акселератора [*pyidal aksyili-rahtura*]
gas-permeable lenses газо-проницаемые линзы [*gaza-pranitsa-yemee-ye leenzee*]
gas station бензозаправочная станция [*byinza-za-prahvuchna-ya stantsi-ya*]
gas tank бензобак [*byinza-bak*]
gastroenteritis гастроэнтерит [*gastra-en-tyireet*]

gate ворота [*varota*]; (*at airport*) выход [*veekhut*]

gauge измерительный прибор [*iz-myiree-tyilnee pree-bor*]

gay (*homosexual*) гомосексуалист [*gama-seksoo-aleest*]

gear передача [*pyiri-dacha*]; the gears keep sticking переключение передач застревает [*pyiri-klyoocheni-ye pyiri-dach za-stryiva-yet*]

gearbox коробка передач [*karopka pyiri-dach*]; I have gearbox trouble у меня плохо работает коробка передач [*oo minya plokhuh rabota-yet karopka pyiri-dach*]

gear lever, gear shift рычаг переключения передач [*richag pyiri-klyoocheni-ya pyiri-dach*]

general delivery до востребования [*da vass-tryebuvani-ya*]

generous: that's very generous of you вы очень великодушны [*vee ochin vyilika-dooshnee*]

gentleman (*man*) мужчина (*m*) [*moozh-cheena*]; that gentleman over there вот этот мужчина там [*vot ettut moozh-cheena tam*]; he's such a gentleman он настоящий джентельмен [*on nasta-yash-chee jen-tyil-myen*]

gents (*toilet*) мужской туалет [*moozh-skoy too-a-lyet*]

genuine настоящий [*nasta-yash-chee*]

Georgia Грузия [*groozi-ya*]

German немецкий [*nyi-myetskee*]; do you speak German? вы говорите по-немецки? [*vee gavareet-ye pa nyi-myetskee*]

German measles краснуха [*krasnookha*]

Germany Германия [*gyirmahni-ya*]

get: have you got ...? у вас есть? [*oo vass yist*]; how do I get to ...? как пройти в/на ...? [*kak pratee v/na*]; where can I get it from? где можно это достать? [*gdye mozh-nuh ettuh dastat*]; can I get you a drink? что вы будете пить? [*shto vee boodit-ye peet*]; will you get it for me? достаньте это для меня, пожалуйста [*dastahn-tye ettuh dlya minya pa-zhahlsta*]; when do we get there? когда мы будем там? [*kagda mee boo-dyim tam*]; I've got to ... мне надо ... [*mnye nahduh*]; I've got to go мне надо пойти [*mnye nahduh ptee*]; where do I get off? где мне выходить? [*gdye mnye vikhadeet*]; it's difficult to get to трудно туда пойти [*troodnuh tooda ptee*]; when I get up (*in morning*) когда я встаю [*kagda ya fsta-yoo*]

ghastly страшный [*strash-nee*]

ghost привидение [*pree-vyi-dyeni-ye*]

giddy: I feel giddy у меня кружится голова [*oo minya kroozhitsa galava*]

gift подарок [*padahruk*]

gigantic огромный [*agromnee*]

gin джин [*jin*]; a gin and tonic джин с тоником [*jin stonikum*]

girl (*little girl*) девочка [*dyevuchka*]; (*young woman*) девушка [*dyevooshka*]

girlfriend подруга [*padrooga*]

give давать/дать [*davaht/daht*]; will you give me ...? дайте пожалуйста ... [*di-tye pa-zhahlsta*]; I'll give you 1 rouble я вам дам один рубль [*ya vam dam adeen roobl*]; I gave it to him я дал это ему [*ya dahl ettuh yimoo*]; will you give it back? вы это мне вернёте? [*vee ettuh mnye vyir-nyo-tye*]; would you give this to ...? передайте, пожалуйста ... [*pyiri-di-tye pa-zhahlsta*]

glad рад [*raht*]

glamorous: a glamorous woman обаятельная женщина [*aba-yah-tyilna-ya zhensh-china*]

gland железа [*zhi-lyiza*]

glandular fever воспаление желёз [*vaspa-lyeni-ye zhi-lyoss*]

glasnost гласность (*f*) [*glahsnust*]

glass (*material*) стекло [*styiklo*]; (*drinking*) стакан [*stakan*]; (*for wine*) рюмка [*ryoomka*]; glass of water стакан воды [*stakan vadee*]

glasses (*spectacles*) очки [*achkee*]

gloves перчатки [*pyirchatkee*]

glue (*noun*) клей [*klyay*]

gnat комар [*kamar*]

go (*on foot*) идти/ходить [*eed-tee/khadeet*]; (*by transport*) ехать/ездить [*yekhat/yezdeet*]; we want to go to ... мы хотим пойти/поехать в ... [*mee khateem ptee/pa-yekhat v*]; I'm going there tomorrow я пойду/поеду туда завтра [*ya pidoo/pa-yedoo tooda zaftra*]; when does it go? (*bus etc*) когда отходит? [*kagda at-khodit*]; where are you going? куда вы идёте? [*kooda vee ee-dyo-tye*]; let's go пошли/поехали [*pashlee/ pa-yekhalee*]; he's gone его здесь нет [*yivo zdyiss nyet*]; it's all gone всё кончилось [*fsyo konchiluss*]; I went there yesterday я был там вчера [*ya beel tam fchira*]; go away!

уходите! [ōōkhadee-tye]; it's gone off (milk etc) прокисло [prakee-sluh]; (meat) протухло [pratōōkh-luh]; we're going out to the theatre tonight сегодня вечером мы идём в театр [syivo-dnya vye-chirum mee ee-dyom ftyi-ahtr]; do you want to go out tonight? вы хотите пойти куда-нибудь сегодня вечером? [vee khatee-tye ptee kooda-nibōōt syivo-dnya vyechirum]; has the price gone up? цена повысилась? [tsina pavee-seelass]

goal (sport) гол [gol]

goat коза [kaza]

goat's cheese козий сыр [kozee seer]

god бог [bokh]

gold золото [zolutuh]

golf гольф [golf]

golf clubs клюшки для гольфа [klyōōshkee dlya golfa]

golf course площадка для игры в гольф [plash-chatka dlya eegree vgolf]

good хороший [kharoshee]; good! хорошо! [khara-sho]; that's no good это не годится [ettuh nye gadeetsa]; good heavens! господи! [gospudee]

goodbye до свидания [da svidani-ya]

good-looking красивый [kra-seevee]

gooey (food etc) липкий [leepkee]

goose гусь (m) [gōōss]

gooseberry крыжовник [krizhovnik]

gorgeous великолепный [vyilika-lyepnee]

government правительство [pravee-tyilst-vuh]

gradually постепенно [pa-styi-pyexnuh]

grammar грамматика [grammahtika]

gram(me) грамм [gram]; see page 120

granddaughter внучка [vnōōchka]

grandfather дедушка [dyedooshka]

grandmother бабушка [bah-booshka]

grandson внук [vnōōk]

grapefruit грейпфрут [gryayp-frōōt]

grapefruit juice грейпфрутовый сок [gryayp-frōōtuwee sok]

grapes виноград [veenagraht]

grass трава [trava]

grateful благодарный [blaga-darnee]; I'm very grateful to you (man) я вам очень благодарен [ya vam ochin blaga-daryin]; (woman) я вам очень благодарна [ya vam ochin blaga-darna]

gravy соус [so-ōōss]

gray серый [sye-ree]; (hair) седой [syidoy]

grease (for car) смазка [smaska]; (on food) жир [zheer]

greasy (food) жирный [zheernee]

great (large) большой [bal-shoy]; Peter the Great Пётр Великий [pyotr vyilee-kee]; that's great! вот это здорово! [vot ettuh zdoruv-uh]

Great Britain Великобритания [vyilika-britani-ya]

greedy жадный [zhadnee]

green зелёный [zyi-lyonee]

green card (car insurance) международная автомобильная страховка [myizhdōō-narodna-ya avta-mabeelna-ya strakhofka]

greengrocer овощной магазин [avash-chnoy magazeen]

grey серый [syeree]; (hair) седой [syidoy]

grilled жареный [zha-ryinee]

gristle хрящ [khryashch]

grocer продовольственный магазин [pradavolst-vyinnee magazeen]

ground земля [zim-lya]; on the ground на земле [na zim-lye]; on the ground floor на первом этаже [na pyervum ettazh-e]

ground beef рубленое мясо [rōōb-lyinuh-ye mya-suh]

group группа [grōōpa]

group insurance страховка группы [strakhofka grōōpee]

group leader руководитель группы [rookavadee-tyil grōōpee]

guarantee (noun) гарантия [garanti-ya]; is it guaranteed? это с гарантией? [ettuh zgaranti-yay]

guardian (of child) опекун [a-pyikōōn]

guest (man) гость [gost]; (woman) гостья [gost-ya]

guesthouse пансион [pan-sion]

guest room комната для гостей [komnata dlya ga-styay]

guide (noun) гид [geet]

guidebook путеводитель [pōō-tyivadee-tyil]

guilty виновный [veenovnee]

guitar гитара [gitara]

gum (in mouth) десна [dyisna]; (chewing gum) жевательная резинка [zhivah-tyilna-ya ryizeenka]

gun винтовка [vintofka]

gymnasium гимнастический зал [gimnastee-chiskee zahl]

gyn(a)ecologist гинеколог [gi-nyikoluk]

H

hair волосы [*volussee*]

hairbrush щётка для волос [*shchotka dlya valoss*]

haircut стрижка [*streezhka*]; just an ordinary haircut please сделайте, пожалуйста, обыкновенную стрижку [*zdyelɪ-tye pa-zhahlsta abiknavyennōō-yōō streezhkōō*]

hairdresser парикмахер [*parik-makh-yir*]

hairdryer (*small*) фен [*fyen*]; (*in salon*) сушилка для волос [*soo-sheelka dlya valoss*]

hair gel брильянтин [*bri-lyanteen*]

hair grip шпилька [*shpeelka*]

half половина [*palaveena*]; half an hour полчаса [*palchassa*]; a half portion полпорции [*palportsi-ee*]; half a litre/liter поллитра [*pal-leetra*]; half as much вдвое меньше [*vdvo-ye myensh-e*]; half as much again в полтора раза больше [*fpaltara rahza bolsh-e*]; see page 119

halfway: halfway to Leningrad на полпути к Ленинграду [*na palpootee klyinin-grahdōō*]

ham ветчина [*vyit-cheena*]

hamburger булочка с рубленой котлетой [*bōōluchka zrōō-blyinoy kat-lyetoy*]

hammer (*noun*) молоток [*malatok*]; hammer and sickle серп и молот [*syerp ee molut*]

hand рука [*rooka*]; will you give me a hand? вы мне поможете? [*vee mnye pamozhit-ye*]

handbag (дамская) сумочка [(*damskaya*) *sōōmuchka*]

hand baggage ручная кладь [*roochna-ya klat*]

handbrake ручной тормоз [*roochnoy tormuz*]

handkerchief носовой платок [*na-savoy platok*]

handle (*noun*) ручка [*rōōchka*]; will you handle it? вы займётесь этим? [*vee zɪmyo-tyiss ettim*]

hand luggage ручная кладь [*roochna-ya klat*]

handmade ручная работа [*roochna-ya rabota*]

handsome красивый [*kra-seevee*]

hanger (*for clothes*) вешалка [*vyeshalka*]

hangover похмелье [*pakh-mye-lye*]; I've got a terrible hangover у меня разболелась голова от похмелья [*ōō minya razba-lyelass galava at pakh-mye-lya*]

happen случаться/случиться [*slōōchahtsa/ slōōcheetsa*]; how did it happen? как это случилось? [*kak ettuh slōōcheeluss*]; what's happening? что случается? [*shto slōōcha-yitsa*]; it won't happen again это больше не повторится [*ettuh bolsh-e nye paftareetsa*]

happy счастливый [*s-chast-leevee*]; we're not happy with the room номер нас не устраивает [*no-myir nass nye oostra-yiva-yit*]

harbo(u)r порт [*port*]

hard твёрдый [*tvyordee*]; (*difficult*) трудный [*trōōdnee*]

hard-boiled egg яйцо вкрутую [*yɪtso fkrootōō-yōō*]

hard lenses твёрдые контактные линзы [*tvyordee-ye kantakt-nee-ye linzee*]

hardly едва [*yidva*]; hardly ever очень редко [*ochin ryetkuh*]

hardware store хозяйственный магазин [*kha-zyɪst-vyinnee magazeen*]

harm (*noun*) вред [*vryet*]

hassle: it's too much hassle не стоит труда [*nye sto-yit trooda*]; a hassle-free trip поездка без осложнений [*pa-yezdka byez a-slazh-nyenee*]

hat (*woman's*) шляпа [*shlyahpa*]; (*man's*) шапка [*shapka*]

hate ненавидеть/возненавидеть [*nyinavee-dyit/vaz-nyinavee-dyit*]; I hate ... я ненавижу ... [*ya nyi-naveezhōō*]

have: do you have ...? у вас есть ...? [*ōō vass yist*]; can I have ...? дайте, пожалуйста ... [*dɪ-tye pa-zhahlsta*]; can

I have some water? дайте мне, пожалуйста, воды [*dɪ-tye mnye pa-zhahlsta vadee*]; I have ... у меня есть... [*ōō minya yist*]; I don't have ... у меня нет ... [*ōō minya nyet*]; can we have breakfast in our room? мы можем завтракать у себя в номере? [*mee mozhem zaftrakat ōō sibya vno-myir-ye*]; have another возьмите ещё [*vazmeet-ye yish-cho*]; I have to leave early мне надо рано уйти/уехать [*mnye nahduh rahnuh ōō-eetee/ōō-yekhat*]; do I have to ...? разве нужно ...? [*rahz-vye nōōzhnuh*]; *see page 116*

hay fever сенная лихорадка [*syinna-ya leekha-ratka*]

he он [*on*]; is he here? он здесь? [*on zdyiss*]; where does he live? где он живёт [*gdye on zhi-vyot*]; *see page 111*

head голова [*galava*]; we're heading for Moscow мы едем в Москву [*mee yedyem vmask-vōō*]

headache головная боль [*galavna-ya bol*]

headlights фары [*faree*]

headphones наушники [*na-ōōshnikee*]

head waiter метрдотель (*m*) [*myitr-da-tyel*]

head wind встречный ветер [*fstryechnee vye-tyir*]

health здоровье [*zdarov-ye*]; your health! за ваше здоровье! [*za vash-e zdarov-ye*]

healthy здоровый [*zdarovee*]

hear: can you hear me? вы меня слышите? [*vee minya sleeshit-ye*]; I can't hear you я не слышу вас [*ya nye sleeshōō vass*]; I've heard about it мне сказали об этом [*mnye skazahlee ab ettum*]

hearing aid слуховой аппарат [*slookha-voy apparaht*]

heart сердце [*syerdts-e*]

heart attack инфаркт [*infarkt*]

heat жара [*zhara*]; not in this heat! в такую жару! [*ftakōō-yōō zharōō*]

heated rollers бигуди [*bigoodye*]

heater обогреватель (*m*) [*aba-gryivah-tyil*]

heating отопление [*atap-lyeni-ye*]

heat rash сыпь (*f*) [*seep*]

heat stroke солнечный удар [*sol-nyichnee oodar*]

heatwave жара [*zhara*]

heavy тяжёлый [*tya-zholee*]

hectic лихорадочный [*leekha-raduchnee*]

heel (*of foot*) пятка [*pyatka*]; (*of shoe*) каблук [*kablōōk*]; could you put new

heels on these? пожалуйста, поставьте набойки на эти туфли [*pa-zhahlsta pastahf-tye na-boykee na ettee tōōflee*]

heelbar ремонт обуви [*ryimont oboovee*]

height (*of person*) рост [*rost*]; (*of mountain*) высота [*vissata*]

helicopter вертолёт [*vyirta-lyot*]

hell: oh hell! чёрт возьми! [*chort vazmee*]; go to hell! иди к чёрту! [*eedee kchortōō*]

hello привет [*pree-vyet*]; (*on phone*) алло [*allo*]

helmet (*for motorcycle*) шлем [*shlyem*]

help (*verb*) помогать/помочь [*pamagat/pamoch*]; can you help me? помогите мне, пожалуйста [*pamageet-ye mnye pa-zhahlsta*]; thanks for your help спасибо за помощь [*spa-see-buh za pomushch*]; help! помогите! [*pamageet-ye*]

helpful: he was very helpful он был очень любезен [*on beel ochin lyōō-bye-zyin*]; that's helpful это полезно [*ettuh pa-lyeznuh*]

helping (*of food*) порция [*portsi-ya*]

hepatitis гепатит [*gyipa-teet*]

her: I don't know her я её не знаю [*ya yi-yo nye zna-yōō*]; will you send it to her? пошлите ей это, пожалуйста [*pashleet-ye yay ettuh pa-zhahlsta*]; it's her это она [*ettuh ana*]; with her с ней [*snyay*]; for her для неё [*dlya nyi-yo*]; that's her suitcase это её чемодан [*ettuh yi-yo chimadan*]; *see page 112*

herbs травы [*trahvee*]

here здесь [*zdyiss*]; here you are (*giving something*) возьмите, пожалуйста [*vazmeet-ye pa-zhahlsta*]; here he comes вот он идёт [*vot on ee-dyot*]

Hermitage Эрмитаж [*ermitahsh*]

hers её [*yi-yo*]; that's hers это её [*ettuh yi-yo*]; *see page 110*

hey! эй! [*ay*]

hi! привет! [*pree-vyet*]

hiccups икота [*eekota*]

hide: I have nothing to hide мне нечего скрывать [*mnye nyechivuh skrivaht*]

hideous ужасный [*ōōzhah-snee*]

high высокий [*vissokee*]

highbeam дальний свет фар [*dalnee svyet far*]

highchair детский стульчик [*dyetskee stōōl-chik*]

highway автострада [*avtastrada*]

hiking путешествие пешком [*poo-tyishestvi-ye pyishkom*]

hill гора [*gara*]; it's further up the hill выше в гору [*veesh-e vgoroō*]

hillside склон горы [*sklon garee*]

hilly холмистый [*khalmee-stee*]

him: I don't know him я его не знаю [*ya yivo nye zna-yōō*]; will you send this to him? пошлите ему это, пожалуйста [*pashleet-ye yimōō ettuh pa-zhahlsta*]; it's him это он [*ettuh on*]; with him с ним [*sneem*]; for him для него [*dlya nyi-vo*]; *see page 112*

hip бедро [*byidro*]

hire брать/взять напрокат [*braht/vzyat na-prakaht*]; can I hire a car? я хочу взять машину напрокат [*ya khachōō vzyat masheenōō na-prakaht*]; do you hire them out? вы их даёте напрокат? [*vee eekh da-yot-ye na-prakaht*]

his: it's his drink это его напиток [*ettuh yivo napeetuk*]; it's his это его [*ettuh yivo*]; *see page 110*

history: the history of Moscow история Москвы [*istori-ya maskvee*]

hit ударять/ударить [*ōōda-ryat/ōōdareet*]; he hit me он ударил меня [*on ōōdaril minya*]; I hit my head я ударился головой [*ya ōōdaril-sa galavoy*]

hitch: is there a hitch? в чём задержка? [*fchom za-dyerzhka*]

hitch-hike путешествовать на попутных машинах [*poo-tyishest-vuvat na pa-pōōtnikh masheenakh*]

hitch-hiker человек, который путешествует на попутных машинах [*chila-vyek katoree pōō-tyishest-vooyit na pa-pōōtnikh masheenakh*]

hit record популярный диск [*papoo-lyarnee deesk*]

hole дыра [*dirra*]

holiday отдых [*ot-dikh*]; (*festival*) праздник [*prahzd-nik*]; (*school, college*) каникулы [*kanee-kōōlee*]; I'm on holiday я отдыхаю [*ya at-dikha-yōō*]

Holland Голландия [*galandi-ya*]

home (*house*) дом [*dom*]; at home (*in my house*) дома [*doma*]; (*in my country*) на родине [*na rodin-ye*]; I go home tomorrow я поеду домой завтра [*ya pa-yedōō damoy zaftra*]; home sweet home в гостях хорошо, а дома лучше [*vga-styakh khara-sho a doma lōōch-e*]

home address домашний адрес [*damashnee ah-dryess*]

homemade домашнего изготовления [*damash-nyivuh izgatav-lyeni-ya*]

homesick: I'm homesick я тоскую по родине [*ya taskōō-yōō pa rodin-ye*]

honest честный [*chestnee*]

honestly? серьёзно? [*syi-ryoznuh*]

honey мёд [*myot*]

honeymoon медовый месяц [*myidovee mye-syats*]; it's our honeymoon это наше свадебное путешествие [*ettuh nash-e svah-dyibnuh-ye pōō-tyishestvi-ye*]

hood (*of car*) капот [*kapot*]

hoover (*tm*) пылесос [*pi-lyi-soss*]

hope надеяться [*na-dye-yatsa*]; I hope so я надеюсь, что это так [*ya na-dye-yōōss shto ettuh tak*]; I hope not я надеюсь, что это не так [*ya na-dye-yōōss shto ettuh nye tak*]

horn (*of car*) сигнал [*signal*]

horrible ужасный [*ōōzhah-snee*]

hors d'oeuvre закуска [*zakōōska*]

horse лошадь (*f*) [*losh-at*]

horse riding езда верхом [*yizda vyirkhom*]

hose (*for car radiator*) шланг [*shlang*]

hospital больница [*balneetsa*]

hospitality гостеприимство [*ga-styepri-eemst-vuh*]; thank you for your hospitality спасибо за гостеприимство [*spa-see-buh za ga-styepri-eemst-vuh*]

hostel общежитие [*ab-shezheeti-ye*]

hot (*to touch*) горячий [*ga-ryachee*]; (*weather*) жаркий [*zharkee*]; (*spicy etc*) острый [*ostree*]; I'm hot мне жарко [*mnye zharkuh*]; something hot to eat что-нибудь горячего [*shto-nibōōt ga-ryachiv-uh*]; it's very hot today сегодня очень жарко [*syivo-dnya ochin zharkuh*]

hotdog булочка с горячей сосиской [*bōōluchka zga-ryachay sa-seeskoy*]

hotel гостиница [*gastee-nitsa*]; at my hotel у меня в гостинице [*ōō minya vgastee-nits-e*]

hotel clerk администратор [*admini-strahtur*]

hotplate (*on cooker*) плитка [*pleetka*]

hot-water bottle грелка [*gryelka*]

hour час [*chass*]; on the hour ровно в час [*rovnuh fchass*]

house дом [*dom*]

housewife домохозяйка [*damakha-zyıka*]

house wine столовое вино [*stalovuh-ye vino*]

hovercraft судно на воздушной подушке [*sōōdnuh na vaz-dōōshnoy padōōsh-kye*]

how как [*kak*]; **how many?** сколько? [*skol-kuh*]; **how much?** сколько стоит? [*skol-kuh sto-yit*]; **how often?** как часто? [*kak chastuh*]; **how are you?** как дела? [*kak dyila*]; **how do you do?** как поживаете? [*kak pazhiva-yit-ye*]; **how about a beer?** хотите кружку пива? [*khateet-ye kroozhkoo peeva*]; **how nice!** как хорошо! [*kak khara-sho*]; **would you show me how to?** покажите, пожалуйста, как это сделать [*pa-kazheet-ye pa-zhahlsta kak ettuh zdyelat*]

humid влажный [*vlahzh-nee*]

humidity влажность [*vlahzh-nust*]

humo(u)r: where's your sense of humo(u)r? шуток не понимаете? [*shootuk nye paneeta-yit-ye*]

hundredweight *see page 121*

Hungary Венгрия [*vyengri-ya*]

hungry голодный [*galodnee*]; **I'm hungry** (man) я голоден [*ya goluh-dyen*]; (woman) я голодна [*ya galadna*]

hurry: I'm in a hurry я спешу [*ya spyishoo*]; **hurry up!** быстрее! [*bist-rye-ye*]; **there's no hurry** это не спешно [*ettuh nye spyesh-nuh*]

hurt: it hurts это болит [*ettuh baleet*]; **my back hurts** у меня болит спина [*oo minya baleet speena*]

husband: my husband мой муж [*moy moosh*]

hydrofoil судно на подводных крыльях [*soodnuh na padvod-nikh kree-lyakh*]

I

I я [*ya*]; **I am English** (man) я англичанин [*ya ang-gleechah-nin*]; (woman) я англичанка [*ya ang-gleechanka*]; **I live in Manchester** я живу в Манчестере [*ya zhivoo vmanchester-ye*]; *see page 111*

ice лёд [*lyot*]; **with ice** со льдом [*sal-dom*]; **with ice and lemon** со льдом и лимоном [*sal-dom ee leemonum*]

ice cream мороженое [*marozhenuh-ye*]

ice-cream cone рожок [*razhok*]

iced coffee кофе со льдом [*koff-ye sal-dom*]

ice hockey хоккей на льду [*kha-kyay nal-doo*]

ice lolly фруктовое мороженое [*frook-tovuh-ye marozhenuh-ye*]

ice rink каток [*katok*]

ice skates коньки [*kankee*]

ice-skating катание на коньках [*katahni-ye na kankakh*]

icicle сосулька [*sa-soolka*]

icon икона [*eekona*]

icy ледяной [*lyi-dyanoy*]

idea идея [*ee-dye-ya*]; **good idea!** здорово придумано! [*zdoruvuh pridooman-uh*]

ideal идеальный [*i-dyi-ahlnee*]

identity papers удостоверение личности [*oodasta-vyi-ryeni-ye leech-nustee*]

idiot идиот [*idee-ot*]

idyllic идиллический [*idil-leechiskee*]

if если [*ye-slee*]; **if you could** если можете [*ye-slee mozhit-ye*]; **if not** если нет [*ye-slee nyet*]

ignition зажигание [*za-zhigahni-ye*]

ill больной [*bal-noy*]; **I am ill** (man) я болен [*ya bo-lyen*]; (woman) я больна [*ya balna*]

illegal незаконный [*nyi-zakonnee*]

illegible неразборчивый [*nyi-razborchivee*]

illness болезнь (f) [*ba-lyezn*]

imitation (leather etc) искусственный [*isskoost-vyinnee*]

immediately немедленно [*nyi-myed-lyinnuh*]

immigration иммиграция [*immi-grahtsi-ya*]

import (verb) ввозить/ввезти [*v-vazeet/v-vyiztee*]; (noun) импорт [*import*]

important важный [*vazhnee*]; **it's very important** это очень важно [*ettuh ochin vazhnuh*]; **it's not important** это неважно [*ettuh nyi-vazhnuh*]

impossible невозможный [*nyivaz-mozhnee*]

impressive впечатляющий [*fpyichat-lya-yoosh-chee*]

improve улучшать/улучшить [*ooloochaht/ ooloocheet*]; **it's improving** это намного лучше [*ettuh nam-noguh looch-e*]; **I want to improve my Russian** я хочу усовершенствовать свой русский [*ya khachōō ōossa-vyirshenst-vuvat svoy rooskee*]

improvement улучшение [*ōolōocheni-ye*]

in: in my room в моей комнате [*vma-yay komnat-ye*]; in the town centre в центре города [*ftsent-rye goruda*]; in America в Америке [*va-myerik-ye*]; in one hour's time через час [*che-ryiz chass*]; in August в августе [*vahvgoost-ye*]; in English по-английски [*pa ang-gleeskee*]; in Russian по-русски [*pa rooskee*]; is he in? он дома? [*on doma*]

inch *see page 120*

include включать/включить [*fklyōōchaht/ fklyōōcheet*]; is that included in the price? это засчитано в цену? [*ettuh zas-cheetanuh ftsenōō*]

incompetent неспособный [*nyi-spassobnee*]

inconvenient неудобный [*nyi-ōōdobnee*]

increase (*noun*) увеличение [*ōō-vyilicheni-ye*]

incredible невероятный [*nyi-vyira-yatnee*]

indecent неприличный [*nyi-preeleech-nee*]

independent (*adjective*) независимый [*nyi-zavee-seemee*]

India Индия [*indi-ya*]

Indian (*man*) индиец [*indee-yets*]; (*woman*) индианка [*indi-yanka*]; (*adjective*) индийский [*indeeskee*]

indicator (*on car*) указатель (*m*) [*ōōkazah-tyil*]

indigestion расстройство желудка [*ras-stroyst-vuh zhelōōtka*]

indoor pool закрытый бассейн [*zakreetee ba-syayn*]

indoors в помещении [*fpa-myisheni-ee*]

industry промышленность (*f*) [*prameesh-lyinnust*]

inefficient (*person*) неспособный [*nyi-spassobnee*]; (*thing*) неэффективный [*nyi-effekteevnee*]

infection заражение [*zarazheni-ye*]

infectious инфекционный [*infyiktsi-onnee*]

inflammation воспаление [*vasspa-lyeni-ye*]

inflation инфляция [*in-flyatsi-ya*]

informal неофициальный [*nyi-afitsi-ahlnee*]

information информация [*informahtsi-ya*]

information desk справочный стол [*sprahvuchnee stol*]

information office справочное бюро [*sprahvuch-nuh-ye byooro*]

injection инъекция [*in-yektsi-ya*]

injured раненый [*rah-nyinee*]; she's been injured она ушиблась [*ana ōōsheeblass*]

injury рана [*rahna*]

in-law: my in-laws моя родня [*ma-ya rad-nya*]

innocent невинный [*nyi-veennee*]

inquisitive любознательный [*lyōōba-znah-tyilnee*]

insect насекомое [*na-syikomuh-ye*]

insect bite укус насекомого [*oo-kōōss na-syikomuv-uh*]

insecticide инсектицид [*insekti-tseet*]

insect repellent средство от насекомых [*sryedst-vuh at na-syikomikh*]

inside: inside the tent в палатке [*fpalaht-kye*]; let's sit inside давайте посидим в комнате [*davı-tye pa-seedeem vkomnat-ye*]

insincere неискренний [*nyi-eesk-ryinnee*]

insist: I insist on it я настаиваю на этом [*ya nasta-eeva-yōō na ettum*]

insomnia бессонница [*byis-sonnitsa*]

instant coffee растворимый кофе [*rastvareemee koff-ye*]

instead вместо [*vmyestuh*]; I'll have that one instead я возьму это вместо этого [*ya vazmōō ettuh vmyestuh ettuvuh*]; instead of ... вместо ... . [*vmyestuh*]

insulating tape изоляционная лента [*eeza-lyats-yonna-ya lyenta*]

insulin инсулин [*in-sōōleen*]

insult (*noun*) оскорбление [*askarb-lyeni-ye*]

insurance страхование [*strakha-vahni-ye*]

insurance company страховое общество [*strakha-vo-ye ob-shistvuh*]; please write the name of your insurance company here пожалуйста, напишите здесь название вашего страхового общества [*pa-zhahlsta na-pisheet-ye zdyiss nazvahni-ye vashevuh strakha-vovuh ob-shistva*]

insurance policy страховой полис [*strakha-voy poliss*]

intellectual (*noun*) интеллигент [*in-tyilli-gent*]

intelligent умный [*ōōmnee*]

intentionally: I didn't do it intentionally я это не сделал умышленно [*ya ettuh nye zdyelal ōōmeesh-lyinnuh*]

interest: places of interest достопримечательности [*dasta-pree-myichah-tyil-nustee*]

interested: I'm very interested in ... меня
очень интересует ... [*minya ochin in-tyiri-soo-yit*]

interesting интересный [*in-tyi-ryessnee*];
that's very interesting это очень
интересно [*ettuh ochin in-tyi-ryessnuh*]

international международный
[*myizhdoo-narodnee*]

international driving licence/driver's
license международные права
[*myizhdoo-narodnee-ye prava*]

interpret переводить/перевести [*pyiri-vadeet/pyiri-vyistee*]; would you interpret
for us? можете перевести для нас?
[*mozhit-ye pyiri-vyistee dlya nass*]

interpreter (*man*) переводчик [*pyiri-vodchik*]; (*woman*) переводчица [*pyiri-vodchitsa*]

intersection перекрёсток [*pyiri-kryostuk*]

interval (*during play etc*) антракт [*antrakt*]

into в, на [*v, na*]; I'm not into that (*don't like*) мне не нравится это [*mnye nye nrahvitsa ettuh*]

introduce: may I introduce ...?
разрешите познакомить ... [*raz-ryisheet-ye pazna-komeet*]

introvert интроверт [*intra-vyert*]

invalid инвалид [*invaleet*]

invalid chair кресло для инвалидов
[*krye-sluh dlya invaleeduff*]

invitation приглашение [*priglasheni-ye*];
thank you for the invitation спасибо за
приглашение [*spa-see-buh za priglasheni-ye*]

invite приглашать/пригласить
[*priglashat/ priglasseet*]; can I invite you
out? можно пригласить вас? [*mozhnuh priglasseet vass*]

involved: I don't want to get involved мне
не хочется вмешиваться [*mnye nye khochitsa vmyeshivat-sa*]

iodine йод [*yot*]

Iran Иран [*eeran*]

Ireland Ирландия [*eerlandi-ya*]

Irish ирландский [*eerlant-skee*]

iron (*material*) железо [*zhi-lyezuh*]; (*for clothes*) утюг [*oo-tyook*]; can you iron
these for me? пожалуйста, отутюжьте
это для меня [*pa-zhahlsta atoo-tyoozh-tye ettuh dlya minya*]

Iron Curtain железный занавес [*zhi-lyeznee zahna-vyess*]

ironmonger хозяйственный магазин
[*kha-zyıst-vyinnee magazeen*]

is *see page 116*

island остров [*ostruff*]

isolated изолированный [*izalee-ruvannee*]

it: is it ...? это ...? [*ettuh*]; where is it? где
это? [*gdye ettuh*]; it's her это она [*ettuh ana*]; it was ... это было ... [*ettuh beeluh*]; that's just it (*just the problem*) вот
это и есть проблема [*vot ettuh ee yist prab-lyema*]; that's it (*that's right*) вот именно
[*vot ee-myennuh*]

Italy Италия [*eetahli-ya*]

itch: it itches чешется [*cheshitsa*]

itinerary маршрут [*marsh-root*]

J

jack (*for car*) домкрат [*dam-kraht*]

jacket пиджак [*pid-zhak*]

jam варенье [*va-ryen-ye*]; a traffic jam
пробка [*propka*]; I jammed on the brakes
я резко затормозил [*ya ryezkuh za-tarmazeel*]

January январь (*m*) [*yanvar*]

jaundice желтуха [*zhiltookha*]

jaw челюсть (*f*) [*che-lyoost*]

jazz джаз [*jazz*]

jazz club джазовый клуб [*jazzuvee kloop*]

jealous ревнивый [*ryiv-neevee*]; he's
jealous он ревнует [*on ryivnoo-yit*]

jeans джинсы [*jeensee*]

jellyfish медуза [*myidooza*]

jetlag: I'm suffering from jetlag у меня
после полёта нарушение суточного
ритма организма [*oo minya poss-lye pa-lyota na-roosheni-ye sootuch-nuvuh reetma arganeezma*]

jetty пристань (*m*) [*pree-stan*]

Jew (*man*) еврей [*yivray*]; (*woman*) еврейка
[*yiv-ryayka*]

jewel(le)ry ювелирные изделия [*yoo-vyileerni-ye iz-dyeli-ya*]

Jewish еврейский [*yiv-ryay-skee*]

jiffy: just a jiffy одну минуточку [*adnoo minootachkoo*]

job работа [*rabota*]; just the job! (*just right*) в
самый раз [*fsahmee rass*]; it's a good job

you told me! хорошо, что вы мне сказали об этом [*khara-sho shto vee mnye skazahlee ab ettum*]

jogging оздоровительный бег трусцой [*azdaravee-tyilnee byek trooss-tsoy*]

join: I'd like to join (*club etc*) я хочу стать членом [*ya khachōō staht chlyenum*]; can I join you? (*sit with*) можно присоединиться к вам? [*mozhnuh pree-sa-yidineetsa kvam*]; do you want to join us? (*go with*) хотите пойти с нами? [*khateet-ye ptee snahmee*]; (*sit with*) хотите присоединиться к нам? [*khateet-ye pree-sa-yidineetsa k-nam*]

joint (*in body*) сустав [*soostaff*]

joke шутка [*shōōtka*]; you've got to be joking! вы должно быть шутите [*vee dalzhno beet shōōteet-ye*]; it's no joke это не шутка [*ettuh nye shōōtka*]

jolly: it was jolly good было очень хорошо [*beeluh ochin khara-sho*]; jolly good! вот и хорошо! [*vot ee khara-sho*]

journey поездка [*pa-yezdka*]; have a good journey! счастливого пути! [*s-chastlee-vuvuh pootee*]

jug кувшин [*koovsheen*]; a jug of water кружка воды [*krōōzhka vadee*]

July июль (*m*) [*eeyōōl*]

jump прыгать/прыгнуть [*preegat/preegnōōt*]; you made me jump вы меня испугали [*vee minya isspōō-gahlee*]; jump in! (*to car*) садитесь, подвезу! [*sadee-tyiss pad-vyizōō*]

jumper свитер [*svee-tyir*]

jump leads, jumper cables подводящий провод [*padva-dyash-chee provut*]

junction распутье [*rasspōōt-ye*]; (*crossroads*) перекрёсток [*pyiri-kryostuk*]

June июнь (*m*) [*eeyōōn*]

junior: Mr Jones junior мистер Джоунс младший [*mist-yer 'jones' mladshee*]

junk (*rubbish*) старьё [*sta-ryo*]

just: just one только один [*tol-kuh adeen*]; just me только я [*tol-kuh ya*]; just for me исключительно для меня [*iss-klyoochee-tyil-nuh dlya minya*]; just a little только немножко [*tol-kuh nyim-nozhkuh*]; just here как раз тут [*kak rass tōōt*]; not just now не сейчас [*nye syichass*]; that's just right это в самый раз [*ettuh fsahmee rass*]; it's just the same это то же самое [*ettuh to zhe sahmuh-ye*]; he was here just now он как раз здесь был [*on kak raz zdyiss beel*]; I've only just arrived я только что приехал [*ya tol-kuh shto pree-yekhal*]

K

kagul куртка от дождя [*kōōrtka at dazh-dya*]

Kazakhstan Казахстан [*kazakh-stan*]

keen: I'm not keen мне не хочется [*mnye nye khochitsa*]

keep: can I keep it? можете мне это дать? [*mozhit-ye mnye ettuh daht*]; please keep it это для вас [*ettuh dlya vass*]; keep the change оставьте себе сдачу [*astahf-tye sibye zdachōō*]; will it keep? (*food*) это не испортится? [*ettuh nye issportitsa*]; it's keeping me awake это мне мешает спать [*ettuh mnye myisha-yit spaht*]; it keeps on breaking постоянно ломается [*pasta-yannuh lama-yitsa*]; I can't keep anything down (*food*) меня всё время рвёт [*minya fsyo vrye-mya rvyot*]

kerb край тротуара [*krı trotoo-ara*]

kerosene (*for stoves etc*) керосин [*kyira-seen*]

ketchup томатный кетчуп [*tamahtnee kyet-chup*]

kettle чайник [*chınik*]

key ключ [*klyōōch*]

KGB КГБ [*ka-ge-be*]

kid: the kids дети [*dyetee*]; I'm not kidding я не шучу [*ya nye shoochōō*]

kidneys почки [*pochkee*]

kill убивать/убить [*ōōbivaht/ōōbeet*]; my feet are killing me у меня жутко болят ноги [*ōō minya zhōōtkuh ba-lyaht nogee*]

kilo кило [*kilo*]; see page 120

kilometre, kilometer километр [*kila-myetr*]; see page 120

kind: that's very kind очень любезно с вашей стороны [*ochin lyōō-byez-nuh zvashay staranee*]; this kind of . . . . . . такого рода [*takova roda*]

kiosk киоск [*kee-osk*]

Kirgizia Киргизия [*kirgizi-ya*]

kiss (*noun*) поцелуй [*patsiloo-ee*]; (*verb*) целовать/поцеловать [*tsila-vat/pa-tsila-vat*]

kitchen кухня [*kookh-nya*]

Kleenex (*tm*) бумажный платочек [*boomahzh-nee platochek*]

knee колено [*ka-lyenuh*]

kneecap коленная чашечка [*ka-lyenna-ya chashich-ka*]

knickers трусики [*troo-sikee*]

knife нож [*nosh*]

knitting вязание [*vyazahni-ye*]

knitting needle вязальная игла [*vyazalna-ya eegla*]

knock: there's a knocking noise from the engine мотор стучит [*mator stoocheet*];

he's had a knock on the head его ударили по голове [*yivo oo-dahrilee pa gala-vye*]; he's been knocked over by a car его сбила машина [*yivo zbeela masheena*]

knot (*in rope*) узел [*oo-zyil*]

know (*somebody, something*) знать [*znaht*]; I don't know я не знаю [*ya nye zna-yoo*]; do you know a good restaurant? вы знаете где найти хороший ресторан? [*vee zna-yit-ye gdye ntee kharoshee ryistaran*]; who knows? кто знает? [*kto zna-yit*]; I didn't know that я этого не знал [*ya ettuvuh nye znahl*]; I don't know him я его не знаю [*ya yivo nye zna-yoo*]

Kremlin Кремль (*m*) [*kryeml*]

L

label ярлык [*yarleek*]

laces (*for shoes*) шнурки [*shnoorkee*]

lacquer (*for hair*) лак для волос [*lak dlya valoss*]

ladies (*room*) женский туалет [*zhenskee too-a-lyet*]

lady дама [*dahma*]; ladies and gentlemen! дамы и господа! [*dahmee ee gaspada*]

lager светлое пиво [*svyetluhye peevuh*]

lake озеро [*o-zyiruh*]

lamb ягнёнок [*yag-nyonuk*]

lamp лампа [*lampa*]; (*in street*) фонарь (*m*) [*fanar*]

lamppost фонарный столб [*fanarnee stolp*]

lampshade абажур [*abazhoor*]

land (*not sea*) суша [*soosha*]; when does the plane land? когда самолёт приземляется? [*kagda sama-lyot preezimlya-yitsa*]

landscape пейзаж [*pyay-zash*]

lane (*on motorway*) ряд [*ryat*]; a country lane дорожка [*daroshka*]

language язык [*yazik*]

language course языковой курс [*yazikavoy koorss*]; a Russian language course курс русского языка [*koorss rooskuh-vuh yazika*]

large большой [*bal-shoy*]

laryngitis ларингит [*laran-geet*]

last последний [*pa-slyednee*]; when's the last bus? когда отходит последний автобус? [*kagda at-khodit pa-slyednee avto-*

booss]; one last drink последняя рюмка [*pa-slyed-nya-ya ryoomka*]; when were you last in Leningrad? когда вы были в Ленинграде в последний раз? [*kagda vee beelee vlyinin-grahd-ye fpa-slyednee rass*]; last year в прошлом году [*fproshlum gadoo*]; last Wednesday в прошлую среду [*fproshloo-yoosryedoo*]; last night вчера вечером [*fchira vyechirum*]; at last! наконец-то! [*naka-nyets-tuh*]; how long does it last? как долго это продолжается? [*kak dolguh ettuh pradalzha-yitsa*]

last name фамилия [*fameeli-ya*]

late поздно [*pozd-nuh*]; sorry I'm late извините за опоздание [*izvinee-tye za apaz-dahni-ye*]; don't be late смотрите, не опоздайте [*smatree-tye nye apazdı-tye*]; the bus was late автобус опоздал [*avto-booss apaz-dahl*]; I'll be back late я вернусь поздно [*ya vyirnooss pozd-nuh*]; it's getting late уже поздно [*oozh-e pozd-nuh*]; is it that late! вот как поздно [*ya nye za-myetil shto tak pozd-nuh*]; it's too late now теперь уже слишком поздно [*tyi-pyer oozh-e sleesh-kum pozd-nuh*]; I'm a late riser обычно я встаю поздно [*abeech-nuh ya fsta-yoo pozd-nuh*]

lately за последнее время [*za pa-slyed-nye-ye vrye-mya*]

later позже [*pozh-e*]; later on потом [*patom*]; I'll come back later я вернусь позже [*ya vyirnooss pozh-e*]; see you later увидимся позже [*ōo-veedeemsa pozh-e*]; no later than Tuesday не позднее вторника [*nye pozd-nye-ye ftornika*]

latest: the latest news последние новости [*pa-slyedni-ye novustee*]; at the latest самое позднее [*samuh-ye paz-dnye-ye*]

Latvia Латвия [*latvi-ya*]

laugh смеяться/засмеяться [*smyi-yahtsa/za-smyi-yahtsa*] don't laugh не смейтесь [*nye smyay-tyiss*]; it's no laughing matter это не шутка [*ettuh nye shōotka*]

launderette, laundromat прачечная-автомат [*prachechna-ya avta-maht*]

laundry (clothes) бельё [*byi-lyo*]; (place) прачечная [*prachechna-ya*]; could you get the laundry done? можете сдать бельё в стирку? [*mozhit-ye zdat byi-lyo fsteerkōo*]

lavatory уборная [*ōoborna-ya*]

law закон [*zakon*]; against the law противозаконно [*prateeva-zakon-nuh*]

lawn газон [*gazon*]

lawyer юрист [*yōoreest*]

laxative слабительное [*slabee-tyilnuh-ye*]

lay-by стоянка на обочине [*sta-yanka na abochin-ye*]

laze around: I just want to laze around я хочу бездельничать [*ya khachōo byiz-dyelnichat*]

lazy ленивый [*lyinee-vee*]; don't be lazy не ленитесь [*nye lyinee-tyiss*]; a nice lazy holiday приятный спокойный отдых [*pri-yahtnee spa-koynee otdikh*]

lead (electric) провод [*provut*]; where does this road lead? куда ведёт эта дорога? [*kōoda vyi-dyot etta daroga*]

leaf лист [*leest*]

leaflet брошюра [*brashōora*]; do you have a leaflet on ...? у вас есть брошюра о ...? [*ōo vass yist brashōora a*]

leak (noun) течь (f) [*tyech*]; the roof leaks крыша протекает [*kreesha pra-tyika-yit*]

learn: I want to learn Russian я хочу учиться русскому языку [*ya khachōo ōocheetsa rooskamōo yazikōo*]

learner: I'm just a learner я всего лишь ученик [*ya fsyivo leesh ōocheneek*]

least: I'm not in the least interested я совсем не интересуюсь [*ya sa-fsyem nye in-tyi-ryi-sōo-yōoss*]; at least 100 по крайней мере 100 [*pa krı-nye mye-rye sto*]

leather кожа [*kozha*]

leave: when does the bus leave? когда отходит автобус? [*kagda at-khodit avto-booss*]; I leave tomorrow я уезжаю завтра [*ya ōo-yizha-yōo zaftra*]; he left this morning он уехал сегодня утром [*on ōo-yekhal syivo-dnya ōōtrum*]; may I leave this here? можно это здесь оставить? [*mozhnuh ettuh zdyiss astah-veet*]; I left my bag in the bar я оставил свою сумку в баре [*ya astahvil sva-yōo soomkōo vbar-ye*]; she left her bag here она оставила сумку здесь [*ana astahvila soomkōo zdyiss*]; leave the window open please пожалуйста, оставьте окно открытым [*pa-zhahlsta astahf-tye akno at-kreetim*]; there's not much left осталось совсем немного [*astahluss sa-fsyem nyem-noguh*]; I've hardly any money left у меня почти что кончились деньги [*ōo minya pachtee shto konchileess dyen-gee*]; I'll leave it up to you решение ваше [*ryi-sheni-ye vash-e*]

lecherous развратный [*razvraht-nee*]

left левый [*lyevee*]; on/to the left налево [*na-lyevuh*]

left-hand drive (car) (машина) с левосторонним управлением [(*masheena*) *slyiva-staron-nim ōopra-vlyeni-yem*]

left-handed левша [*lyivsha*]

left-luggage office камера хранения [*ka-myira khra-nyeni-ya*]

leg нога [*naga*]

legal (juridical) юридический [*yōori-deechiskee*]; (permitted by law) законный [*zakonnee*]

legal aid юридическая консультация [*yōori-deechiska-ya kan-sōoltahtsi-ya*]

lemon лимон [*leemon*]

lemonade лимонад [*leemanat*]

lemon tea чай с лимоном [*chı sleemonum*]

lend: would you lend me your ...? одолжите, пожалуйста, ваш ... [*adalzhee-tye pa-zhahlsta vash*]

Leningrad Ленинград [*lyinin-graht*]

Lenin Library Библиотека имени Ленина [*biblia-tyeka ee-myinee lyenina*]

Lenin's Mausoleum Мавзолей Ленина [*mavza-lyay lyenina*]

lens (camera) объектив [*ab-yikteef*]; (contact) контактная линза [*kantaktna-ya linza*]

lens cap крышка объектива [*kreeshka ab-yikteeva*]

Lent великий пост [*vyileekee posst*]

lesbian лесбиянка [*lyizbi-yanka*]

less: less than an hour меньше часа [*myensh-e chassa*]; much less гораздо меньше [*garazduh myensh-e*]; less cold менее холодный [*mye-nye-ye khalodnee*]

lesson урок [*oorok*]; do you give lessons? вы даёте уроки? [*vee da-yot-ye oorokee*]

let: would you let me use it? разрешите мне пользоваться этим? [*raz-ryishee-tye mnye pol-zuvatsa ettim*]; will you let me know? дайте мне, пожалуйста, знать [*dı-tye mnye pa-zhahlsta znaht*]; I'll let you know я вам дам знать [*ya vam dam znaht*]; let me try дайте мне попробовать [*dı-tye mnye pa-probuvat*]; let me go! пустите меня! [*pōosteet-ye minya*]; let's leave now давайте уйдём сейчас [*davı-tye ōoee-dyom syay-chass*]; let's not go yet давайте останемся ещё [*davı-tye asta-nyimsa yish-cho*]; will you let me off at ...? высадите меня, пожалуйста, в/на ... [*vee-sadeet-ye minya pa-zahlsta v/na*]; room to let сдаётся комната [*zda-yotsa komnata*]

letter (*in mail*) письмо [*pi-smo*]; (*of alphabet*) буква [*bōokva*]; are there any letters for us? письма для нас есть? [*pee-sma dlya nass yist*]

letterbox почтовый ящик [*pach-tovee yash-chik*]

lettuce салат [*salaht*]

level crossing переезд [*pyiri-yezd*]

lever (*noun*) рычаг [*richak*]

liable: to be liable (*responsible*) нести ответственность [*nyistee at-vyetst-vyinnust*]

liberated: a liberated woman эмансипированная женщина [*eman-sipeeruvanna-ya zhensh-china*]

library библиотека [*biblia-tyeka*]

licence, license лицензия [*leetsenzi-ya*]; (*permit*) разрешение [*raz-ryisheni-ye*]

license plate (*on car*) номерной знак [*namyirnoy znak*]

lid крышка [*kreeshka*]

lie (*untruth*) ложь (f) [*lozh*]; to (*tell a*) lie лгать/солгать [*lgaht/salgaht*]; to lie (*down*) ложиться/лечь [*lazheetsa/lyech*]; to be lying (*down*) лежать [*lyizhaht*]; can he lie down for a while? разрешите ему чуть-чуть прилечь? [*raz-ryisheet-ye yimōo chōot-chōot pree-lyech*]; I want to go and lie down мне хочется прилечь [*mnye khochitsa pree-lyech*]

lie-in: I'm going to have a lie-in tomorrow я встану завтра попозже [*ya fstahnōo zaftra papozh-e*]

life жизнь (f) [*zheezn*]; not on your life! ни в коем случае! [*nee fko-yem slōochı-ye*]; that's life! такова жизнь [*takava zheezn*]

lifebelt спасательный пояс [*spassah-tyilnee po-yass*]

lifeboat спасательная шлюпка [*spassah-tyilna-ya shlyōopka*]

lifeguard телохранитель (m) [*tyila-khranee-tyil*]

life insurance страхование жизни [*strakha-vahni-ye zheeznee*]

life jacket спасательный жилет [*spassah-tyilnee zhee-lyet*]

lift (*in hotel etc*) лифт [*leeft*]; could you give me a lift? можете меня подвезти? [*mozhit-ye minya pad-vyiztee*]; do you want a lift? вас подвезти? [*vass pad-vyiztee*]; thanks for the lift спасибо, что подбросили [*spa-see-buh shto pad-brosee-lee*]; I got a lift меня подвезли [*minya pad-vyizlee*]

light (*noun*) свет [*svyet*]; (*not heavy*) лёгкий [*lyokh-kee*]; the light was on свет горел [*svyet ga-ryel*]; do you have a light? у вас есть прикурить? [*ōo vass yist pree-kooreet*]; a light meal закуска [*zakōoska*]; light blue светло-голубой [*svyetluh ga-looboy*]

light bulb электрическая лампочка [*e-lyik-treechiska-ya lampuchka*]

lighter (*cigarette*) зажигалка [*zazhigalka*]

lighthouse маяк [*ma-yak*]

light meter экспонометр [*ekspano-myitr*]

lightning молния [*molni-ya*]

like: I'd like a ... мне бы хотелось ... [*mnye bee kha-tyeluss*]; I'd like to ... я хотел бы ... [*ya kha-tyel bee*]; would you like a ...? хотите ...? [*khateet-ye*]; would you like to come with us? хотите пойти с нами? [*khateet-ye pıtee snahmee*]; I'd like to me бы хотелось [*mnye bee kha-tyeluss*]; I like it мне нравится [*mnye nrahvitsa*]; I like you вы мне нравитесь [*vee mnye nrahvi-tyiss*]; I don't like it мне не нравится [*mnye nye nrahvitsa*]; he doesn't like it ему не нравится [*yimōo nye nrahvitsa*]; do you like ...? вам нравится ...? [*vam nrahvitsa*]; I like swimming я люблю плавать [*ya lyōob-lyōo plahvat*]; OK, if you like ладно, если хотите [*lahdnuh, *ye-slee khateet-ye*]; what's it like there? как это там? [*kak ettuh tam*]; do it like this это надо сделать так [*ettuh nahduh zdyelat tak*]; one like that такое же [*tako-yezh-e*]

lilo надувной матрац [*na-doovnoy matrats*]

lime cordial, lime juice сок лайма [*sok lıma*]

line (*on paper*) строка [*straka*]; (*telephone*) линия [*leeni-ya*]; (*of people*) очередь (*f*) [*ochi-ryit*]; would you give me a line? (*telephone*) соедините меня, пожалуйста [*sa-yedineet-ye minya pa-zhahlsta*]

linen (*for beds*) бельё [*byi-lyo*]

linguist лингвист [*lingveest*]; I'm no linguist мне трудно даются языки [*mnye trŏŏdnuh da-yŏŏtsa yazikee*]

lining подкладка [*pad-klahtka*]

lip губа [*gooba*]

lip brush щёточка для нанесения губной помады [*shotuchka dlya na-nyisseni-ye goobnoy pamahdee*]

lip pencil карандаш для губ [*karandash dlya gŏŏp*]

lip salve гигиеническая губная помада [*gee-gee-eneechiska-ya goobna-ya pamahda*]

lipstick губная помада [*goobna-ya pamahda*]

liqueur ликёр [*li-kyor*]

liquor алкоголь (*m*) [*alkagol*]

liquor store винный магазин [*veennee magazeen*]

list список [*spee-suk*]

listen: I'd like to listen to ... мне хочется послушать ... [*mnye khochitsa pa-slŏŏshat*]; listen! слушайте! [*slŏŏshı-tye*]

Lithuania Литва [*litva*]

litre, liter литр [*leetr*]; see page 121

litter (*rubbish*) мусор [*mŏŏssur*]

little немного [*nyem-noguh*]; just a little, thanks чуть-чуть, пожалуйста [*chŏŏt-chŏŏt pa-zhahlsta*]; just a very little только совсем немножко [*tol-kuh sa-fsyem nyem-nozhkuh*]; a little cream чуточку сливок [*chŏŏtuch-kŏŏ sleevuk*]; a little more добавьте немного [*dabahf-tye nyem-noguh*]; a little better немного лучше [*nyem-noguh lŏŏch-e*]; that's too little (*not enough*) недостаточно [*nyi-dastahtuch-nuh*]

live жить [*zheet*]; I live in ... я живу в ... [*ya zhivŏŏ v*]; where do you live? где вы живёте? [*gdye vee zhi-vyo-tye*]; where does

he live? где он живёт? [*gdye on zhi-vyot*]; we live together мы живём вместе [*mee zhi-vyom vmyest-ye*]

lively (*person, town*) живой [*zhivoy*]

liver (*in body*) печень (*f*) [*pyechin*]

lizard ящерица [*yash-cheritsa*]

loaf буханка хлеба [*bookhanka khlyeba*]

lobby (*of hotel*) вестибюль (*m*) [*vyisti-byŏŏl*]

lobster омар [*amar*]

local: a local newspaper местная газета [*myestna-ya ga-zyeta*]; a local restaurant близлежащий ресторан [*bleez-lyizhahsh-chee ryistaran*]; a local wine местное вино [*myestnuh-ye veeno*]

lock (*noun*) замок [*zamok*]; it's locked заперто [*zah-pyertuh*]; I locked myself out of my room ключ от комнаты остался внутри [*klyŏŏch at kom-natee astalsa vnŏŏtree*]

locker (*for luggage etc*) шкафчик [*shkafchik*]

log: I slept like a log я крепко спал [*ya kryepkuh spahl*]

lollipop леденец [*lyi-dyi-nyets*]

London Лондон [*lundun*]

lonely одинокий [*adinokee*]; are you lonely? вы чувствуете себя одиноким? [*vee chŏŏstvŏŏ-yit-ye sibya adinokim*]

long длинный [*dleennee*]; how long does it take? как долго это длится? [*kak dolguh ettuh dleetsa*]; is it a long way? это далеко? [*ettuh da-lyiko*]; a long time долго [*dolguh*]; I won't be long я скоро вернусь [*ya skoruh vyirnŏŏss*]; don't be long не задерживайтесь [*nye za-dyerzhivı-tyiss*]; that was long ago это было давно [*ettuh beeluh davno*]; I'd like to stay longer мне бы хотелось остаться дольше [*mnye bee kha-tyeluss astahtsa dolsh-e*]; long time no see! сколько лет, сколько зим! [*skol-kuh lyet skol-kuh zeem*]; so long! пока! [*paka*]

long-distance call междугородный или международный телефонный разговор [*myizhdŏŏ-garodnee eelee myizhdŏŏ-narodnee tyili-fonnee razgavor*]

loo: where's the loo? где туалет? [*gdye too-a-lyet*]; I want to go to the loo мне нужно в туалет [*mnye nŏŏzhnuh ftoo-a-lyet*]

look: that looks good смотрится хорошо [*smotritsa khara-sho*]; you look tired у вас усталый вид [*ŏŏ vass ŏŏ-stahlee veet*]; I'm just looking, thanks спасибо, мне ничего не нужно, я только хочу посмотреть [*spa-see-buh mnye nee-chivo nye noozhnuh ya tol-kuh khachoo pasma-tryet*]; **you don't look your age** вы хорошо сохранились [*vee khara-sho sa-khraneeleess*]; **look at him** посмотрите на него [*pasmatree-tye na nyivo*]; **I'm looking for . . .** я ищу . . . [*ya ish-choo*]; **look out!** осторожно! [*asta-rozhnuh*]; **can I have a look?** можно посмотреть? [*mozh-nuh pasma-tryet*]; **can I have a look around?** можно посмотреть, что здесь имеется? [*mozh-nuh pasma-tryet shto zdyiss ee-mye-yitsa*]

loose: **the button is loose** пуговица плохо держится [*pooguvitsa plokhuh dyerzhitsa*]; **the handle is loose** ручка плохо держится [*roochka plokhuh dyerzhitsa*]

loose change мелочь (*f*) [*myeluch*]

lorry грузовик [*groozaveek*]

lorry driver водитель грузовика [*vadee-tyil groozaveeka*]

lose терять/потерять [*tyi-ryat/pa-tyiryat*]; **I've lost my . . .** я потерял свой . . . [*ya pa-tyi-ryal svoy*]; **I'm lost** я заблудился [*ya zabloodeel-sa*]

lost-property office, lost and found бюро находок [*byooro nakhoduk*]

lot: **a lot, lots** много [*mnoguh*]; **not a lot** не так уж много [*nye tak oozh mnoguh*]; **a lot of money** много денег [*mnoguh dyenyek*]; **a lot of women** много женщин [*mnoguh zhensh-chin*]; **a lot cooler** намного прохладней [*nam-noguh prakhlahd-nyay*]; **I like it a lot** мне очень нравится [*mnye ochin nrahvitsa*]; **is it a lot further?** это намного дальше? [*ettuh*

nam-noguh dalsh-e]; **I'll take the** (*whole*) **lot** я возьму всё [*ya vazmoo fsyo*]

lotion лосьон [*la-syon*]

loud громкий [*gromkee*]; **the music is too loud** музыка играет слишком громко [*moozika eegrah-yet sleesh-kum gromkuh*]

lounge (*in house, hotel*) гостиная [*gasteenaya*]

lousy отвратительный [*atvratee-tyilnee*]

love: **I love you** я вас люблю [*ya vass lyooblyoo*]; **he's fallen in love** он влюбился [*on vlyoo-beelsa*]; **I love the Soviet Union** мне нравится Советский Союз [*mnye nrahvitsa sa-vyetskee sa-yooss*]

lovely замечательный [*za-myichah-tyilnee*]

low низкий [*neezkee*]

low beam ближний свет фар [*bleezhnee svyet far*]

LP долгоиграющая грампластинка [*dalga-eegrah-yoosh-cha-ya gram-plastinka*]

luck судьба [*sood-ba*]; **hard luck!** не везёт! [*nye vyi-zyot*]; **good luck!** желаю успеха! [*zhila-yoo oo-spyekha*]; **just my luck!** мне никогда не везёт [*mnye nee-kagda nye vyizyot*]; **it was pure luck** просто повезло [*prostuh pa-vyizlo*]

lucky: **that's lucky!** везёт же! [*vyi-zyotzhe*]

lucky charm талисман [*talisman*]

luggage багаж [*bagahsh*]

lumbago люмбаго [*lyoom-bahguh*]

lump (*medical*) опухоль (*f*) [*opookhul*]

lunch обед [*a-byet*]

lungs лёгкие [*lyokh-kee-ye*]

luxurious роскошный [*raskoshnee*]

luxury роскошь (*f*) [*roskush*]

M

mad сумасшедший [*sooma-shedshee*]

madam госпожа [*gaspazha*]

magazine журнал [*zhoornal*]

magnificent великолепный [*vyilika-lyepnee*]

maid горничная [*gornichna-ya*]

maiden name девичья фамилия [*dyeveech-ya fameeli-ya*]

mail (*noun*) почта [*pochta*]; **is there any mail for me?** есть для меня письма? [*yist dlya minya peesma*]; **where can I mail**

this? где могу это отправить? [*gdye magoo ettuh at-prahveet*]

mailbox почтовый ящик [*pachtovee yash-chik*]

main главный [*glahv-nee*]; **where's the main post office?** где главпочтамт? [*gdye glaf-pachtamt*]

main road (*in town*) главная улица [*glahvna-ya oolitsa*]; (*trunk road*) главная магистраль (*f*) [*glahvna-ya ma-gistrahl*]

make делать/сделать [*dyelat/zdyelat*]; **do you make this yourself?** вы сами изготовляете это? [*vee sahmee izgatav-lya-yit-ye ettuh*]; it's very well made это очень добротно сделано [*ettuh ochin dabrot-nuh zdyelan-uh*]; what does that make altogether? сколько всё это, вместе взятое? [*skol-kuh fsyo ettuh vmyest-ye vzyatuh-ye*]; I make it only 5 roubles у меня выходит 5 рублей [*ōō minya vikhodit pyat roob-lyay*]

make-up косметика [*kaz-myetika*]

make-up remover крем для снятия косметики [*kryem dlya snyati-ya kaz-myetikee*]

male chauvinist pig мужской шовинист [*mōōzh-skoy shavineest*]

man (*male*) мужчина [*mōōzh-cheena*]; (*human being*) человек [*chila-vyek*]

manager заведующий [*za-vyedoo-yōōsh-chee*]; may I see the manager? позовите, пожалуйста, заведующего [*pazaveet-ye pa-zhahlsta za-vyedoo-yōōsh-chivuh*]

manicure маникюр [*mani-kyōōr*]

many многие [*mnogi-ye*]

map карта [*karta*]; it's not on this map на карте этого нет [*na kart-ye ettuv-uh nyet*]

marble (*noun*) мрамор [*mrah-mur*]

March март [*mart*]

marijuana марихуана [*marikhoo-ahna*]

mark: there's a dirty mark on it на этом пятно [*na ettum pyatno*]; could you mark it on the map for me? можете отметить это место на карте, пожалуйста? [*mozhit-ye at-myeteet ettuh myestuh na kart-ye pa-zhahlsta*]

market (*noun*) рынок [*reenuk*]

marmalade апельсиновое варенье [*a-pyil-seenuvuh-ye va-ryeni-ye*]

married: are you married? (*said to woman*) вы замужем? [*vee zah-moozhem*]; (*said to man*) вы женаты? [*vee zhinahtee*]; I'm married (*woman*) я замужем [*ya zah-moozhem*]; (*man*) я женат [*ya zhinaht*]

mascara тушь для ресниц и бровей [*toosh dlya ryi-sneets ee bra-vyay*]

mast мачта [*machta*]

masterpiece шедевр [*she-dyevr*]

matches спички [*speech-kee*]

material (*cloth*) ткань (*f*) [*tkan*]

matter: it doesn't matter неважно [*nyi-vazhnuh*]; what's the matter в чём дело? [*fchom dyeluh*]

mattress матрац [*matrats*]

mausoleum мавзолей [*mavza-lyay*]

maximum (*noun*) максимум [*maksimoom*]

May май [*mı*]

may: may I take one? можно взять? [*mozh-nuh vzyat*]; may I? можно? [*mozh-nuh*]; may I have another bottle? дайте мне, пожалуйста, ещё бутылку [*dı-tye mnye pa-zhahlsta yish-cho boo-teelkōō*]

maybe может быть [*mozhit beet*]; maybe not может и нет [*mozhit ee nyet*]

mayonnaise майонез [*mı-a-nyess*]

me: come with me идёмте со мной [*ee-dyom-tye samnoy*]; it's for me это для меня [*ettuh dlya minya*]; it's me это я [*ettuh ya*]; me too я тоже [*ya tozh-e*]; *see page 112*

meal: that was an excellent meal еда была отличная [*yida bila at-leechna-ya*]; does that include meals? цена включает и питание? [*tsina fklyoo-cha-yit ee pitahni-ye*]

mean: what does this word mean? что значит это слово? [*shto znachit ettuh slov-uh*]; what does he mean? что он хочет сказать? [*shto on khochit skazat*]

measles корь (*f*) [*kor*]; German measles краснуха [*kra-snōōkha*]

measurements размеры [*raz-myeree*]

meat мясо [*mya-suh*]

mechanic: do you have a mechanic here? здесь есть механик? [*zdyiss yist myi-khahnik*]

medicine медицина [*myidi-tseena*]

medieval средневековый [*sryid-nyi-vyikovee*]

medium (*adjective*) средний [*sryed-nee*]

medium-rare довольно хорошо прожаренный, но ещё с кровью [*da-volnuh khara-sho pra-zhah-ryinnuh no yish-cho skrov-yōō*]

medium-sized среднего размера [*sryed-nyivuh raz-myera*]

meet: pleased to meet you рад познакомиться [*raht pazna-komitsa*]; where shall we meet? где мы встретимся? [*gdye mee fstrye-timsa*]; let's meet up again давайте встретимся ещё [*davı-tye fstrye-timsa yish-cho*]

meeting (*business, committee etc*) заседание [*za-syidahni-ye*]; (*encounter, rendez-vous*) встреча [*fstryecha*]

meeting place место встречи [*myestuh fstryechee*]

melon дыня [*deen-ya*]; (*water melon*) арбуз [*arbōōss*]

melt таять/растаять [*ta-yat/rass-ta-yat*]

member член [*chlyen*]; I'd like to become a member я хочу стать членом [*ya khachóo staht chlyen-um*]

men (*males*) мужчины [*móozh-cheenee*]; (*human beings*) люди [*lyóodee*]

mend: can you mend this? можете это починить? [*mozhit-ye ettuh pachineet*]

men's room мужской туалет [*moozh-skoy too-a-lyet*]

mention: don't mention it не за что [*nye-za-shtuh*]

menu меню [*myin-yóo*]; may I have the menu please? дайте мне, пожалуйста, меню [*di-tye mnye pa-zhahlsta myin-yóo*]

mess: it's a mess ужасный беспорядок [*óo-zhah-snee byispa-ryahduk*]

message: are there any messages for me? мне что-нибудь передавали? [*mnye shto-nee-bóot pyiri-davahlee*]; I'd like to leave a message for . . . можете передать . . .? [*mozhi-tye pyiri-daht*]

metal (*noun*) металл [*myital*]

metre, meter метр [*myetr*]; *see page 120*

midday: at midday в полдень [*fpol-dyin*]

middle: in the middle посередине [*pa-syiri-deen-ye*]; in the middle of the road посередине дороги [*pa-syiri-deen-ye darogee*]

midnight: at midnight в полночь [*fpol-nuch*]

might: I might want to stay another 3 days может быть, я захочу остаться ещё на 3 дня [*mozhit beet ya za-khachóo astahtsa yish-cho na tree dnya*]; you might have warned me! вы могли меня хотя бы предупредить! [*vee maglee minya kha-tya bee pryidóo-pryideet*]

migraine мигрень (*f*) [*mee-gryen*]

mild умеренный [*oo-myeryenee*]

mile миля [*mee-lya*]; that's miles away! это страшно далеко! [*ettuh strash-nuh da-lyiko*]; *see page 120*

military (*adjective*) военный [*va-yennee*]

milk молоко [*malako*]

milkshake молочный коктейль [*maloch-nee kak-tyayl*]

millimetre, millimeter миллиметр [*milli-myetr*]

minced meat рубленое мясо [*róo-blyinuh-ye mya-suh*]

mind: I don't mind я не прочь [*ya nye proch*]; would you mind if I . . .? вы не возражаете если я . . .? [*vee nye vaz-razhah-yit-ye ye-slee ya*]; never mind не волнуйтесь! [*nye val-nóoi-tyiss*]; I've changed my mind я передумал [*ya pyiri-dóomal*]

mine: it's mine это моё [*ettuh ma-yo*]; *see page 110*

mineral water минеральная вода [*minirahlna-ya vada*]

minimum минимум [*minimoom*]

mint (*sweet*) мятная конфета [*myatna-ya kan-fyeta*]

minus минус [*meenooss*]; minus 3 degrees минус 3 градуса [*meenooss tree grah-doossa*]

minute минута [*minóota*]; in a minute через минуту [*che-ryiz minóotoo*]; just a minute минуточку [*minóotuch-kóo*]

mirror зеркало [*zyerka-luh*]

Miss госпожа [*gaspazha*]; Miss! девушка [*dyevooshka*]

miss: I miss you я соскучился по вас [*ya sa-skóochilsa pa vass*]; there's a . . . missing здесь недостаёт . . . [*zdyiss nye-dasta-yot*]; we missed the bus мы опоздали на автобус [*mee apaz-dahlee na avto-booss*]

mist туман [*too-mahn*]

mistake ошибка [*a-sheepka*]; I think there's a mistake here произошла ошибка [*pra-izashla a-sheepka*]

misunderstanding недоразумение [*nyi-darazoo-myeni-ye*]

mixture смесь (*f*) [*smyess*]

mix-up: there's been some sort of mix-up with . . . вышла какая-то путаница с . . . [*veeshla kaka-ya-tuh póotanitsa s*]

modern современный [*sa-vryi-myennee*]

modern art современное искусство [*sa-vryi-myennuh-ye iss-kóost-vuh*]

moisturizer увлажняющий лосьон [*óo-vlazh-nya-yóosh-chee la-syon*]

Moldavia Молдавия [*maldahvi-ya*]

moment момент [*ma-myent*]; I won't be a moment минуточку [*minóotuch-kóo*]

monastery монастырь (*m*) [*mana-steer*]

Monday понедельник [*pa-nyi-dyelnik*]

money деньги [*dyen-gee*]; I don't have any money у меня нет денег [*óo minya nyet dye-nyek*]; do you take English/American money? можно заплатить в фунтах/долларах? [*mozh-nuh za-plateet v-foontakh/dollar-akh*]

Mongolia Монголия [*mang-goli-ya*]

month месяц [*mye-syats*]

monument памятник [*pam-yatnik*]

moon луна [*lóona*]

moped мопед [*ma-pyet*]

more больше [*bolsh-e*]; may I have some more? можно взять ещё? [*mozh-nuh vzyat yish-cho*]; more water, please дайте ещё воды, пожалуйста [*dt-tye yish-cho vadee pa-zhahlsta*]; no more, thanks спасибо, больше не хочу [*spa-see-buh bolsh-e nye khachoo*]; more expensive дороже [*darozh-e*]; more than 10 более 10 [*bo-lye-ye dyi-syatee*]; more than that более чем это [*bo-lye-ye chem ettuh*]; a lot more гораздо больше [*garahz-duh bolsh-e*]; not any more больше нет [*bolsh-e nyet*]; I'm not staying there any more я там уже не проживаю [*ya tam oozh-e nye prazhiva-yoo*]

morning утро [*ōōtruh*]; good morning доброе утро [*dobruh-ye ōōtruh*]; this morning сегодня утром [*syivo-dnya ōōtrum*]; in the morning утром [*ōōtrum*]

Moscow Москва [*maskva*]

mosquito комар [*kamar*]

most: I like this one most мне больше всего нравится это [*mnye bol-she fsyi-vo nrahvitsa ettuh*]; most of the time большая часть времени [*balsha-ya chast vrye-myinee*]; most hotels большинство гостиниц [*balshin-stvo gastee-nits*]

mother: my mother моя мать [*ma-ya mat*]

motif (*in pattern*) узор [*ōōzor*]

motor двигатель (*f*) [*dveega-tyil*]

motorbike мотоцикл [*mata-tseekl*]

motorboat моторная лодка [*matorna-ya lotka*]

motorist автомобилист [*avtamabee-leest*]

motorway автострада [*avta-strada*]

motor yacht моторная яхта [*matorna-ya yakh-ta*]

mountain гора [*gara*]; up in the mountains в горах [*vga-rakh*]; a mountain village горный посёлок [*gornee pa-syoluk*]

mouse мышь (*f*) [*meesh*]

moustache усы [*oo-see*]

mouth рот [*rot*]

move: he's moved to another hotel он переселился в другую гостиницу [*on pyiri-syileel-sa vdroo-goo-yoo gastee-nitsoo*];

could you move your car? вы можете переставить свою машину? [*vee mozhit-ye pyiri-stahvit sva-yoo masheenoo*]

movie фильм [*film*]; let's go to the movies пойдёмте в кино [*pt-dyom-tye fkeeno*]

movie camera кинокамера [*keena-kah-myira*]

movie theater кинотеатр [*keena-tyi-ahtr*]

moving: a very moving tune очень трогательная мелодия [*ochin troga-tyilna-ya myilodi-ya*]

Mr господин [*gaspadeen*]

Mrs госпожа [*gaspazha*]

Ms госпожа [*gaspazha*]

much много [*mnoguh*]; much better намного лучше [*nam-noguh looch-e*]; much cooler намного прохладней [*nam-noguh prakhlad-nyay*]; not much немного [*nyem-noguh*]; not so much не так много [*nye tak mnoguh*]

muffler (*on car*) глушитель (*m*) [*glooshee-tyil*]

mug: I've been mugged на меня напали [*na minya na-pahlee*]

muggy сырой [*siroy*]

mumps свинка [*sveenka*]

mural стенная роспись [*styinna-ya ross-peess*]

muscle мышца [*meesh-tsa*]

museum музей [*moo-zyay*]

mushroom гриб [*greep*]

music музыка [*mōōzika*]; guitar music гитарная музыка [*gitarna-ya mōōzika*]; do you have the sheet music for . . .? у вас есть ноты . . .? [*ōō vass yist notee*]

musician музыкант [*moozikant*]

must: I must . . . (*man*) я должен . . . [*ya dolzhen*]; (*woman*) я должна . . . [*ya dalzhna*]; I mustn't drink . . . мне нельзя пить . . . [*mnye nyil-zya peet*]; you mustn't forget не забудьте! [*nye za-bōōd-tye*]

mustache усы [*oo-see*]

mustard горчица [*garcheetsa*]

my: my (*hotel*) room мой номер [*moy no-myir*]; see page 110

myself: I'll do it myself я сделаю сам [*ya zdyela-yoo sahm*]

N

nail (*of finger*) ноготь (*m*) [*nogut*]; (*in wood*) гвоздь (*m*) [*gvozd*]

nail clippers ножницы для ногтей [*nozhnitsee dlya nag-tyay*]

nailfile пилка для ногтей [*peelka dlya nag-tyay*]

nail polish лак для ногтей [*lak dlya nag-tyay*]

nail polish remover жидкость для снятия лака [*zheetkust dlya snyati-ya laka*]

nail scissors ножницы для ногтей [*nozh-nitsee dlya nag-tyay*]

naked голый [*golee*]

name (*first name*) имя [*ee-mya*]; (*surname*) фамилия [*fameeli-ya*]; **what's your name?** как вас зовут? [*kak vass zavoot*]; **what's its name?** как это называется? [*kak ettuh naziva-yitsa*]; **my name is . . .** меня зовут . . . [*minya zavoot*]

nap: he's having a nap он спит [*on speet*]

napkin салфетка [*sal-fyetka*]

nappy пелёнка [*pyi-lyonka*]

narrow узкий [*oozkee*]

nasty отвратительный [*atvratee-tyilnee*]; (*injury*) опасный [*apah-snee*]

national национальный [*natsion-ahlnee*]

nationality национальность (*f*) [*natsion-ahlnust*]

natural естественный [*yiss-tyest-vyinnee*]

naturally (*of course*) конечно [*ka-nyeshnuh*]

nature (*trees etc*) природа [*preeroda*]

nausea тошнота [*tashnata*]

near близко [*bleezkuh*]; **is it near here?** это близко отсюда? [*ettuh bleezkuh at-syooda*]; **near the window** около окна [*okuluh akna*]; **do you go near . . .?** вы проедете мимо . . .? [*vee pra-ye-dye-tye meemuh*]; **where is the nearest. . .?** где ближайший . . . ? [*gdye bleezhsh-chee*]

nearby недалеко [*nyida-lyiko*]

nearly почти [*pachtee*]

neat (*room etc*) чистый [*cheestee*]; (*drink*) неразбавленный [*nyi-razbahv-lyinnee*]

necessary необходимый [*nyi-ab-khadeemee*]; **is it necessary to . . .?** нужно . . .? [*noozh-nuh*]; **it's not necessary** не надо [*nye nah-duh*]

neck шея [*she-ya*]; (*of dress, shirt*) воротник [*varatneek*]

necklace ожерелье [*azhe-rye-lye*]

necktie галстук [*galstook*]

need: I need a . . . мне надо . . . [*mnye nah-duh*]; **do I need a . . .?** нужно ли мне . . .? [*noozh-nuh lee mnye*]; **it needs more salt** нужно добавить соли [*noozh-nuh dabahveet solee*]; **there's no need** нет необходимости [*nyet nyi-ab-khadeemustee*]; **there's no need to shout!** необязательно кричать! [*nyi-abyazah-tyilnuh kreechat*]

needle иголка [*eegolka*]

negative (*film*) негатив [*nyigateef*]

neighbo(u)r сосед [*sa-syet*]

neighbo(u)rhood соседство [*sa-syedst-vuh*]

neither: neither of us никто из нас [*nee-kto iz nass*]; **neither one** (*of them*) никто из них [*nee-kto iz neekh*]; **neither . . . nor . . .** ни . . . ни . . . [*nee . . . nee . . .*]; **neither do I** я тоже [*ya tozh-e*]; **neither does he** он тоже [*on tozh-e*]

nephew: my nephew мой племянник [*moy plyim-yahnik*]

nervous нервный [*nyervnee*]

net (*fishing*) сеть (*f*) [*syet*]; (*tennis*) сетка [*syetka*]

nettle крапива [*krapeeva*]

neurotic невротический [*nyi-vrateechiskee*]

neutral (*gear*) нейтральная передача [*nyay-tralna-ya pyiri-dacha*]

never никогда [*nee-kagda*]

new новый [*novee*]

news новости [*novustee*]; **is there any news?** есть какие-нибудь новости? [*yist kakee-ye-niboot novustee*]

newspaper газета [*ga-zyeta*]; **do you have any English newspapers?** у вас есть английские газеты? [*ōō vass yist anglee-skee-ye ga-zyetee*]

newsstand газетный киоск [*ga-zyetnee kee-osk*]

New Year Новый год [*novee got*]; **Happy New Year!** С Новым Годом! [*snovim godum*]

New Year's Eve канун Нового года [*kanōōn novuv-uh goda*]

New York Нью-Йорк [*nyōō york*]

New Zealand Новая Зеландия [*nova-ya zyelandi-ya*]

New Zealander (*man*) новозеландец [*nava-zyiland-yits*]; (*woman*) новозеландка [*nava-zyilandka*]; (*adjective*) новозеландский [*nava-zyiland-skee*]

next следующий [*slyedoo-yōōsh-chee*]; **next week/Monday** на следующей неделе/в следующий понедельник [*na slyedoo-yōōsh-chay nyi-dye-lye/fslyedoo-yōōsh-chee pa-nyi-dyelnik*]; **it's at the next corner** на ближайшем углу [*na blee-zhzsh-chem oo-glōō*]; **next to the post office** рядом с почтой [*ryadum spochtoy*]; **the one next to that** то, что рядом с этим [*to shto ryadum settim*]

nextdoor (*adverb*) рядом [*ryadum*]; (*adjective*) соседний [*sa-syednee*]

next of kin ближайший родственник [*bleezhzsh-chee rodst-vyinnik*]

nice хороший [*kharoshee*]; **that's very nice** (*food, drink*) это очень вкусно [*ettuh ochin fkōō-snuh*]; **that's very nice of you** очень мило с вашей стороны [*ochin meeluh zvashay staranee*]

nickname прозвище [*prozveesh-che*]

niece: my niece моя племянница [*ma-ya plyi-myannitsa*]

night ночь (*f*) [*noch*]; **for one night** на одну ночь [*na adnōō noch*]; **for three nights** на три ночи [*na tree nochee*]; **good night** спокойной ночи [*spakoynoy nochee*]; **at night** ночью [*noch-yōō*]

nightcap (*drink*) стакан чего-то на ночь [*stakan chivo-tuh na-noch*]

nightclub ночной клуб [*nachnoy klōōp*]

nightdress ночная рубашка [*nachna-ya roobashka*]

night flight ночной полёт [*nachnoy pa-lyot*]

nightmare кошмар [*kashmar*]

night porter ночной портье [*nachnoy par-tyay*]

nit (*bug*) гнида [*gneeda*]

no нет [*nyet*]; **I've no money** у меня нет денег [*ōō minya nyet dye-nyek*]; **there's no more** больше нет [*bolsh-e nyet*]; **no more than . . .** не больше чем . . . [*nye bolsh-e chem*]; **oh no!** (*refusal*) ни в коем случае! [*nee fko-yem slōō-chu-ye*]; (*upset*) не может быть! [*nye mozhit beet*]

nobody никто [*nee-kto*]

noise шум [*shōōm*]

noisy шумный [*shōōm-nee*]; **it's too noisy here** здесь слишком шумно [*zdyiss sleesh-kum shōōm-nuh*]

non-alcoholic безалкогольный [*byiz-alkagolnee*]

none (*people*) никто [*nee-kto*]; (*things*) ничто [*nee-shto*]; **none of them knows** никто из них не знает [*nee-kto iz nikh ne zna-yit*]

nonsense ерунда [*yiroonda*]

non-smoking (*compartment, section of plane*) для некурящих [*dlya nyi-koo-ryash-cheekh*]

non-stop (*bus, train*) безостановочный [*byiz-astanovuchnee*]; **non-stop flight** беспосадочный полёт [*byiss-pasaduch-nee pa-lyot*]

no-one никто [*nee-kto*]

nor: nor do I я тоже [*ya tozh-e*]; **nor does he** он тоже [*on tozh-e*]

normal нормальный [*narmalnee*]; (*customary*) обычный [*abeechnee*]

north север [*sye-vyir*]; **in the north** на севере [*na sye-vyir-ye*]; **to the north of . . .** к северу от . . . [*ksye-vyirōō at*]

northeast северо-восток [*sye-vyira-vastok*]; **in the northeast** на северо-востоке [*na sye-vyira-vastok-ye*]

Northern Ireland Северная Ирландия [*sye-vyirna-ya eerlandi-ya*]

northwest северо-запад [*sye-vyiruh-zahpat*]; **in the northwest** на северо-западе [*na sye-vyiruh-zahpad-ye*]

Norway Норвегия [*nar-vyegi-ya*]

nose нос [*noss*]; **my nose is bleeding** у меня из носа течёт кровь [*ōō minya iz nossa tyichot kroff*]

not не [*nye*]; **I don't smoke** я не курящий [*ya nye koo-ryash-chee*]; **he didn't say anything** он ничего не сказал [*on nee-chivo nye skazal*]; **it's not important** это неважно [*ettuh nyi-vazhnuh*]; **not that one** не тот [*nye tot*]; **not for me** не для меня [*nye dlya minya*]; see page 117

note (*banknote*) банкнота [*banknota*]; (*written message*) записка [*zapeeska*]

notebook записная книжка [*zapeesna-ya k-neezh-ka*]

nothing ничего [*nee-chivo*]

November ноябрь (*m*) [*na-yabr*]

now сейчас [*syay-chass*]; **not now** не сейчас [*nye syay-chass*]

nowhere нигде [*nee-gdye*]

nuisance: **he's being a nuisance** он пристаёт ко мне [*on preesta-yot kam-nye*]

numb (*limb etc*) онемевший [*a-nyi-myevshee*]

number (*figure*) число [*chislo*]; (*house, telephone*) номер [*no-myir*]; **number plate** номерной знак [*na-myirnoy znak*]

nurse медсестра [*myid-syistra*]

nursery (*at airport etc*) детская комната [*dyetska-ya komnata*]

nut орех [*a-ryekh*]; (*for bolt*) гайка [*gıka*]

nutter: **he's a nutter** он спятил [*on spyateel*]

O

oar весло [*vyislo*]

obligatory обязательный [*a-byazah-tyilnee*]

obnoxious несносный [*nyi-snosnee*]

obvious: **that's obvious** само собой разумеется [*samo saboy razoom-ye-yitsa*]

occasionally иногда [*inagda*]

o'clock *see page 119*

October октябрь (*m*) [*ak-tyabr*]

October Revolution Великая Октябрьская Социалистическая Революция [*vyileeka-ya ak-tyabr-ska-ya satsiali-steechiska-ya ryiva-lyōōtsi-ya*]

odd (*strange*) странный [*strannee*]; (*number*) нечётный [*nyi-chotnee*]

odometer счётчик пройденных километров [*schot-chik proy-dyennikh kila-myetruff*]

of: **the name of the hotel** название гостиницы [*nazvahni-ye gastee-nitsee*]; **have one of mine** возьмите одно из моих [*vazmeet-ye adno iz ma-yeekh*]; *see page 106*

off: **20% off** на 20% ниже обычной цены [*na dvad-tsat pra-tsentuff neezh-e abeech-noy tsinee*]; **the lights were off** свет был выключен [*svyet beel vee-klyōōchen*]; **just off the main road** недалеко от главной дороги [*nyida-lyiko ot glahvnoy darogee*]

offend: **don't be offended** не обижайтесь [*nye abizhı-tyiss*]

office (*place of work*) контора [*kantora*]

officer (*said to policeman*) товарищ милиционер [*tavarishch militsia-nyer*]

official (*noun*) служащий [*slōōzhash-chee*]; **is that official?** это официально? [*ettuh afitsi-ahlnuh*]

off-season: **in the off-season** вне сезона [*vnye syizona*]

often часто [*chastuh*]; **not often** не часто [*nye chastuh*]

oil (*for car, for salad*) масло [*mah-sluh*]; (*crude oil*) нефть (*f*) [*nyeft*]; **we're losing oil** у нас утечка масла [*ōō nass ōō-tyechka mah-sla*]; **will you change the oil?** поменяйте, пожалуйста, масло в моторе [*pa-myin-yı-tye pa-zhahlsta mah-sluh vmator-ye*]; **the oil light's flashing** масляный манометр горит [*mah-slyanee mana-myetr gareet*]

oil painting картина написанная маслом [*karteena na-pee-sanna-ya mah-slum*]

oil pressure масляное давление [*mah-slyanuh-ye da-vlyeni-ye*]

ointment мазь (*f*) [*mahss*]

OK ладно [*lahdnuh*]; **are you OK?** всё в порядке? [*fsyo fpa-ryat-kye*]; **that's OK thanks** всё в порядке, спасибо [*fsyo fpa-ryat-kye spa-see-buh*]; **that's OK by me** (*man*) я согласен [*ya saglah-syin*]; (*woman*) я согласна [*ya saglah-sna*]

old старый [*stahree*]; **how old are you?** сколько вам лет? [*skol-kuh vam lyet*]

old-age pensioner пенсионер [*pyen-si-anyer*]

old-fashioned старомодный [*stara-modnee*]

old town старая часть города [*stahra-ya chast goruda*]

olive маслина [*masleena*]

olive oil оливковое масло [*aleefkuh-vuh-ye mah-sluh*]

omelet(t) омлет [*am-lyet*]

on на [*na*]; **on the roof** на крыше [*na kreesh-e*]; **on the beach** на пляже [*na* *plyazh-e*]; on Friday в пятницу [*fpyat-nitsōō*]; on television по телевизору [*pa tyili-veezurōō*]; I don't have it on me я не взял с собой [*ya nye vzyal s-saboy*]; the drinks are on me я заплачу за напитки [*ya za-plachōō za na-peetkee*]; a book on Moscow книга о Москве [*k-neega a mask-vye*]; the warning light comes on включается предупредительный сигнал [*fklyoo-chah-yitsa pryidoo-pryidee-tyilnee signal*]; the light was on свет был включён [*svyet beel fklyoo-chon*]; what's on at the cinema today? что идёт сегодня в кино? [*shto ee-dyot syivo-dnya fkeeno*]; it's just not on! это просто несправедливо [*ettuh prostuh nyispra-vyid-leevuh*]

once (*one time*) один раз [*adeen raz*]; (*formerly*) прежде [*pryezh-dye*]; at once (*immediately*) сразу же [*srahzōō zhe*]

one один [*adeen*]; that one тот [*tot*]; the green one зелёный [*zi-lyonee*]; the one with the black skirt on особа в чёрной юбке [*asoba fchornoy yōōp-kye*]

onion лук [*lōōk*]

only только [*tolkuh*]; only one только один [*tol-kuh adeen*]; the only one единственный [*yideenst-vyinnee*]; only once всего раз [*fsyivo rass*]; it's only 9 o'clock всего 9 часов [*fsyivo dye-vyat chassoff*]; I've only just arrived я только что приехал [*ya tolkuh shto pree-yekhal*]

open (*adjective*) открытый [*atkreetee*]; when do you open? когда вы открываете? [*kagda vee atkriva-yet-ye*]; in the open (*outdoors*) на открытом воздухе [*na atkreetum vozdookh-ye*]; it won't open не открывается [*nye atkriva-yitsa*]

opening times часы работы [*chassee rabotee*]

opera опера [*o-pyira*]

operation (*med*) операция [*a-pyirahtsi-ya*]

operator (*telephone*) телефонистка [*tyili-faneest-ka*]

opportunity возможность (*f*) [*vaz-mozhnust*]

opposite: opposite the church напротив церкви [*naprotif tserkvee*]; it's directly opposite это прямо напротив [*ettuh pryamuh naprotif*]

oppressive (*heat*) томительный [*tamee-tyilnee*]

optician оптик [*optik*]

optimistic оптимистический [*aptimis-teechiskee*]

optional необязательный [*nyi-a-byazah-tyilnee*]

or или [*eelee*]

orange (*fruit*) апельсин [*a-pyil-seen*]; (*colour*) оранжевый [*a-ranzhivee*]

orange juice апельсиновый сок [*a-pyil-seenuvee sok*]

orchestra оркестр [*ar-kyestr*]

order: could we order now? можно заказать? [*mozhnuh zakazaht*]; we've already ordered мы уже заказали [*mee ōōzh-e zakazahlee*]; I didn't order that я этого не заказывал [*ya ettuvuh nye za-kahzival*]; it's out of order (*lift etc*) не работает [*nye rabota-yet*]

ordinary обычный [*abeechnee*]

organization (*company*) организация [*arganee-zahtsi-ya*]

organize организовать [*arganee-zavat*]; could you organize it? можете устроить это? [*mozhit-ye oostro-yit ettuh*]

original оригинальный [*ariginahl-nee*]; is it an original? это подлинник? [*ettuh podleennik*]

ornament украшение [*ōōkrasheni-ye*]

Orthodox православный [*prava-slahvnee*]; an Orthodox church православная церковь [*prava-slahvna-ya tserkuff*]

ostentatious показной [*pakaznoy*]

other другой [*drōōgoy*]; the other waiter другой официант [*drōōgoy afitsi-ant*]; the other one другой [*drōōgoy*]; do you have any others? у вас есть другие? [*ōō vass yist drōōgee-ye*]; some other time, thanks спасибо, как-нибудь в другой раз [*spa-see-buh, kak-neebōōt vdrōōgoy rass*]

otherwise иначе [*inahch-e*]

ouch! ай! [*ı*]

ought: he ought to be here soon он должен здесь скоро быть [*on dolzhen zdyiss skoruh beet*]

ounce *see page 121*

our: our hotel наша гостиница [*nasha gastee-nitsa*]; our suitcases наши чемоданы [*nashee chima-dahnee*]; *see page 111*

ours наш [*nash*]; that's ours это наше [*ettuh nash-e*]; *see page 111*

out: he's out его нет [*yivo nyet*]; get out! вон отсюда! [*von at-syōōda*]; I'm out of money у меня нет денег [*ōō minya nyet dye-nyek*]; a few kilometres out of town в нескольких километрах от города [*vnye-skol-kikh kila-myetrakh at goruda*]

outboard (*motor*) подвесной мотор [*pad-vyisnoy mator*]

outdoors на открытом воздухе [*na at-kreetum vozdookh-ye*]

outlet (*elec*) розетка [*ra-zyetka*]

outside (*adjective*) наружный [*narōozh-nee*]; (*adverb*) наружу [*narōo-zhōo*]; can we sit outside? можно посидеть на улице? [*mozh-nuh pa-syi-dyet na ōolits-e*]

outskirts: on the outskirts of ... на окраине города ... [*na akra-een-ye goruda*]

oven духовка [*dōokhofka*]

over: over here вот здесь [*vot zdyiss*]; over there вон там [*von tam*]; over 100 за 100 [*za sto*]; she's trembling all over она вся дрожит [*ana fsya drazheet*]; our holiday's over наш отпуск кончается [*nash otpoosk kancha-yitsa*]

overcharge: you've overcharged me вы с меня слишком много взяли [*vee sminya sleesh-kum mnoguh vzyalee*]

overcoat пальто [*palto*]

overcooked переваренный [*pyiri-vah-ryinnee*]

overexpose (*photograph*) передержать [*pyiri-dyirzhat*]

overheat: the engine's overheating мотор перегревается [*mator pyiri-gryiva-yitsa*]

overland: to travel overland путешествовать по суше [*pōo-tyishest-vuvat pa sōosh-e*]

overlook: overlooking the park с видом на парк [*zveedum na park*]

overnight journey ночное путешествие [*nachno-ye pōo-tyishest-vee-ye*]

oversleep: I overslept я проспал [*ya praspahl*]

overtake обгонять/обогнать [*abgan-yat/abagnat*]

overweight (*person*) грузный [*grōoznee*]

own: my own ... мой собственный ... [*moy sobst-vyinnee*]; are you on your own? (*to man*) вы один? [*vee adeen*] (*to woman*) вы одна? [*vee adna*]; I'm on my own (*man*) я один [*ya adeen*]; (*woman*) я одна [*ya adna*]

owner владелец [*vla-dye-lyits*]

oyster устрица [*ōostreetsa*]

Р

Pacific Ocean Тихий океан [*teekhee ak-e-an*]

pack: a pack of cigarettes пачка сигарет [*pachka siga-ryet*]; I'll go and pack я пойду укладывать вещи [*ya pidōo ōoklahdivat vyesh-chee*]

package (*at post office*) бандероль (*f*) [*ban-dyirol*]

package tour туристическая поездка [*tooristee-chiska-ya pa-yezdka*]

packed lunch лёгкий завтрак [*lyokh-kee zaftrak*]

packed out: the place was packed out там было битком набито [*tam beeluh bitkom na-beetuh*]

packet пачка [*pachka*]; a packet of cigarettes пачка сигарет [*pachka siga-ryet*]

paddle (*noun*) весло [*vyislo*]

padlock (*noun*) висячий замок [*vyi-syachee zamok*]

page (*of book*) страница [*straneetsa*]; could you page ...? можете вызвать ...? [*mozhit-ye veez-vat*]

pain боль (*f*) [*bol*]; I have a pain here у меня болит здесь [*ōo minya baleet zdyiss*]

painful: it is painful это больно [*ettuh bolnuh*]

painkiller болеутоляющее средство [*ba-lyi-ōota-lya-yōosh-che-ye sryedst-vuh*]

paint (*noun*) краска [*kraska*]; I want to do some painting (*artist*) я хочу написать картину [*ya khachōo napee-saht karteenōo*]

paintbrush (*artist's*) кисть (*f*) [*keest*]

painting живопись (*f*) [*zhiva-peess*]

pair: a pair of ... пара ... [*pahra*]

pajamas пижама [*peezhama*]

Pakistan Пакистан [*pakistan*]

Pakistani (*man*) пакистанец [*pakistan-yits*]; (*woman*) пакистанка [*pakistanka*]; (*adjective*) пакистанский [*pakistanskee*]

pal (*male*) приятель (*m*) [*pree-ya-tyil*]; (*female*) приятельница [*pree-ya-tyilnitsa*]

palace дворец [*dva-ryets*]

pale бледный [*blyednee*]; pale blue светло-голубой [*svyitla-galooboy*]

palm tree пальма [*palma*]

palpitations сильное сердцебиение [*seelnuh-ye syirtse-bee-yeni-ye*]

pancake блин [*bleen*]

panic: don't panic не впадайте в панику [*nye fpadı-tye fpahnikōō*]

panties трусики [*trōō-sikee*]

pants (*trousers*) брюки [*bryōōkee*]; (*underpants*) трусы [*troo-see*]

panty girdle дамский пояс [*damskee poyass*]

pantyhose колготки [*kalgotkee*]

paper бумага [*boomahga*]; (*newspaper*) газета [*ga-zyeta*]; a piece of paper кусок бумаги [*koo-sok boomahgee*]

paraffin керосин [*kyira-seen*]

parallel: parallel to ... параллельно ... [*para-lyelnuh*]

parasol зонтик от солнца [*zontik at solntsa*]

parcel посылка [*pa-seelka*]

pardon (me)? простите? [*prasteet-ye*]

parents: my parents мои родители [*ma-yee radee-tyilee*]

park (*noun*) парк [*park*]; where can I park? куда можно поставить машину? [*kōōda mozh-nuh pastahveet masheenōō*]; there's nowhere to park некуда поставить машину [*nye-kooda pastahveet masheenōō*]

parking lights стояночные фонари [*sta-yanuchnee-ye fanaree*]

parking lot стоянка автомобилей [*sta-yanka avtamabee-lyay*]

parking place: there's a parking place! вот место для стоянки! [*vot myestuh dlya sta-yankee*]

part (*noun*) часть (*f*) [*chast*]

partner партнёр [*part-nyor*]

party (*group, political*) партия [*parti-ya*]; (*celebration*) вечеринка [*vyichirinka*]; let's have a party давайте устроим вечеринку [*davı-tye ōōstro-yim vyichirinkōō*]

party member член партии [*chlyen parti-ee*]

pass (*in mountains*) перевал [*pyiri-vahl*]; (*verb : overtake*) обгонять/обогнать [*abga-nyat/abagnat*]; he passed out он потерял сознание [*on pa-tyi-ryal saznani-ye*]; he made a pass at me он заигрывал со мной [*on za-eegrival samnoy*]

passable (*road*) открытый для проезда [*atkreetee dlya pra-yezda*]

passenger пассажир [*passazheer*]

passport паспорт [*pahsspurt*]

past: in the past в прошлом [*fproshlum*]; just past the bank за банком [*za bankum*]

pastry (*dough*) тесто [*tyestuh*]; (*small cake*) пирожное [*pirozhnuh-ye*]

patch: could you put a patch on this? можете поставить на это заплату? [*mozhit-ye pastahveet na ettuh zaplahtōō*]

pâté паштет [*pash-tyet*]

path тропинка [*trapeenka*]

patient: be patient будьте терпеливы [*bōōd-tye tyir-pyileevee*]

patronymic отчество [*ot-chistvuh*]

pattern узор [*oozor*]; a dress pattern выкройка для платья [*vee-kroyka dlya plah-tya*]

paunch пузо [*pōōzuh*]

pavement тротуар [*tratoo-ar*]

pay платить/заплатить [*plateet/zaplateet*]; can I pay, please? можно рассчитаться? [*mozh-nuh rass-chitahtsa*]; it's already paid for за это уже заплатили [*za ettuh ōōzh-e zaplateelee*]; I'll pay for this я заплачу за это [*ya zaplachōō za ettuh*]

pay phone телефон-автомат [*tyilifon-avtamaht*]

peace (*not war*) мир [*meer*]; (*calm*) покой [*pakoy*]; leave me in peace! оставьте меня в покое! [*astaf-tye minya fpako-ye*]

peaceful мирный [*meernee*]

peach персик [*pyer-sik*]

peanuts арахис [*arakhiss*]

pear груша [*grōōsha*]

pearl жемчуг [*zhemchōōk*]

peas горох [*garokh*]

peculiar своеобразный [*sva-ye-abraznee*]

pedal педаль (*f*) [*pyidal*]

pedestrian пешеход [*pyishi-khot*]

pedestrian crossing пешеходный переход [*pyishi-khodnee pyiri-khot*]

pedestrian precinct пешеходная зона [*pyishi-khodna-ya zona*]

peeping Tom человек с нездоровым любопытством [*chila-vyek znyi-zdarovim lyooba-peetstvum*]

peg (*for washing*) прищепка [*preesh-chepka*]; (*for tent*) колышек [*kolishek*]

pen ручка [*roochka*]; do you have a pen? у вас есть ручка? [*ōō vass yist roochka*]

pencil карандаш [*karandash*]

penfriend знакомый по переписке [*znakomee pa pyiri-peesk-ye*]

penicillin пенициллин [*pyini-tsileen*]

penknife перочинный ножик [*pyira-cheennee nozhik*]

pen pal знакомый по переписке [*znakomee pa pyiri-peesk-ye*]

pensioner пенсионер [*pyinsi-a-nyer*]

people люди [*lyōōdee*]; a lot of people много людей [*mnoguh lyoo-dyay*]; the Russian people русские [*rooskee-ye*]

people's (*adjective*) народный [*narodnee*]

pepper (*spice*) перец [*pye-ryits*]; green pepper зелёный перец [*zi-lyonee pye-ryits*]; red pepper красный перец [*krahsnee pye-ryits*]

peppermint (*sweet*) мятная конфета [*myatna-ya kan-fyeta*]

per: per night за ночь [*za noch*]; how much per hour? какова стоимость в час? [*kakova sto-yimust fchass*]

per cent процент [*pratsent*]

perestroika перестройка [*pyiri-stroyka*]

perfect совершенный [*sa-vyirshennee*]

perfume духи [*dookhee*]

perhaps может быть [*mozhit beet*]

period (*of time*) срок [*srok*]; (*menstruation*) месячные [*mye-syachnee-ye*]

perm перманент [*pyirma-nyent*]

permit разрешение [*raz-ryisheni-ye*]

person человек [*chila-vyek*]

pessimistic пессимистический [*pyissi-myi-steechiskee*]

petrol бензин [*byinzeen*]

petrol can бензиновая канистра [*byinzeenuva-ya kaneestra*]

petrol station бензозаправочная станция [*byinza-zaprah-vuchna-ya stantsi-ya*]

petrol tank (*in car*) бензобак [*byinza-bak*]

pharmacy аптека [*ap-tyeka*]

phone *see* telephone

photogenic фотогеничный [*fata-gyineechnee*]

photograph фотография [*fata-grafi-ya*]; would you take a photograph of us? сфотографируйте нас, пожалуйста [*sfata-grafeeroo-itye nass pa-zhahlsta*]

photographer фотограф [*fato-graf*]

phrase: a useful phrase полезное выражение [*pa-lyeznuh-ye vee-razheni-ye*]

phrasebook разговорник [*razgavornik*]

pianist пианист [*pianeest*]

piano пианино [*pianeenuh*]; (*grand piano*) рояль (*m*) [*ra-yal*]

pickpocket вор-карманник [*vor-karmannik*]

pick up: when can I pick them up? когда прийти за ними? [*kagda preetee za neemee*]; will you come and pick me up? можете за мной заехать? [*mozhit-ye zamnoy za-yekhat*]

picnic (*noun*) пикник [*pikneek*]

picture картина [*karteena*]

pie пирог [*pirok*]

piece кусок [*koo-sok*]; a piece of bread кусок хлеба [*koo-sok khlyeba*]

pig свинья [*sveen-ya*]

pigeon голубь (*m*) [*goloop*]

piles (*medical*) геморрой [*gyima-roy*]

pile-up (*crash*) авария [*avari-ya*]

pill таблетка [*ta-blyetka*]; I'm on the pill я принимаю противозачаточные таблетки [*ya prini-ma-yōō prativa-zachahtuchni-ye ta-blyetkee*]

pillarbox почтовый ящик [*pachtovee yash-chik*]

pillow подушка [*padōōshka*]

pillow case наволочка [*navuluchka*]

pin (*noun*) булавка [*boolafka*]

pineapple ананас [*ananass*]

pineapple juice ананасовый сок [*anana-suvee sok*]

pink розовый [*rozuvee*]

pint *see page 121*

pipe (*for smoking*) трубка [*trōōpka*]; (*for water*) трубопровод [*trooba-pravot*]

pipe cleaner ёршик для трубки [*yorshik dlya trōōpkee*]

pipe tobacco табак для трубки [*tabak dlya trōōpkee*]

pity: it's a pity жаль [*zhahl*]

pizza пицца [*peetsa*]

place (*noun*) место [*myestuh*]; is this place taken? это место занято? [*ettuh myestuh zah-nyatuh*]; would you keep my place for me? займите мне место [*zimeet-ye mnye myestuh*]; at my place у меня (дома) [*ōō minya (doma)*]; at Ivan's (*place*) у Ивана (дома) [*ōō eevahna (doma)*]

place mat подставка [*padstafka*]

plain (*food etc*) простой [*prastoy*]; (*not patterned*) без узора [*byez oozora*]

plane (*aircraft*) самолёт [*sama-lyot*]

plant (*botanic*) растение [*ras-tyeni-ye*]; (*factory*) завод [*zavot*]

plaster cast гипсовая повязка [*geepsuva-ya pa-vyazka*]

plastic (*adjective*) пластический [*plasteechiskee*]

plastic bag полиэтиленовая сумка [*palieti-lyenuva-ya soomka*]

plate тарелка [*ta-ryelka*]

platform платформа [*platforma*]; which platform, please? скажите, пожалуйста, какая платформа? [*skazheet-ye pa-zhahlsta kaka-ya platforma*]

play играть/сыграть [*eegraht/sigraht*]; (*noun: in theatre*) пьеса [*pyessa*]

playboy повеса [*pa-vyessa*]

playground детская площадка [*dyetska-ya plash-chatka*]

pleasant приятный [*pree-yahtnee*]

please пожалуйста [*pa-zhahlsta*]; yes please пожалуйста [*pa-zhahlsta*]; could you please ...? можете, пожалуйста ...? [*mozhit-ye pa-zhahlsta*]

pleasure: with pleasure с удовольствием [*sooda-volstvi-em*]

plenty: plenty of ... много ...? [*mnoguh*]; that's plenty, thanks спасибо, достаточно [*spa-see-buh dastatuch-nuh*]

pleurisy плеврит [*plyivreet*]

pliers плоскогубцы [*plaska-goop-tsee*]

plonk (*wine*) вино [*veeno*]; (*cheap wine*) дешёвое вино [*dyishovuh-ye veeno*]

plug (*elec*) штепсельная вилка [*shtyep-syilna-ya veelka*]; (*for car*) свеча зажигания [*svyicha zazhigani-ya*]; (*in sink*) пробка [*propka*]

plughole (*in sink*) отверстие в раковине [*at-vyerstvi-ye vrahkuveen-ye*]; (*in bath*) отверстие в ванне [*at-vyerstvi-ye v-van-nye*]

plum слива [*sleeva*]

plumber водопроводчик [*vada-pravodchik*]

plus плюс [*plyooss*]

p.m.: at 2 p.m. в 2 часа дня [*vdva chassa dnya*]; at 10 p.m. в 10 часов вечера [*vdye-syat chassoff vyechera*]

pneumonia воспаление лёгких [*vaspa-lyeni-ye lyokh-kikh*]

poached egg яйцо-пашот [*yitso-pashot*]

pocket карман [*karman*]; in my pocket в моём кармане [*vma-yom karman-ye*]

pocketbook бумажник [*boo-mazhnik*]

pocketknife карманный складной нож [*karman-nee skladnoy nosh*]

podiatrist педикюрша [*pyidi-kyoorsha*]

point: could you point to it? можете указать пальцем на это? [*mozhit-ye ookazaht pahl-tsem na ettuh*]; four point six четыре целых и шесть десятых [*chiteer-ye tselikh ee shest dyi-syahtikh*]; there's no point не имеет смысла [*nye ee-mye-yet smeessla*]

points (*in car*) контакт [*kantakt*]

poisonous ядовитый [*yada-veetee*]

Poland Польша [*polsha*]

police полиция [*pa-leetsi-ya*]; (*in USSR*) милиция [*mi-leetsi-ya*]; call the police! вызовите милицию! [*vee-zaveet-ye mileetsi-yoo*]

policeman полицейский [*palee-tsayskee*]; (*in USSR*) милиционер [*mileetsi-a-nyer*]

police station (*in USSR*) отделение милиции [*at-dyi-lyeni-ye mileetsee*]

polish (*noun*) глянец [*glya-nyits*]; will you polish my shoes? можете почистить мои туфли? [*mozhit-ye pa-cheesteet mayee tooflee*]

polite вежливый [*vyezh-leevee*]

politician политик [*paleetik*]

politics политика [*paleetika*]

polluted загрязнённый [*za-gryaz-nyonnee*]

pond пруд [*proot*]

pony пони [*ponee*]

pool (*for swimming*) бассейн [*ba-syayn*]

poor (*not rich*) бедный [*byednee*]; (*quality*) плохой [*pla-khoy*]; poor old Vanya! бедный Ваня! [*byednee van-ya*]

Pope папа римский [*papa reemskee*]

pop music поп-музыка [*pop-moozika*]

pop singer (*man*) поп-певец [*pop-pyi-vyets*]; (*woman*) поп-певица [*pop-pyi-veetsa*]

popular популярный [*papoo-lyarnee*]

population население [*na-syi-lyeni-ye*]

pork свинина [*svineena*]

port (*for boats*) порт [*port*]; (*drink*) портвейн [*part-vyayn*]

porter (*in hotel*) швейцар [*shvyay-tsar*]; (*at station etc*) носильщик [*na-seelsh-chik*]

portrait портрет [*par-tryet*]

Portugal Португалия [*partoo-gahli-ya*]

poser (*phoney person*) позёр [*pa-zyor*]

posh шикарный [*shikarnee*]

possibility возможность (*f*) [*vaz-mozhnust*]

possible возможный [*vaz-mozhnee*]; is it possible to ...? можно ...? [*mozh-nuh*] as far as possible насколько возможно [na-skolkuh vaz-mozh-nuh]; as soon as possible как можно скорее [kak mozh-nuh ska-rye-ye]; as early as possible как можно раньше [kak mozh-nuh ransh-e]

post (noun: mail) почта [pochta]; could you post this letter? пожалуйста, отправьте это письмо [pa-zhahlsta at-prahft-ye ettuh pee-smo]

postbox почтовый ящик [pachtovee yash-chik]

postcard открытка [at-kreetka]

poster (illustrated) плакат [plakaht]; (announcement) афиша [afeesha]

poste restante до востребования [davass-tryeba-vani-ya]

post office почта [pochta]

pot котёлок [katyilok]; (earthenware) горшок [garshok]

potato картофель (m) [karto-fyil]

potato chips хрустящий картофель [khroo-styash-chee karto-fyil]

potato salad картофельный салат [karto-fyilnee salaht]

pottery (objects) гончарные изделия [gancharni-ye iz-dyeli-ya]; (workshop) гончарная мастерская [gancharna-ya ma-styirska-ya]

pound (money) фунт стерлинг [foont styerling]; (weight) фунт [foont]; see page 121

pour: it's pouring down дождь идёт как из ведра [dozhd ee-dyot kak iz vydra]

powder (for face) пудра [poodra]

powdered milk молочное порошок [malochnee parashok]

power (authority) власть (f) [vlast]; nuclear power атомная энергия [atumna-ya en-yergi-ya]

power cut отключение электроэнергии [at-klyoocheni-ye e-lyektra-en-yergee]

power point розетка [ra-zyetka]

power station электростанция [e-lyektra-stantsi-ya]

practise, practice: I need to practise мне надо упражняться [mnye nahduh oo-pryazh-nyatsa]

pram детская коляска [dyetska-ya ka-lyaska]

prawns креветки [kryi-vyetkee]

prefer: I prefer white wine я предпочитаю белое вино [ya pryid-pachita-yoo byeluh-ye veeno]

preferably: preferably not tomorrow лучше не завтра [looch-e nye zaftra]

pregnant беременная [byi-rye-myinna-ya]

prescription (for chemist) рецепт [ryizept]

present (gift) подарок [padaruk]; here's a present for you этот подарок для вас [ettut padaruk dlya vass]; at present теперь [tyi-pyer]

president (of country) президент [pryizi-dyent]; (chairman) председатель (m) [pryid-syidah-tyil]

press: could you press these trousers? можете погладить эти брюки? [mozhit-ye pa-glahdeet ettee bryookee]

pretty прелестный [pryi-lyesnee]; it's pretty expensive довольно дорого [davolnuh doruguh]

price цена [tsena]

priest священник [svyash-chennik]

prime minister премьер-министр [pryim-yer-mineestr]

print (noun: picture) гравюра [gra-vyoora]

printed matter печатный материал [pyichaht-nee ma-tyiri-al]

priority (in driving) приоритет [pree-ari-tyet]

prison тюрьма [tyoorma]

private частный [chastnee]; private bath отдельная ванная [at-dyelna-ya vanna-ya]

prize приз [preez]

probably вероятно [vyira-yahtnuh]

problem проблема [prab-lyema]; I have a problem у меня проблема [oo minya prab-lyema]; no problem! ничего! [nee-chivo]

program(me) программа [pra-gramma]

promise (verb) обещать [a-byish-chat]; is that a promise? обещаете? [a-byish-cha-yit-ye]

pronounce: how do you pronounce this? как произнести это? [kak pra-iz-nyistee ettuh]; I can't pronounce it я не могу это произнести [ya nye magoo ettuh pra-iz-nyistee]

properly: you haven't repaired it properly вы не починили это как следует [vee nye pachinee-lee ettuh kak slyedoo-yet]

prostitute проститутка [prasti-tootka]

protect защищать/защитить [zash-chish-chat/ zash-chiteet]

protein remover (for contact lenses) раствор для чистки контактных линз [rastvor dlya cheestkee kantakt-nikh linz]

Protestant протестантский [*pratyistantskee*]

proud гордый [*gordee*]

prunes чернослив [*chirna-sleef*]

public (*adjective*) общественный [*abshchest-vyinnee*]

public convenience туалет [*too-a-lyet*]

public holiday всенародный праздник [*fsye-narodnee prazd-nik*]

pudding пудинг [*poodink*]

pull тянуть [*tyanōot*]; he pulled out without indicating он выехал, не сигналя [*on vee-yekhal nye signal-ya*]

pullover свитер [*svee-tyir*]

pump (*noun*) насос [*na-soss*]

punctual пунктуальный [*poonk-too-ahlnee*]

puncture (*noun*) прокол [*prakol*]

pure (*silk etc*) натуральный [*natoorahlnee*]; (*alcohol*) чистый [*cheestee*]

purple фиолетовый [*fee-a-lyetuvee*]

purse (*for money*) кошелёк [*kashi-lyok*]; (*handbag*) сумочка [*soomuchka*]

push толкать [*tal-kat*]; don't push! не толкайтесь! [*nye tal-kı-tyiss*]

push-chair складная детская коляска [*skladna-ya dyetska-ya ka-lyaska*]

put (*stand*) ставить/поставить [*stahveet/pa-staveet*]; (*lay*) класть/положить [*klahst/pala-zheet*]; where can I put ...? куда мне поставить/положить ...? [*kōoda mnye pa-stahveet/pala-zheet*]; could you put the lights on? можете включить свет? [*mozhit-ye fklyoo-cheet svyet*]; will you put the light out? выключите, пожалуйста, свет [*vee-klyoocheet-ye pazhahlsta svyet*]; you've put the price up вы повысили цену [*vee pa-veesilee tsenōo*]; could you put us up for the night? мы можем у вас остановиться на ночь? [*mee mozhem ōo vass astana-veetsa na-noch*]

pyjamas пижама [*peezhama*]

Q

quality качество [*kah-chistvuh*]; poor quality низкого качества [*neezkuv-uh kah-chistva*]; good quality высокого качества [*vissokuv-uh kah-chistva*]

quarantine карантин [*karanteen*]

quart *see page 121*

quarter четверть (*f*) [*chet-vyirt*]; quarter of an hour четверть часа [*chet-vyirt chassa*]

quay причал [*preechal*]

quayside: on the quayside на пристани [*na pree-stanee*]

question вопрос [*vapross*]; that's out of the question об этом не может быть и речи [*ab ettum nye mozhit beet ee ryechee*]

queue (*noun*) очередь (*f*) [*ochi-ryid*]; there was a big queue там была длинная очередь [*tam beela dleenna-ya ochi-ryid*]

quick быстрый [*beestree*]; that was quick! как быстро! [*kak beestruh*]; which is the quickest way? какой самый короткий путь? [*kakoy sahmee karotkee pōot*]

quickly быстро [*beestruh*]

quiet (*place, hotel*) тихий [*teekhee*]; be quiet! тише! [*teesh-e*]

quinine хинин [*khineen*]

quite: quite a lot довольно много [*davolnuh mnoguh*]; it's quite different это совсем не то [*ettuh sav-syem nye to*]; I'm not quite sure я не совсем уверен [*ya nye sav-syem ōo-vye-ryin*]

R

rabbit кролик [*krolik*]

race (*for horses*) скачки [*skachkee*]; (*cars*) гонки [*gonkee*]; I'll race you there давай

побежали наперегонки [*davı pa-byizhahlee na-pyiri-gankee*]

racket (*sport*) ракетка [*ra-kyetka*]

radiator (*of car*) радиатор [*radi-ahtur*]; (*in room*) батарея [*bata-rye-ya*]

radio радио [*rahdee-uh*]; **on the radio** по радио [*pa rahdee-uh*]

rag (*for cleaning*) тряпка [*tryapka*]

rail: by rail поездом [*po-yizdum*]

railroad, railway железная дорога [*zhilyezna-ya daroga*]

railroad crossing переезд [*pyiri-yezd*]

rain (*noun*) дождь (m) [*dozhd*]; **in the rain** под дождём [*pad dazh-dyom*]; **it's raining** идёт дождь [*ee-dyot dozhd*]

rain boots резиновые сапоги [*ryizeenuhvuh-ye sapagee*]

raincoat плащ [*plashch*]

rape (*noun*) изнасилование [*izna-seeluvaniye*]

rare (*object etc*) редкий [*ryetkee*]; (*steak*) недожаренный [*nyida-zhah-ryinnee*]

rash (*on skin*) сыпь (f) [*seep*]

raspberry малина [*maleena*]

rat крыса [*kreessa*]

rate (*for changing money*) валютный курс [*va-lyootnee koorss*]; **what's the rate for the pound?** каков курс фунта стерлингов? [*kakoff koorss foonta styerling-uff*]; **what are your rates?** (*at car hire etc*) сколько стоит прокат? [*skol-kuh sto-yit prakaht*]

rather: it's rather late довольно поздно [*davolnuh pozd-nuh*]; **I'd rather ...** я предпочёл бы ... [*ya pryid-pachol bee*]; **I'd rather have rice** я предпочитаю рис [*ya pryid-pachitah-yoo reess*]

raw (*meat etc*) сырой [*siroy*]

razor бритва [*breetva*]

razor blade лезвие бритвы [*lyezvi-ye breetvee*]

reach: within easy reach неподалёку [*nyipada-lyokoo*]

read читать/прочитать [*cheetat/pra-cheetat*]; **I can't read this** я не могу прочесть, что здесь написано [*ya nye magoo pra-chest shto zdyiss napee-sanuh*]; **could you read it out?** можете прочесть вслух? [*mozhit-ye pra-chest fslookh*]

ready готовый [*gatovee*]; **when will it be ready?** когда это будет готово? [*kagda ettuh bood-yit gatovuh*]; **I'll go and get ready** я пойду собираться [*ya paidoo sabee-rahtsa*]; **I'm not ready yet** я ещё не собрался [*ya yish-cho nye sabrahlsa*]

real настоящий [*nasta-yash-chee*]

really действительно [*dyayst-vee-tyilnuh*]; **I really must go** (*man*) я непременно должен уходить [*ya nyi-pryi-myennuh dolzhin oo-khadeet*]; (*woman*) я непременно должна уходить [*ya nyi-pryi-myennuh dalzh-na oo-khadeet*]; **is it really necessary?** это действительно необходимо? [*ettuh dyayst-vee-tyil-nuh nyi-abkha-deemuh*]

rear: at the rear сзади [*zadee*]; **rear wheels** задние колёса [*zadni-ye ka-lyossa*]

rearview mirror зеркало заднего вида [*zyerka-luh zahd-nyivuh veeda*]

reasonable (*prices etc*) недорогой [*nyidaragoy*]; **be reasonable** будьте благоразумны [*bood-tye blagarazoomnee*]

receipt квитанция [*kvitantsi-ya*]

recently недавно [*nyi-dahvnuh*]

reception (*in hotel*) регистратура [*ryigistratoora*]; (*for guests*) приём [*pree-yom*]

receptionist регистратор [*ryi-gistrahtur*]

recipe рецепт [*retsept*]; **can you give me the recipe for this?** у вас есть рецепт этого блюда? [*oo vass yist retsept ettuvuh blyooda*]

recognize узнавать/узнать [*ooznavaht/oo-znaht*]; **I didn't recognize it** я не узнал это [*ya nye ooznahl ettuh*]

recommend: could you recommend ...? вы можете мне порекомендовать ...? [*vee mozhit-ye mnye pa-ryika-myindavaht*]

record (*music*) пластинка [*plasteenka*]

record player проигрыватель (m) [*pra-eegrivah-tyil*]

red красный [*krah-snee*]

Red Army Красная Армия [*krah-sna-ya armi-ya*]

Red Square Красная площадь [*krah-sna-ya plosh-chat*]

reduction (*in price*) снижение цен [*snee-zheni-ye tsen*]; (*discount*) скидка [*skeetka*]

red wine красное вино [*krah-snuh-ye veeno*]

refreshing освежающий [*a-svyizhah-yoosh-chee*]

refrigerator холодильник [*khala-deelnik*]

refund возмещение [*vaz-myish-cheni-ye*]; **do I get a refund?** я получу возмещение? [*ya paloochoo vaz-myish-cheni-ye*]

region область (f) [*oblast*]

registered: by registered mail заказным [*zakazneem*]

registration number номерной знак [*na-myirnoy znak*]

relative: my relatives мои родственники [*ma-yee rodst-vyennikee*]

relaxing: it's very relaxing здесь очень спокойная обстановка [*zdyiss ochin spakoyna-ya ab-stanofka*]

reliable надёжный [*na-dyozhnee*]

religion религия [*ryileegi-ya*]

remains (*historical*) развалины [*razvahleenee*]

remember: I don't remember я не помню [*ya nye pom-nyoo*]; I remember я помню [*ya pom-nyoo*]; do you remember? вы помните? [*vee pom-neet-ye*]

remote отдалённый [*atda-lyonnee*]

rent (*noun: for apartment etc*) квартирная плата [*kvarteerna-ya plahta*]; (*verb: car etc*) брать/взять на прокат [*braht/vzyaht na prakaht*]; I'd like to rent a bike/car я хочу взять напрокат велосипед/машину [*ya khachoo vzyaht naprakaht vyi-lyassi-pyet/masheenoo*]

rental car машина, выдаваемая напрокат [*masheena vidava-yima-ya naprakaht*]

repair (*verb*) чинить/починить [*chineet/pachineet*]; can you repair it? можете это починить? [*mozhit-ye ettuh pachineet*]

repeat повторять/повторить [*pavta-ryaht/ pavtareet*]; could you repeat that? повторите, пожалуйста [*pavtareet-ye pa-zhahlsta*]

representative (*of company*) представитель (*m*) [*pryid-stavee-tyil*]

request (*noun*) просьба [*prossba*]

rescue спасать/спасти [*spa-saht/spastee*]

reservation предварительный заказ [*pryidvaree-tyilnee zakass*]; I have a reservation у меня предварительный заказ [*oo minya pryidvaree-tyilnee zakass*]

reserve заказывать/заказать заранее [*za-kahzivat/zakazaht zarahn-ye-ye*]; I reserved a room in the name of . . . я заказал номер на имя . . . [*ya zakazahl no-myir na ee-mya*]; can I reserve a table for tonight? можете для меня забронировать столик на сегодня? [*mozhit-ye dlya minya za-braneeruvat stolik na syivo-dnya*]

rest (*repose*) отдых [*ot-dikh*]; (*remainder*) остаток [*astahtuk*]; I need a rest мне нужно отдохнуть [*mnye noozh-nuh at-dakh-noot*]; the rest of the group остальные члены группы [*astalni-ye chlyenee. groopee*]

restaurant ресторан [*ryistaran*]

rest room туалет [*too-a-lyet*]

retired: I'm retired я на пенсии [*ya na pyensi-ee*]

return: a return to Zagorsk обратный билет до Загорска [*abratnee bi-lyet do zagorska*]; (*verb*) возвращать/вернуть [*vaz-vrashchat/ vyirnoot*]; I'll return it to you tomorrow я верну вам это завтра [*ya vyirnoo vam ettuh zaftra*]; I am returning to England я возвращаюсь в Англию [*ya vaz-vrashcha-yooss vang-glee-yoo*]

returnable (*deposit*) подлежащий возврату [*pad-lyizhash-chee vaz-vrahtoo*]

reverse charge call телефонный вызов за счёт вызываемого [*tyili-fonnee veezuff za s-chot viziva-yimuvuh*]

reverse gear задний ход [*zahdnee khot*]

revolting отвратительный [*atvratee-tyilnee*]

revolution революция [*ryiva-lyootsi-ya*]

revolutionary (*noun*) революционер [*ryiva-lyootsia-nyer*]

rheumatism ревматизм [*ryiv-mateezm*]

rib ребро [*ryibro*]; a cracked rib сломанное ребро [*slomannuh-ye ryibro*]

ribbon лента [*lyenta*]

rice рис [*rees*]

rich (*person*) богатый [*bagahtee*]; (*food*) питательный [*pitah-tyilnee*]

ride: can you give me a ride into town? можете меня подвезти в город? [*mozhit-ye minya pad-vyiztee vgorut*]; thanks for the ride спасибо, что подвезли [*spa-see-buh shto pad-vyizlee*]

ridiculous: that's ridiculous это просто смешно [*ettuh prostuh smyishno*]

right (*correct*) правильный [*prahvilnee*]; (*not left*) правый [*prahvee*]; you're right вы правы [*vee prahvee*]; you were right вы оказались правы [*vee akazahleess prahvee*]; that's right совершенно верно [*sa-vyir-shennuh vyernuh*]; that can't be right этого не может быть [*ettuvuh nye mozhit beet*]; right! хорошо! [*khara-sho*]; is this the right road for . . .? мы на правильной дороге в/на . . .? [*mee na*] *prahvilnoy darog-ye v*/*na*]; on the right направо [*naprahvuh*]; turn right сверните направо [*svyirneet-ye naprahvuh*]; not right now не в данный момент [*nye vdannee ma-myent*]

right-hand drive car машина с рулём справа [*masheena sroo-lyom sprahva*]

ring (*on finger*) кольцо [*kaltso*]; (*verb*) звонить/позвонить [*zvaneet*/*pazvaneet*]; **I'll ring you** я позвоню вам [*ya pazvan-yoo vam*]

ring road кольцевая дорога [*kaltsiva-ya daroga*]

ripe (*fruit*) зрелый [*zryelee*]

rip-off: it's a rip-off это грабёж среди бела дня [*ettuh gra-byozh sryidee byela dnya*]

risky рискованный [*riskovan-nee*]

river река [*ryika*]; by the river у реки [*oo ryikee*]

road дорога [*daroga*]; is this the road to ...? эта дорога ведёт в/на ...? [*etta daroga vyi-dyot v*/*na*]; further down the road дальше по дороге [*dalsh-e pa darog-ye*]

road accident авария [*avari-ya*]

road hog: he's a road hog он занимает всю дорогу [*on zanima-yet fsyoo darogoo*]

road map дорожная карта [*darozhna-ya karta*]

roadside: by the roadside на обочине [*na abochin-ye*]

roadsign дорожный знак [*darozhnee znak*]

roadwork(s) дорожные работы [*darozhnee-ye rabotee*]

roast beef ростбиф [*rost-bif*]

rob: I've been robbed меня ограбили [*minya agrahbilee*]

robe (*housecoat*) халат [*khalaht*]

rock (*stone*) скала [*skala*]; on the rocks (*with ice*) со льдом [*saldom*]

rocky скалистый [*skaleestee*]

roll (*bread*) булочка [*booluchka*]

Roman Catholic (*adjective*) католический [*katalee-chiskee*]

romance романтика [*ramantika*]

Romania Румыния [*roomeeni-ya*]

Rome: when in Rome ... в чужой монастырь со своим уставом не ходят [*fchoozhoy manasteer sasva-yeem oo-stavum nye kho-dyat*]

roof крыша [*kreesha*]; on the roof на крыше [*na kreesh-e*]

roof rack багажник на крыше автомобиля [*bagahzh-nik na kreesh-e avtamabee-lya*]

room (*hotel*) номер [*no-myir*]; (*house*) комната [*komnata*]; do you have any rooms? у вас есть свободные номера? [*oo vass yist svabodni-ye na-myira*]; a room for two people номер на двоих [*no-myir na dva-yeekh*]; a room for three nights номер на три ночи [*no-myir na tree nochee*]; a room with a bathroom номер с отдельной ванной [*no-myir sat-dyelnoy vannoy*]; in my room у меня в номере [*oo minya vno-myir-ye*]; there's no room мест нет [*myest nyet*]

room service обслуживание номеров [*ab-sloozhi-vani-ye na-myiroff*]

rope канат [*kanat*]

rose роза [*roza*]

rosé (*wine*) розовое вино [*rozuvuh-ye veeno*]

rotary движение автотранспорта по кругу [*dvizheni-ye avta-transporta pa kroogoo*]

rough (*sea, crossing*) бурный [*boornee*]; the engine sounds a bit rough мотор звучит совсем нехорошо [*mator zvoochit sa-fsyem nyi-kharasho*]

roughly (*approximately*) приблизительно [*preeblizee-tyilnuh*]

roulette рулетка [*roo-lyetka*]

round (*adjective*) круглый [*krooglee*]; it's my round мой черёд [*moy chi-ryot*]

roundabout движение автотранспорта по кругу [*dvizheni-ye avta-transporta pa kroogoo*]

round-trip: a round-trip ticket to ... билет в ... туда и обратно [*bi-lyet v ... tooda ee abraht-nuh*]

route маршрут [*marsh-root*]; what's the best route? каков кратчайший путь? [*kakoff krat-chishee poot*]

rowboat, rowing boat гребная шлюпка [*gryibna-ya shlyoopka*]

rubber (*material*) резина [*ryizeena*]; (*eraser*) резинка [*ryizinka*]

rubber band резиновая тесьма [*ryizeenuva-ya tyisma*]

rubbish (*waste*) мусор [*moossur*]; (*poor quality goods*) дрянь (*f*) [*dryan*]; that's rubbish! чепуха! [*chipookha*]

rucksack рюкзак [*ryook-zak*]

rude грубый [*groobee*]; he was very rude to me он нагрубил мне [*on na-groobeel mnye*]

rug ковёр [*ka-vyor*]

ruins развалины [*raz-vahleenee*]

rum ром [*rom*]

rum and coke кока-кола с ромом [*koka-kola sromum*]

run (*person*) бегать [*byegat*]; I go running every day я бегаю каждый день [*ya byega-yōō kazh-dee dyin*]; quick, run! давай! бегом! [*davı, byigom*]; how often do the buses run? как часто ходят автобусы? [*kak chastuh kho-dyat avto-boossee*]; he's been run over его задавила машина [*yivo zadaveela masheena*]; I've

run out of gas/petrol у меня кончился бензин [*ōō minya konchilsa byin-zeen*]

rupture (*medical*) грыжа [*greezha*]

Russia Россия [*ra-see-ya*]

Russian (*man*) русский [*rooskee*]; (*woman*) русская [*rooska-ya*]; (*adjective*) русский [*rooskee*]; (*language*) русский язык [*rooskee yazik*]; the Russians русские [*rooski-ye*]; I don't speak Russian я не говорю по-русски [*ya nye gava-ryōō pa-rooskee*]

Russian Orthodox church русская православная церковь [*rooska-ya pravaslavna-ya tserkuff*]

S

saccharine сахарин [*sakhareen*]

sad грустный [*grōostnee*]

saddle седло [*syidlo*]

safe (*not in danger*) находящийся в безопасности [*nakha-dyash-chee-sa vbyiza-pah-snustee*]; (*not dangerous*) безопасный [*byiza-pahsnee*]; will my case be safe here? мой чемодан будет здесь в сохранности? [*moy chimadan bōod-yit zdyiss fsakh-rahnnustee*]; is it safe to drink? это не опасно пить? [*ettuh nye apah-snuh peet*]; is it safe for swimming here? здесь не опасно плавать? [*zdyiss nye apah-snuh plahvat*]; could you put this in your safe? пожалуйста, положите это в сейф [*pa-zhahlsta palazheet-ye ettuh fsayf*]

safety pin английская булавка [*ang-gleeska-ya boolahfka*]

sail (*noun*) парус [*pahrooss*]; can we go sailing? мы можем покататься на парусной лодке? [*mee mozhem pa-katahtsa na pah-roossnoy lot-kye*]

sailor моряк [*ma-ryak*]

salad салат [*salaht*]

salad dressing приправа к салату [*pri-prahva ksalah-tōo*]

sale: is it for sale? это продаётся? [*ettuh prada-yotsa*]; it's not for sale не продаётся [*nye prada-yotsa*]

sales clerk (*male*) продавец [*prada-vyets*]; (*female*) продавщица [*pradafsh-cheetsa*]

salmon лосось (*m*) [*la-soss*]

salt соль (*f*) [*sol*]

salty: it's too salty слишком солёное [*sleeshkum sa-lyonuh-ye*]

same тот же самый [*tot zhe sahmee*]; we're in the same hotel мы в той же самой гостинице [*mee ftoy zhe sahmoy gastee-nits-e*]; one the same as this одинаковый [*a-deenah-kuvee*]; the same again, please то же самое ещё раз, пожалуйста [*tozh-e sahmuh-ye yish-cho rass pa-zhahlsta*]; have a good time - same to you желаю вам всего хорошего - взаимно [*zhila-yōō vam fsyivo kharosheh-vuh - vza-eem-nuh*]; it's all the same to me мне всё равно [*mnye fsyo ravno*]; thanks all the same (*man*) тем не менее я очень благодарен [*tyem nye mye-nye-ye ya ochin blaga-dah-ryen*]; (*woman*) тем не менее я очень благодарна [*tyem nye mye-nye-ye ya ochin blaga-darna*]

samovar самовар [*samavar*]

sand песок [*pyi-sok*]

sandals сандали [*sandahlee*]; a pair of sandals пара сандалей [*para sandahlyay*]

sandwich бутерброд [*boo-tyirbrot*]; a chicken sandwich бутерброд с жареной курицей [*boo-tyirbrot s-zhah-ryenoy kōoritsay*]

sandy песчаный [*pyiss-chanee*]; a sandy beach песчаный пляж [*pyiss-chanee plyahsh*]

sanitary napkin/towel гигиеническая салфетка [*gee-gee-eneechiska-ya sal-fyetka*]

sarcastic язвительный [*yazvee-tyilnee*]

sardines сардины [*sardeenee*]

satellite спутник [*spōotnik*]

satisfactory удовлетворительный [*oodav-lyitva-ree-tyilnee*]; this is not satisfactory это неудовлетворительно [*ettuh nye-oodav-lyitva-ree-tyil-nuh*]

Saturday суббота [*soobbota*]

sauce соус [*so-ooss*]; (*thin, gravy*) подливка [*padleefka*]

saucepan кастрюля [*kast-ryōō-lya*]

saucer блюдце [*blyōōds-e*]

sauna сауна [*sa-oona*]

sausage (*salami*) колбаса [*kalbassa*]; (*frankfurter*) сосиска [*sa-seeska*]

sauté potatoes жареная картошка [*zhah-ryena-ya kartoshka*]

save (*life*) спасать/спасти [*spasaht/spastee*]

savo(u)ry острый [*ostree*]

say: how do you say ... in Russian? как по-русски...? [*kak pa rooskee*]; **what did you say?** что вы сказали? [*shto vee skazahlee*]; **what did he say?** что он сказал? [*shto on skazahl*]; **I said ... я** сказал... [*ya skazahl*]; **he said ... он** сказал [*on skazahl*]; **I wouldn't say no я** не откажусь [*ya nye at-kazhōōss*]

scald: he's scalded himself он ошпарил себя кипятком [*on ashpareel sibya ki-pyatkom*]

scarf (*for neck*) шарф [*sharf*]; (*for head*) платок [*platok*]

scarlet алый [*ahlee*]

scenery пейзаж [*pyay-zash*]

scent (*perfume*) духи [*dookhee*]

schedule расписание [*raspi-sahni-ye*]

scheduled flight рейсовый полёт [*ryay-suvee pa-lyot*]

school школа [*shkola*]; (*university*) университет [*ooni-vyirsi-tyet*]

science наука [*na-ōōka*]

scissors: a pair of scissors ножницы [*nozhnitsee*]

scooter (*motor scooter*) мотороллер [*mataroll-yer*]

scorching: it's really scorching (*weather*) сегодня невыносимо жарко [*syivo-dnya nye-vinasseema zharkuh*]

score: what's the score? какой счёт? [*kakoy s-chot*]

Scot (*man*) шотландец [*shotland-yits*]; (*woman*) шотландка [*shotlantka*]

Scotch (*whisky*) виски [*viskee*]

Scotch tape (*tm*) клейкая лента [*klyayka-ya lyenta*]

Scotland Шотландия [*shotlandi-ya*]

Scottish шотландский [*shotland-skee*]

scrambled eggs яичница-болтунья [*ya-eech-nitsa baltōōn-ya*]

scratch (*noun*) царапина [*tsa-rahpina*]; it's only a scratch это всего лишь царапина [*ettuh fsyivo leesh tsa-rahpina*]

scream кричать/закричать [*kreechaht/zakrichaht*]

screw (*noun*) винт [*vint*]

screwdriver отвёртка [*at-vyortka*]

scrubbing brush щётка [*shchotka*]

scruffy (*appearance*) неопрятный [*nyiapryatnee*]; (*dirty*) грязный [*gryaznee*]

scuba diving нырять со скубой [*ni-ryat sa skōōboy*]

sea море [*mor-ye*]; by the sea у моря [*ōō mor-ya*]

sea air морской воздух [*marskoy voz-dookh*]

seafood морские продукты [*marskee-ye pradooktee*]

seafood restaurant рыбный ресторан [*ribnee ryistaran*]

seafront: on the seafront на приморском бульваре [*na pri-morskum boolvar-ye*]

seagull чайка [*chika*]

search искать/поискать [*iskaht/pa-iskaht*]; I searched everywhere я искал повсюду [*ya iskahl pa-fsyōōdōō*]

search party поисковый отряд [*po-iskovee at-ryat*]

seashell ракушка [*rakōōshka*]

seasick: I get seasick я страдаю морской болезнью [*ya strada-yōō marskoy ba-lyez-nyōō*]

seaside: at the seaside на берегу моря [*na byi-ryigōō mor-ya*]; let's go to the seaside давайте поедем к морю [*davi-tye pa-ye-dyem kmor-yōō*]

season время года [*vrye-mya goda*]; in the high season в разгар сезона [*vrazgar syizona*]; the low season мёртвый сезон [*myortvee syizon*]

seasoning приправа [*priprahva*]

seat место [*myestuh*]; is this anyone's seat? это место свободно? [*ettuh myestuh svabod-nuh*]

seat belt привязной ремень [*pri-vyaznoy ryi-myen*]

sea urchin морской ёж [*marskoy yozh*]

seaweed водоросль (*f*) [*vodarossl*]

secluded уединённый [*ōō-yidi-nyonnee*]

second (*adjective*) второй [*ftaroy*]; (*of time*) секунда [*syikoonda*]; just a second! минуточку! [*minōōtuch-kōō*]; can I have a

second helping? можно мне добавок? [*mozh-nuh mnye dabahvuk*]

second class второго класса [*ftarovuh klassa*]

second-hand подержанный [*padyerzhannee*]

secret (*noun*) секрет [*syi-kryet*]

security check проверка [*pra-vyerka*]

sedative успокаивающее средство [*ōospaka-eeva-yōōsh-cheh-ye sryetst-vuh*]

see видеть/увидеть [*vee-dyet/ōovee-dyet*]; I didn't see it я не видел этого [*ya nye veedyel ettuvuh*]; have you seen my husband? вы не видели моего мужа? [*vee nye veedyelee ma-yivo mōozha*]; I saw him this morning я видел его утром [*ya vee-dyel yivo ōotrum*]; can I see the manager? можно поговорить с начальником? [*mozh-nuh pa-gavareet snachalnikum*]; see you tonight! до вечера! [*da vyechera*]; can I see? можно посмотреть? [*mozh-nuh pasma-tryet*]; oh, I see! понятно! [*pan-yaht-nuh*]; will you see to it? вы уладите это? [*vee ōolahdeet-ye ettuh*]

seldom изредка [*eez-ryetka*]

self-service самообслуживание [*sama-abslōozhivani-ye*]

sell продавать/продать [*pradavat/pradat*]; do you sell ...? у вас есть в продаже ...? [*ōo vass yist fpradahzh-e*]; will you sell it to me? продадите мне это? [*pradadeet-ye mnye ettuh*]

sellotape (*tm*) клейкая лента [*klyayka-ya lyenta*]

send посылать/послать [*pa-silaht/paslaht*]; I want to send this to England я хочу это послать в Англию [*ya khachōo ettuh pa-slaht vang-glee-yōo*]; I'll have to send this food back эту еду надо вернуть на кухню [*ettōo yidōo nahduh vyirnōot na kookh-nyōo*]

senior: Mr Jones senior мистер Джоунс старший [*mister 'jones' starshee*]

senior citizen пенсионер [*pyinsi-a-nyer*]

sensational великолепный [*vyilika-lyepnee*]

sense: I have no sense of direction я плохо ориентируюсь [*ya plokhuh ari-enteeroo-yōoss*]; it doesn't make sense это лишено всякого смысла [*ettuh leesheno fsyakuvuh smeessla*]

sensible разумный [*razōomnee*]

sensitive чувствительный [*choostvee-tyilnee*]

sentimental сентиментальный [*syinti-myintahl-nee*]

separate отдельный [*at-dyelnee*]; can we have separate bills? каждый платит отдельно [*kahzh-dee plahteet at-dyelnuh*]

separated: I'm separated я разведённый [*ya raz-vyi-dyonnee*]

separately отдельно [*at-dyelnuh*]

September сентябрь (*m*) [*syin-tyabr*]

septic септический [*syip-teechiskee*]

serious серьёзный [*syi-ryoznee*]; (*illness*) тяжёлый [*tyazholee*]; I'm serious я не шучу [*ya nye shoochōo*]; you can't be serious! вы, наверно, шутите? [*vee na-vyernuh shōoteet-ye*]; is it serious, doctor? это опасно? [*ettuh apah-snuh*]

seriously: seriously ill тяжело болен [*tyazhilo bo-lyen*]

service: the service is excellent обслуживание отличное [*abslōozhivani-ye atleechnuh-ye*]; could we have some service, please! вы нас можете обслужить! [*vee nass mozhit-ye ab-sloozheet*]; (*church*) богослужение [*baga-sloozheni-ye*]; the car needs a service машина нуждается в техобслуживании [*masheena noozhda-yitsa ftyikh-ab-slōozhivani-ee*]; service charge (*in restaurant*) плата за обслуживание [*plahta za ab-slōozhivani-ye*]

service station станция технического обслуживания [*stantsi-ya tyikh-neechiskuh-vuh ab-slōozhivani-ya*]

serviette салфетка [*sal-fyetka*]

set: it's time we were setting off пора отправляться [*para atprav-lyatsa*]

set menu комплексное меню [*kom-plyiks-nuh-ye myi-nyōo*]

settle up: can we settle up now? можем рассчитаться? [*mozhem rass-chitahtsa*]

several несколько [*nye-skol-kuh*]

sew шить/сшить [*sheet/s-sheet*]; could you sew this back on? пришейте, пожалуйста, это [*prishay-tye pa-zhahlsta ettuh*]

sex (*sexual intercourse*) секс [*seks*]; (*gender*) пол [*pol*]

sexy сексуальный [*syik-soo-ahlnee*]

shade: in the shade в тени [*ftyinee*]

shadow тень (*f*) [*tyen*]

shake: let's shake hands давайте пожмём руки [*davi-tye pazh-myom rōokee*]; she is shaking она дрожит [*ana drazheet*]

shallow (*water*) мелкий [*myelkee*]

shame: what a shame! как жаль! [*kak zhahl*]

shampoo (*noun*) шампунь (*m*) [*shampoon*]; can I have a shampoo and set? помойте, пожалуйста, голову и сделайте причёску [*pa-moy-tye pa-zhahlsta goluvoo ee zdyelı-tye prichoskoo*]

shandy, shandy-gaff смесь пива с лимонадом [*smyess peeva slimanahdum*]

share (*verb: room, table etc*) делиться/поделиться [*dyileetsa/pa-dyileetsa*]; let's share the cost давайте разделим расходы [*davı-tye raz-dyeleem rass-khodee*]

sharp острый [*ostree*]

shattered: I'm shattered (*very tired*) я смертельно устал [*ya smyir-tyelnuh oostahl*]

shave: I need a shave я должен побриться [*ya dolzhen pabreetsa*]; can you give me a shave? побрейте меня, пожалуйста [*pa-bryay-tye minya pazhahlsta*]

shaver бритва [*breetva*]

shaving brush кисточка для бритья [*keestuchka dlya bree-tya*]

shaving foam крем для бритья [*kryem dlya bree-tya*]

shaving point розетка для электрической бритвы [*ra-zyetka dlya e-lyiktree-chiskoy breetvee*]

shaving soap мыло для бритья [*meeluh dlya bree-tya*]

shawl шаль (*f*) [*shahl*]

she она [*ana*]; is she here? она здесь? [*ana zdyiss*]; is she a friend of yours? это ваша знакомая? [*ettuh vasha znakoma-ya*]; *see page 111*

sbeep овца [*aftsa*]

sheet (*for bed*) простыня [*prastee-nya*]

shelf полка [*polka*]

shell раковина [*rakuveena*]

shellfish моллюск [*ma-lyoosk*]

sherry херес [*kheress*]

shingles лишай [*leeshı*]

ship корабль (*m*) [*karabl*]; by ship на корабле [*na karab-lye*]

shirt рубашка [*roobashka*]

shit говно [*gavno*]

shock (*surprise, medical*) шок [*shock*]; (*blow*) удар [*oodar*]; I got an electric shock from the ... меня ударило током от ... [*minya oo-dahril-uh tokum at*]

shock-absorber амортизатор [*amorti-zahtur*]

shocking скандальный [*skandahl-nee*]

shoe туфля [*toof-lya*]; my shoes мои туфли [*mayee tooflee*]; a pair of shoes пара туфель [*pahra too-fyel*]

shoelace шнурок [*shnoorok*]

shoe polish крем для обуви [*kryem dlya o-boovee*]

shoe repairer сапожник [*sapozh-nik*]

shop магазин [*magazeen*]

shopping: I'm going shopping я иду за покупками [*ya eedoo za pa-koopkamee*]

shop window витрина [*veetreena*]

shore (*of sea, lake*) берег [*bye-ryek*]

short (*person*) низкий [*neezkee*]; (*time, journey*) короткий [*karotkee*]; it's only a short distance это недалеко [*ettuh nye-da-lyiko*]

short-change: you've short-changed me вы меня обсчитали [*vee minya abs-sheetahlee*]

short circuit короткое замыкание [*karotkuh-ye zamikahni-ye*]

shortcut: we took a shortcut through the park мы шли напрямик через парк [*mee shlee na-pryameek che-ryiz park*]

shorts шорты [*shortee*]; (*underpants*) трусы [*troo-see*]

should: what should I do? что мне делать? [*shto mnye dyelat*]; he shouldn't be long он скоро вернётся [*on skoruh vyir-nyotsa*]; you should have told me вы должны были мне сказать об этом [*vee dalzhnee beelee mnye skazaht ab ettum*]

shoulder плечо [*plyicho*]

shoulder blade лопатка [*lapatka*]

shout кричать/закричать [*krichaht/-zakri-chaht*]

show: could you show me? можете показать? [*mozhit-ye pakazaht*]; does it show? видно? [*veednuh*]; we'd like to go to a show мы хотим пойти на представление [*mee khateem pıtee na pyid-stav-lyeni-ye*]

shower (*in bathroom*) душ [*doosh*]; a room with shower комната с отдельным душем [*komnata sat-dyelnum dooshem*]

showercap резиновая шапочка [*ryizeenuva-ya shapuchka*]

show-off: don't be a show-off не хвастайся [*nye khva-stıs-ya*]

shrimps креветки [*kryi-vyetkee*]

shrine храм [*khram*]

shrink: it's shrunk in the wash это село при стирке [*ettuh syeluh pree steerk-ye*]

shut закрывать/закрыть [*zakrivaht/zakreet*]; **when do you shut?** когда закрываете? [*kagda zakrivah-yit-ye*]; **when do they shut?** когда закрывают? [*kagda zakrivah-yōōt*]; **it was shut** было закрыто [*beeluh zakreetuh*]; **shut up!** замолчи! [*zamalchee*]

shutter (*on camera*) затвор объектива [*zatvor a-byek-teeva*]; (*on window*) ставень (*m*) [*stah-vyen*]

shutter release размыкание [*razmikahni-ye*]

shy застенчивый [*za-styenchivee*]

Siberia Сибирь (*f*) [*seebeer*]

sick (*ill*) больной [*balnoy*]; **I'm going to be sick** меня тошнит [*minya tashneet*]

side сторона [*starana*]; **at the side of the road** на обочине [*na abochin-ye*]; **the other side of town** в другом конце города [*vdroogom kants-e goruda*]

side lights подфарники [*pad-farneekee*]

side salad салат [*salaht*]

side street переулок [*pyiri-ōōluk*]

sidewalk тротуар [*trotoo-ahr*]

sidewalk café кафе на открытом воздухе [*kaff-e na atkreetum vozdookh-ye*]

siesta полуденный отдых [*palōō-dyinnee otdikh*]

sight: the sights of ... достопримечательности ... [*dasta-primyi-chah-tyilnustee*]

sightseeing: sightseeing tour осмотр достопримечательностей [*a-smotr dasta-primyi-chah-tyilnust-yay*]; **we're going sightseeing** мы собираемся осматривать достапримичательности [*mee sabira-yimsa a-smahtrivat dasta-primyi-chah-tyil-nustee*]

sign (*roadsign etc*) дорожный знак [*darozhnee znak*]; (*written character*) обозначение [*aba-znacheni-ye*]; **where do I sign?** где подписаться? [*gdye pad-pisahtsa*]

signal: he didn't give a signal (*driver, cyclist*) он не сигналил [*on nye signahleel*]

signature подпись (*f*) [*pod-peess*]

signpost указатель (*m*) [*ōōkazah-tyel*]

silence тишина [*teesheena*]

silencer глушитель (*m*) [*glooshee-tyil*]

silk шёлк [*sholk*]

silly глупый [*glōōpee*]; **that's silly!** это глупо! [*ettuh glōōpuh*]

silver (*noun*) серебро [*syi-ryibro*]; (*adjective*) серебряный [*syi-rye-bryanee*]

silver foil фольга [*folga*]

similar подобный [*padobnee*]

simple (*easy*) простой [*prastoy*]

since: since yesterday со вчерашнего дня [*sa-fcherash-nyivuh dnya*]; **since we got here** с тех пор как мы приехали [*styekh por kak mee pree-yekhalee*]

sincere искренний [*eesk-ryennee*]

sing петь/спеть [*pyet/spyet*]

singer (*man*) певец [*pyi-vyets*]; (*woman*) певица [*pyiveetsa*]

single: a single room отдельный номер [*at-dyelnee no-myir*]; **a single to Peredelkino** билет до Переделкина [*bilyet da pyiri-dyelkina*]; **I'm single** (*man*) я не женат [*ya nye zhinaht*]; (*woman*) я не замужем [*ya nye zah-moozhem*]

sink (*in kitchen*) раковина [*rakuvina*]

sir: excuse me, sir извините, пожалуйста [*izvineet-ye pa-zhahlsta*]

sister: my sister моя сестра [*ma-ya syistra*]

sister-in-law: my sister-in-law моя свояченица [*ma-ya sva-yachenitsa*]

sit: may I sit here? разрешите сюда сесть? [*raz-ryisheet-ye syooda syest*]; **is anyone sitting here?** это место занято? [*ettuh myestuh zah-nyatuh*]

sitting: the second sitting for lunch вторая смена на обед [*ftara-ya smyena na a-byet*]

situation положение [*palazheni-ye*]

size размер [*raz-myer*]; **do you have any other sizes?** у вас есть это в других размерах? [*ōō vass yist ettuh vdroo-geekh raz-myerakh*]

skate (*verb*) кататься на коньках [*katahtsa na kankakh*]; **I can't skate** я не умею кататься на коньках [*ya nye oo-mye-yōō katahtsa na kankakh*]

sketch (*noun*) эскиз [*eskeez*]

ski (*noun*) лыжа [*leezha*]; (*verb*) ходить на лыжах [*khadeet na leezhakh*]; **a pair of skis** лыжи [*leezhee*]

ski boots лыжные ботинки [*leezhnee-ye ba-teenkee*]

skid: I skidded машину занесло [*masheenōō za-nyislo*]

skiing лыжный спорт [*leezhnee sport*]; **we're going skiing** мы идём кататься на лыжах [*mee ee-dyom katahtsa na leezhakh*]

ski instructor тренер по лыжному спорту [*trye-nyer pa leezhnumōō sportōō*]

ski-jumping прыжки на лыжах [*prizhkee na leezhakh*]

ski-lift подъёмник [*pad-yomnik*]

skin кожа [*kozha*]

skin-diving подводное плаванье с аквалангом [*pad-vodnuh-ye plahvan-ye sakva-langum*]; **I go skin-diving** я занимаюсь подводным плаваньем [*ya zani-mah-yōōss pad-vodnim plahvan-yem*]

skinny тощий [*tosh-chee*]

ski-pants лыжные брюки [*leezhnee-ye bryōōkee*]

ski-pass билет на подъёмник [*bi-lyet na pad-yomnik*]

ski pole лыжная палка [*leezhna-ya palka*]

skirt юбка [*yōōpka*]

ski run лыжня [*leezh-nya*]

ski slope лыжный склон [*leezhnee sklon*]

ski wax лыжная мазь [*leezhna-ya mass*]

skull череп [*che-ryep*]

sky небо [*nyebuh*]

sledge сани [*sahnee*]

sleep спать/поспать [*spaht/pa-spaht*]; **I can't sleep** мне не спится [*mnye nye speetsa*]; **did you sleep well?** вы выспались? [*vee vee-spaleess*]; **I need a good sleep** мне надо выспаться [*mnye nahduh vee-spahtsa*]

sleeper (*rail carriage*) спальный вагон [*spalnee vagon*]

sleeping bag спальный мешок [*spalnee myishok*]

sleeping car (*rail*) спальный вагон [*spalnee vagon*]

sleeping pills снотворные таблетки [*snatvornee-ye tab-lyetkee*]

sleepy (*person, town*) сонный [*sonnee*]; **I'm feeling sleepy** мне хочется спать [*mnye khochitsa spaht*]

sleeve рукав [*rookaſ*]

slice (*noun*) ломтик [*lomtik*]

slide (*phot*) слайд [*slɪd*]

slim (*adjective*) стройный [*stroynee*]; **I'm slimming** я хочу похудеть [*ya khachōō pakhoo-dyet*]

slip (*under dress*) комбинация [*kambinahtsi-ya*]; **I slipped** я поскользнулся [*ya paskalz-nōōl-sa*]

slipped disc смещение позвонка [*smyish-cheni-ye pazvanka*]

slippery скользкий [*skolzkee*]; **it's slippery here** здесь скользко [*zdyiss skolzkuh*]

slow медленный [*myed-liynnee*]; **slow down!** (*driving*) тормозите! [*tarma-zeet-ye*]; (*speaking*) говорите медленно [*gavareet-ye myed-lyinnuh*]

slowly медленно [*myed-lyinnuh*]; **could you say it slowly?** можете сказать это медленно? [*mozhit-ye skazaht ettuh myed-lyinnuh*]; **very slowly** очень медленно [*ochin myed-lyinnuh*]

small маленький [*mah-lyenkee*]

small change мелочь (*f*) [*myeluch*]

smallpox оспа [*ospa*]

smart (*clothes*) изящный [*iz-yash-chnee*]

smashing потрясающий [*pa-trya-sa-yōōsh-chee*]

smell: there's a funny smell здесь какой-то странный запах [*zdyiss kakoy-tuh strannee zahpakh*]; **what a lovely smell!** как замечательно пахнет! [*kak za-myichah-tyilnuh pakh-nyet*]; **it smells** какая вонь! [*kaka-ya von*]

smile улыбаться/улыбнуться [*ōō-libahtsa/ōō-libnōōtsa*]; **she's got a nice smile** у неё приятная улыбка [*ōō nyi-yo pri-yahtna-ya ōōlipka*]

smoke курить/закурить [*kooreet/za-kooreet*]; **do you smoke?** вы курите? [*vee kōōreet-ye*]; **do you mind if I smoke?** разрешите закурить? [*raz-ryisheet-ye za-kooreet*]; **I don't smoke** я не курю [*ya nye koo-ryōō*]

smooth (*surface*) гладкий [*glatkee*]

smoothy: he's a real smoothy он слишком такой прилизанный [*on sleeshkum takoy pri-leezannee*]

snack: I'd just like a snack я только хочу перекусить [*ya tolkuh khachōō pyiri-koo-seet*]

snackbar буфет [*boo-fyet*]

snake змея [*zmyi-ya*]

sneakers кеды [*kyedee*]

snob сноб [*snop*]

snorkel трубка акваланга [*trōōpka akva-langa*]

snow (*noun*) снег [*snyek*]; **it's snowing** идёт снег [*ee-dyot snyek*]

snowball снежок [*snyizhok*]

snowflake снежинка [*snyizhinka*]

snowplough, snowplow снего-очиститель (*m*) [*snyiga-achistee-tyil*]

snowstorm метель (*f*) [*myi-tyel*]

so: it's so hot так жарко [*tak zharkuh*]; **it was so beautiful!** было так прекрасно! [*beeluh tak pryikrah-snuh*]; **not so fast** не так быстро [*nye tak beestruh*]; **thank you so much** большое спасибо [*balsho-ye spa-see-buh*]; **it wasn't - it was so!** нет, не так - именно так [*nyet nye tak - ee-myennuh tak*]; **so am/do I** я тоже [*ya tozh-e*]; **how was it? - so-so** ну как? - так себе [*nōō kak - tak si-bye*]

soaked: I'm soaked я промок до нитки [*ya pramok da neetkee*]

soaking solution (*for contact lenses*) раствор для контактных линз [*rastvor dlya kantakt-nikh linz*]

soap мыло [*meeluh*]

soap-powder стиральный порошок [*stiralnee parashok*]

sober трезвый [*tryezvee*]

soccer футбол [*footbol*]

socialism социализм [*satsia-leezm*]

socialist (*noun*) социалист [*satsia-leest*]; (*adjective*) социалистический [*satsia-listee-chiskee*]

sock носок [*na-sok*]

socket (*elec*) розетка [*ra-zyetka*]

soda (*water*) газированная вода [*gazirovanna-ya vada*]

sofa диван [*divan*]

soft мягкий [*myakhkee*]

soft drink безалкогольный напиток [*byiz-alkagolnee napeetuk*]

soft lenses мягкие контактные линзы [*myakhki-ye kantaktnee-ye linzee*]

soldier солдат [*saldat*]

sole (*of shoe*) подошва [*padoshva*]; (*of foot*) ступня [*stoop-nya*]; **could you put new soles on these shoes?** пожалуйста, поставьте новую подмётку на эти туфли [*pa-zhahlsta pa-stahv-tye novōō-yōō pad-myotkōō na ettee tōōflee*]

solid твёрдый [*tvyordee*]

some: may I have some water? дайте мне, пожалуйста, воды [*dı-tye 'mnye pa-zhahlsta vadee*]; **do you have some matches?** у вас есть спички? [*ōō vass yist speechkee*]; **that's some drink!** вот это напиток! [*vot ettuh na-peetuk*]; **some of them** некоторые из них [*nye-katoree-ye iz neekh*]; **can I have some?** можно мне немного? [*mozh-nuh mnye nyim-noguh*]

somebody, someone кто-то [*kto-tuh*]

something что-то [*shto-tuh*]; **something to drink** мне надо что-то выпить [*mnye nahduh shto-tuh veepeet*]

sometime: sometime this afternoon сегодня днём [*syivo-dnya dnyom*]

sometimes иногда [*inagda*]

somewhere где-то [*gdye-tuh*]

son: my son мой сын [*moy seen*]

song песня [*pye-snya*]

son-in-law: my son-in-law мой зять [*moy zyat*]

soon скоро [*skoruh*]; **I'll be back soon** я скоро вернусь [*ya skoruh vyir-nōōss*]; **as soon as you can** как только сможете [*kak tolkuh smozhit-ye*]

sore: it's sore это болит [*ettuh baleet*]

sore throat: I have a sore throat у меня болит горло [*ōō minya baleet gorluh*]

sorry: I'm sorry виноват [*veenavat*]; **sorry?** извините, что вы сказали? [*izvineet-ye shto vee skazahlee*]

sort: what sort of...? что за...? [*shto za*]; **a different sort of...** другой сорт... [*droogoy sort*]; **will you sort it out?** пожалуйста, вы разберитесь [*pa-zhahlsta vee raz-byiree-tyiss*]

soup суп [*sōōp*]

sour (*taste*) кислый [*keeslee*]

south юг [*yōōk*]; **in the south** на юге [*na yōōg-ye*]; **to the south of...** к югу от... [*kyōōgōō at*]

South Africa Южная Африка [*yōōzhna-ya afrika*]

South African (*adjective*) южно-африканский [*yōōzh-nuh-afrikanskee*]; (*man*) южноафриканец [*yōōzh-nuh-afrikahn-yits*]; (*woman*) южноафриканка [*yōōzh-nuh-afrikanka*]

southeast юго-восток [*yōōga-vastok*]; **in the southeast** на юго-востоке [*na yōōga-vastok-ye*]

southwest юго-запад [*yōōga-zahpat*]; **in the southwest** на юго-западе [*na yōōga-zahpad-ye*]

souvenir сувенир [*sōō-vyineer*]

soviet (*noun: council*) совет [*sa-vyet*]

Soviet (*person, adjective*) советский [*sa-vyetskee*]

Soviet Union Советский Союз [*sa-vyetskee sa-yōōss*]

spa (*town*) курорт [*koorort*]

space heater обогреватель (*m*) [*aba-gryivah-tyil*]

spade лопата [*lapahta*]

Spain Испания [*ispani-ya*]

spanner гаечный ключ [*ga-yechnee klyōōch*]

spare part запчасть (*f*) [*zapchast*]

spare tyre/tire запасное колесо [*zapasno-ye ka-lyisso*]

spark(ing) plug свеча зажигания [*svyicha za-zhigahni-ya*]

speak говорить [*gavareet*]; do you speak English? вы говорите по-английски? [*vee gavaree-tye pa-ang-gleeskee*]; I don't speak ... я не говорю ... [*ya nye gavaryōō*]; can I speak to ...? я хочу поговорить с ... [*ya khachōō pa-gavareet s*]; speaking (*on telephone*) я слушаю [*ya slōōsha-yoo*]

special особый [*a-sobee*]; nothing special ничего особенного [*neechivo a-so-byinnu-vuh*]

specialist специалист [*spetsi-aleest*]

special(i)ty специальность (f) [*spetsi-ahlnust*]; the special(i)ty of the house фирменное блюдо [*feer-myinnuh-ye blyōōduh*]

spectacles очки [*achkee*]

speed (*noun*) скорость (f) [*skorust*]; he was speeding он превысил дозволенную скорость [*on pryivee-seel dazvo-lyinnōō-yōō skorust*]

speedboat быстроходный катер [*bistra-khodnee kah-tyer*]

speed limit предельная скорость [*pryi-dyelna-ya skorust*]

speedometer спидометр [*spido-myetr*]

spell: how do you spell it? как это пишется? [*kak ettuh peeshitsa*]

spend тратить/истратить [*trahteet/istrahteet*]; I've spent all my money я истратил все деньги [*ya istrahteel fsye dyen-gee*]

spice пряность (f) [*pryanust*]

spicy острый [*ostree*]

spider паук [*pa-ōōk*]

spin-dryer сушильный барабан [*soo-sheelnee baraban*]

splendid великолепный [*vyilika-lyepnee*]

splint шина [*sheena*]

splinter заноза [*zanoza*]

splitting: I've got a splitting headache у меня ужасно болит голова [*ōō minya ōōzhah-snuh baleet galava*]

spoke спица [*speetsa*]

sponge губка [*gōōpka*]

spoon ложка [*lozhka*]

sport спорт [*sport*]

sport(s) jacket пиджак [*pidzhak*]

spot (*on face etc*) прыщик [*preesh-chik*]; will they do it on the spot? смогут ли они это

сделать сразу? [*smogōōt lee anee ettuh zdyelat srahzōō*]

sprain: I've sprained my ... я растянул себе ... [*ya rast-yanōōl si-bye*]

spray (*for hair*) лак для волос [*lak dlya valoss*]

spring (*season*) весна [*vyi-sna*]; (*of car*) рессора [*ryissora*]; (*in seat*) пружина [*proozheena*]

spy (*noun*) шпион [*shpee-on*]; (*verb*) шпионить [*shpee-onit*]

square (*in town*) площадь (f) [*plosh-chad*]; ten square metres десять квадратных метров [*dye-syat kvadraht-nikh myetruff*]

stain пятно [*pyatno*]

stairs лестница [*lyestnitsa*]

stale (*bread*) чёрствый [*chorstvee*]; (*taste*) безвкусный [*byiz-fkōōsnee*]

stall: the engine keeps stalling двигатель глохнет [*dveega-tyil glokh-nyet*]

stalls (*in theatre*) партер [*par-tyer*]

stamp марка [*marka*]; a stamp for a letter to England, please дайте, пожалуйста, марку для письма в Англию [*dı-tye pa-zhahlsta markōō dlya peesma vang-glee-yōō*]

stand: I can't stand ... я терпеть не могу ... [*ya tyir-pyet nye magōō*]

standard нормальный [*narmalnee*]

star звезда [*zvyizda*]; (*in movies*) кинозвезда [*keena-zvyizda*]

start (*noun*) начало [*na-chahluh*]; (*verb*) начинать/начать [*nachinaht/nachaht*]; when does the film start? когда начинается фильм? [*kagda nachina-yitsa film*]; the car won't start машина не заводится [*masheena nye zavoditsa*]

starter (*of car*) стартёр [*star-tyor*]; (*food*) первое блюдо [*pyervuh-ye blyōōduh*]

starving: I'm starving я умираю от голода [*ya ōōmira-yōō at goluda*]

state (*country*) государство [*ga-sōōdarst-vuh*]; (*adjective*) государственный [*ga-soodarst-vyinnee*]

station (*main line*) вокзал [*vagzal*]; (*metro*) станция [*stantsi-ya*]

statue статуя [*statōō-ya*]

stay: we enjoyed our stay here нам здесь очень понравилось [*nam zdyiss ochin panrahviluss*]; where are you staying? где вы остановились? [*gdye vye astana-veeleess*]; I'm staying at ... я остановился в ... [*ya astana-veelsa v*]; I'd like to stay another week мне бы хотелось остаться ещё неделю [*mnye bee kha-tyeluss astahtsa yish-*

cho *nyi-dyel-yōō*]; **I'm staying in tonight** я буду дома сегодня вечером [*ya bōōdōō doma syivo-dnya vyecherum*]

steak бифштекс [*bif-shtyeks*]

steal красть/украсть [*krahst/ōōkrahst*]; **my bag has been stolen** у меня украли сумочку [*ōō minya ookrahlee soomuch-kōō*]

steep крутой [*krootoy*]

steering рулевое управление [*roo-lyivo-ye ōōprav-lyeni-ye*]; **the steering is slack** рулевое управление слабо затянуто [*roo-lyivo-ye ōōprav-lyeni-ye slahbuh za-tyanoota*]

steering wheel руль (*m*) [*rōōl*]

step (*stair*) ступенька [*stoo-pyenka*]

Steppes степь (*f*) [*styep*]

stereo стерео [*styereo*]

sterling стерлинги [*styerling-gee*]

stew тушёное мясо [*tooshonuh-ye mya-suh*]

steward (*on plane*) стюард [*styōō-art*]

stewardess стюардесса [*styōō-ar-dyessa*]

sticking plaster лейкопластырь (*m*) [*lyayka-plastir*]

sticky: it's sticky это липнет [*ettuh leep-nyet*]

sticky tape клейкая лента [*klyayka-ya lyenta*]

still: I'm still waiting я всё ещё жду [*ya fsyo yish-cho zhdōō*]; **will you still be open?** у вас ещё будет открыто? [*ōō vass yish-cho bōō-dyet atkreetuh*]; **it's still not right** это всё ещё не как положено [*ettuh fsyo yish-cho nye kak palozhinuh*]; **that's better still** это намного лучше [*ettuh nam-noguh lōōch-e*]; **keep still!** не двигайтесь! [*nye dveegɪ-tyiss*]

sting жало [*zhahluh*]; **I've been stung by a bee** меня ужалила пчела [*minya ōō-zhahleela pchila*]

stink (*noun*) вонь (*f*) [*von*]; **it stinks** воняет [*va-nya-yet*]

stockings чулки [*choolkee*]

stolen украденный [*ōōkrah-dyinnee*]; **my wallet's been stolen** у меня украли бумажник [*ōō minya ookrahlee boo-mahzhnik*]

stomach желудок [*zhilōōduk*]; **do you have something for an upset stomach?** у вас есть что-то от расстройства желудка? [*ōō vass yist shto-tuh at ras-stroystva zhilōōtka*]

stomach-ache боль в желудке [*bol vzhi-lōōt-kye*]

stone камень (*m*) [*kah-myin*]; *see page 121*

stop (*bus, tram stop etc*) остановка [*astanofka*]; **where is the bus stop for ...?** где остановка автобуса до ...? [*gdye astanofka avto-boossa da ...*]; **please stop here** (*to taxi driver etc*) пожалуйста, остановите здесь [*pa-zhahlsta astana-veet-ye zdyiss*]; **do you stop near ...?** вы останавливаетесь у ...? [*vee astana-vliva-yit-yes ōō*]; **stop doing that!** перестаньте! [*pyiri-stahn-tye*]

stopover остановка в пути [*astanofka fpootee*]

store (*shop*) магазин [*magazeen*]

stor(e)y (*of building*) этаж [*ettahsh*]

storm буря [*bōō-rya*]

story (*tale*) рассказ [*rasskass*]

stove печь (*f*) [*pyech*]

straight (*road etc*) прямой [*pryamoy*]; **it's straight ahead** идите прямо [*eedee-tye pryah-muh*]; **straight away** немедленно [*nyi-myed-lyinnuh*]; **a straight whisky** неразбавленное виски [*nyi-razbahv-lyinnuh-ye viskee*]

straighten: can you straighten things out? (*sort things out*) можете это уладить? [*mozhit-ye ettuh ōō-lahdeet*]

strange (*odd*) странный [*strannee*]; (*unknown*) незнакомый [*nyi-znakomee*]

stranger (*man*) незнакомец [*nyi-znako-myets*]; (*woman*) незнакомка [*nyi-znakomka*]; **I'm a stranger here** я здесь чужой [*ya zdyiss choozhoy*]

strap (*on watch, on suitcase*) ремень (*m*) [*ryi-myen*]; (*on dress*) бретелька [*bryi-tyelka*]

strawberry клубника [*kloob-neeka*]

streak: could you put streaks in? (*hair*) можете обесцветить пряди волос? [*mozhit-ye a-byiss-tsvyeteet pryadee valoss*]

stream речка [*ryechka*]

street улица [*ōōlitsa*]; **on the street** на улице [*na ōōlits-e*]

street café кафе на открытом воздухе [*kaff-e na atkreetum vozdookh-ye*]

streetcar трамвай [*tramvɪ*]

streetmap план города [*plahn goruda*]

strep throat: I have a strep throat у меня болит горло [*ōō minya baleet gorluh*]

strike: they're on strike они бастуют [*anee bastōō-yōōt*]

string верёвка [*vyi-ryofka*]; **have you got some string?** у вас есть кусок верёвки? [*ōō vass yist koosok vyi-ryofkee*]

striped полосатый [*pala-sahtee*]

striptease стриптиз [*strip-teess*]

stroke: he's had a stroke его разбил паралич [*yivo razbeel para-leech*]

stroll: let's go for a stroll давайте пройдёмся [*davι-tye prι-dyomsa*]

stroller (*for babies*) детская коляска [*dyetska-ya ka-lyaska*]

strong (*person*) сильный [*seelnee*]; (*taste*) резкий [*ryezkee*]; (*drink*) крепкий [*kryepkee*]; (*curry*) острый [*ostree*]

stroppy (*official, waiter*) сварливый [*svar-leevee*]

stuck: the key's stuck ключ не поворачивается в замке [*klyōoch nye pava-rahchiva-yetsa vzahm-kye*]

student (*male*) студент [*stoo-dyent*]; (*female*) студентка [*stoo-dyentka*]

stupid глупый [*glōopee*]; that's stupid это глупо [*ettuh glōopuh*]

sty(e) (*in eye*) ячмень на глазу [*yach-myen na glazōo*]

subtitles субтитры [*soob-teetree*]

suburb пригород [*pree-gurut*]

subway (*underground*) метро [*myitro*]

successful: were you successful? вам повезло? [*vam pa-vyizlo*]

suddenly вдруг [*vdrōok*]

sue: I intend to sue я намереваюсь подать в суд [*ya na-myeriva-yōoss pa-daht fsōot*]

suede замша [*zahmsha*]

sugar сахар [*sahkhar*]

suggest: what do you suggest? что вы предлагаете? [*shto vee pryidlaga-yet-ye*]

suit (*noun*) костюм [*ka-styōom*]; it doesn't suit me мне это не идёт [*mnye ettuh nye ee-dyot*]; it suits you вам это идёт [*vam ettuh ee-dyot*]; that suits me fine меня это вполне устраивает [*minya ettuh fpal-nye oostra-eeva-yet*]

suitable подходящий [*padkha-dyash-chee*]

suitcase чемодан [*chimadan*]

sulk: he's sulking он дуется [*on dōo-yetsa*]

sultry (*weather*) знойный [*znoynee*]

summer лето [*lyetuh*]; in the summer летом [*lyetum*]

sun солнце [*sonts-e*]; in the sun на солнце [*na sonts-e*]; out of the sun в тени [*ftyinee*]

sunbathe загорать [*zagaraht*]

sunblock (*cream*) средство против загара [*sryedst-vuh protif zagara*]

sunburn солнечный ожог [*sol-nyichnee azhog*]

Sunday воскресенье [*vass-kryi-seni-ye*]

sunglasses очки от солнца [*achkee at sontsa*]

sun lounger (*chair*) топчан [*tapchan*]

sunny: if it's sunny если будет хорошая погода [*yeslee bōod-yet kharosha-ya pagoda*]; a sunny day солнечный день [*sol-nyechnee dyin*]

sunrise восход солнца [*vass-khot sontsa*]

sunset закат [*zakaht*]

sunshade зонтик от солнца [*zontik at son-tsa*]

sunshine солнечный свет [*sol-nyechnee svyet*]

sunstroke солнечный удар [*sol-nyechnee oodar*]

suntan загар [*zagar*]

suntan lotion лосьон для загара [*la-syon dlya zagara*]

suntanned загорелый [*zaga-ryelee*]

suntan oil масло для загара [*mah-sluh dlya zagara*]

super превосходный [*pryivass-khodnee*]; super! высший сорт! [*veeshee sort*]

superb великолепный [*vyilika-lyepnee*]

supermarket универсам [*oonivyir-sam*]

supper ужин [*ōozhin*]

supplement (*extra charge*) дополнение [*dapal-nyeni-ye*]

suppose: I suppose so должно быть, да [*dalzhno beet da*]

suppository суппозиторий [*soopozee-toree*]

sure: I'm sure (*man*) я уверен [*ya oo-vye-ryen*]; are you sure? вы уверены? [*vee oo-vye-ryenee*]; she's sure она уверена [*ana oo-vye-ryena*]; sure! конечно! [*ka-nyesh-nuh*]

surname фамилия [*fameeli-ya*]

surprise удивление [*oodiv-lyeni-ye*]; (*gift etc*) сюрприз [*syoor-preez*]; to my surprise к моему удивлению [*kma-yemōo oodiv-lyeni-yōo*]

surprising: that's not surprising не удивительно [*nye oodivee-tyilnuh*]

suspension (*car*) подвес [*pad-vyess*]

swallow глотать/проглатывать [*glataht/pra-glahtivaht*]

swearword сквернословие [*skvyirna-slovi-ye*]

sweat потеть/вспотеть [*pa-tyet/fspa-tyet*]; (*noun*) пот [*pot*]; covered in sweat вспотевший [*fspa-tyefshee*]

sweater свитер [*svee-tyer*]

sweatshirt спротивный свитер [*sparteev-nee svee-tyir*]

Sweden Швеция [*shvyetsi-ya*]

sweet (*taste*) сладкий [*slatkee*]; (*dessert*) сладкое [*slahtkuh-ye*]

sweets конфеты [*kan-fyetee*]

swelling опухоль (*f*) [*opookhul*]

sweltering: it's sweltering душно [*dōosh-nuh*]

swerve: I had to swerve я должен был свернуть [*ya dolzhin beel svyirnōot*]

swim плавать/плыть [*plahvat/pleet*]; I'm going for a swim пойду поплаваю [*pıdōo pa-plahva-yōo*]; do you want to go for a swim? хотите поплавать? [*khateet-ye pa-plahvat*]; I can't swim я не умею плавать [*ya nye oo-mye-yōo plahvat*]

swimming плавание [*plavani-ye*]; I like swimming я люблю плавать [*ya lyoo-blyōo plahvat*]

swimming costume купальник [*koopalnik*]

swimming pool бассейн [*ba-syayn*]

swimming trunks плавки [*plahʃkee*]

switch (*noun*) выключатель (*m*) [*vi-klyoo-chah-tyil*]; could you switch it on? можете включить? [*mozhit-ye ʃklyoo-cheet*]; could you switch it off? можете выключить? [*mozhit-ye vee-klyoocheet*]

Switzerland Швейцария [*shvyay-tsari-ya*]

swollen опухший [*apōokh-shee*]

swollen glands опухшие желёзки [*apōokh-shi-ye zhi-lyozkee*]

sympathy симпатия [*simpahti-ya*]

synagogue синагога [*sinagoga*]

synthetic синтетический [*sin-tyitee-chiskee*]

T

table стол [*stol*]; (*small*) столик [*stolik*]; a table for two столик на два места [*stolik na dva myesta*]; at our usual table у нашего обычного столика [*ōo nashevuh a-beechnuvuh stolika*]

tablecloth скатерть (*f*) [*ska-tyert*]

table tennis настольный теннис [*nastolnee tyennis*]

table wine столовое вино [*stalovuh-ye veeno*]

tactful тактичный [*tak-teechnee*]

Tadzhikistan Таджикистан [*tajikistan*]

tailback (*of traffic*) пробка [*propka*]

tailor портной [*partnoy*]

take брать/взять [*braht/vzyaht*]; will you take this to room 12? отнесите это в номер 12 [*at-nyisseet-ye ettuh vno-myir dvye-nahd-sat*]; will you take me to the airport? можете меня отвезти в аэропорт? [*mozhit-ye minya at-vyiztee va-erraport*]; do you take credit cards? можно заплатить кредитной карточкой? [*mozhnuh za-plateet kryideet-noy kartuch-koy*]; OK, I'll take it ладно, беру [*lahdnuh byirōo*]; how long does it take? сколько времени длится? [*skolkuh vrye-myinee dleetsa*]; it'll take 2 hours это займёт два часа [*ettuh zı-myot dva chassa*]; is this seat taken? это место занято? [*ettuh myestuh zah-*

nyatuh]; food to take away готовое блюдо на вынос [*gatovuh-ye blyōoduh na veenus*]; will you take this back, it's broken эта вещь сломалась, я хочу её вернуть [*etta vyeshch slamahlass, ya khachōo yiyo vyirnōot*]; could you take it in at the side? (*dress, jacket*) можете ушить немного в талии? [*mozhit-ye oosheet nyem-noguh ʃtahlee*]; when does the plane take off? когда вылетает самолёт? [*kagda vee-lyita-yet sama-lyot*]; can you take a little off the top? (*to hairdresser*) подстригите немного спереди [*padstree-geet-ye nyem-noguh spyiridee*]

talcum powder тальк [*talk*]

talk (*verb*) разговаривать [*razga-varivat*]

tall высокий [*vissokee*]

tampax (*tm*) тампон [*tampon*]

tampons тампоны [*tamponee*]

tan (*noun*) загар [*zagar*]; I want to get a good tan я хочу хорошо загореть [*ya khachōo khara-sho zaga-ryet*]

tank (*of car*) бак [*bak*]

tap кран [*krahn*]

tape (*cassette*) магнитофонная кассета [*magneeta-fonna-ya ka-syeta*]; (*sticky*) клейкая лента [*klyayka-ya lyenta*]

tape measure рулетка [*roo-lyetka*]

tape recorder магнитофон [*magneeta-fon*]

taste (*noun*) вкус [*fkōoss*]; **can I taste it?** можно попробовать? [*mozh-nuh pa-probuvat*]; **it has a peculiar taste** это оставляет дурной вкус во рту [*ettuh asta-vlya-yet doornoy fkōoss vartōo*]; **it tastes very nice** это очень вкусно [*ettuh ochin fkōoss-nuh*]; **it tastes revolting** это отвратительно на вкус [*ettuh atvratee-tyilnuh na fkōoss*]

taxi такси [*taksee*]; **will you get me a taxi?** найдите мне такси, пожалуйста [*n-deet-ye mnye taksee pa-zhahlsta*]

taxi-driver водитель такси [*vadee-tyil taksee*]

taxi rank, taxi stand стоянка такси [*sta-yanka taksee*]

tea чай [*chı*]; **tea for two please** две чашки чаю, пожалуйста [*dvye chashkee cha-yōo pa-zhahlsta*]; **could I have a cup of tea?** чашку чаю, пожалуйста [*chashkōo cha-yōo pa-zhahlsta*]

teabag мешочек чая [*myishochek cha-ya*]

teach: could you teach me? научите меня, пожалуйста [*na-oocheet-ye minya pa-zhahlsta*]; **could you teach me Russian?** вы можете научить меня русскому? [*vee mozhit-ye na-oocheet minya rooskumōo*]

teacher (*man*) учитель [*ōochee-tyil*] (*m*); (*woman*) учительница [*ōochee-tyilnitsa*]

team команда [*kamanda*]

teapot чайник [*chınik*]

tea towel кухонное полотенце [*kōochunnuh-ye palta-tyents-e*]

teenager подросток [*padrostuk*]

teetotal: he's teetotal он непьющий [*on nyi-ṗyōosh-chee*]

telegram телеграмма [*tyili-gramma*]; **I want to send a telegram** я хочу послать телеграмму [*ya khachōo pa-slaht tyili-grammōo*]

telephone телефон [*tyili-fon*]; **I want to make a telephone call** я хочу заказать телефонный разговор [*ya khachōo zakazaht tyili-fonnee razgavor*]

telephone box/booth телефонная будка [*tyili-fonna-ya bōotka*]

telephone directory телефонный справочник [*tyili-fonnee sprahvuch-nik*]

telephone number номер телефона [*no-myir tyili-fona*]; **what's your telephone number?** какой ваш номер телефона? [*kakoy vash no-myir tyili-fona*]

telephoto lens телефотографический объектив [*tyili-fata-grafeechiskee ab-yekteef*]

television (*set*) телевизор [*tyili-veezur*]; (*medium*) телевидение [*tyili-vee-dyini-ye*]; **I'd like to watch television** я хочу смотреть телевизор [*ya khachōo sma-tryet tyili-veezur*]; **is the match on television?** матч показывают по телевизору? [*match pa-kahziva-yet pa tyili-veezurōo*]

tell: could you tell him . . .? скажите ему, пожалуйста . . . [*skazheet-ye yimōo pa-zhahlsta*]

temperature температура [*tyim-pyira-tōora*]; **he has a temperature** у него температура [*ōo nyivo tyim-pyira-tōora*]

temporary временный [*vrye-myennee*]

tennis теннис [*tyenniss*]

tennis ball теннисный мяч [*tyenniss-nee myach*]

tennis court теннисный корт [*tyenniss-nee kort*]; **can we use the tennis court?** можно играть на корте? [*mozh-nuh eegraht na kor-tye*]

tennis racket теннисная ракетка [*tyennissna-ya ra-kyetka*]

tent палатка [*palahtka*]

term (*university*) семестр [*syi-myestr*]

terminus (*rail*) конечная станция [*kan-yechna-ya stantsi-ya*]; (*tram, bus*) конечная остановка [*ka-nyechna-ya astanofka*]

terrace терраса [*tyirassa*]; **on the terrace** на террасе [*na tyirass-ye*]

terrible ужасный [*ōozhah-snee*]

terrific колоссальный [*kala-sahlnee*]

testicle яичко [*ya-eech-kuh*]

than чем [*chem*]; **smaller than** меньше чем [*myensh-e chem*]

thanks, thank you спасибо [*spa-see-buh*]; **thank you very much** большое спасибо [*balsho-ye spa-see-buh*]; **thank you for everything** спасибо за всё [*spa-see-buh za fsyo*]; **no thanks** спасибо, не хочу [*spa-see-buh nye khachōo*]

that: that woman та женщина [*ta zhensh-cheena*]; **that man** тот мужчина [*tot moozh-cheena*]; **that coat** то пальто [*to palto*]; **I hope that . . .** я надеюсь, что . . . [*ya na-dye-yōoss shto*]; **that's perfect** это отлично [*ettuh atleech-nuh*]; **is that . . .?** это . . .? [*ettuh*]; **that's it** (*that's right*) вот именно [*vot ee-myennuh*]; **is it that expensive?** это так дорого? [*ettuh tak doruguh*]

thaw (*noun*) оттепель (*f*) [*ot-tye-pyil*]
the *see page 104*
theater, theatre театр [*tyi-ahtr*]
their их [*ikh*]; *see page 111*
theirs их [*ikh*]; *see page 111*
them: for them для них [*dlya nikh*]; with them с ними [*sneemee*]; I gave it to them я дал это им [*ya dahl ettuh eem*]; who? - them кто? - они [*kto anee*]; *see page 112*
then (*at that time*) в то время [*fto vrye-mya*]; (*after that*) потом [*patom*]
there там [*tam*]; over there вон там [*von tam*]; up there вон наверху [*von na-vyirkhōō*]; is there ...? имеется ли ...? [*ee-mye-yitsa lee*]; are there ...? имеются ли ...? [*ee-mye-yōōtsa lee*]; there is ... имеется [*ee-mye-yitsa*]; there are ... имеются [*ee-mye-yōōtsa*]; there you are (*giving something*) вот вам [*vot vam*]
thermal spring горячий источник [*ga-ryachee istochnik*]
thermometer градусник [*grah-doossnik*]
thermos flask термос [*tyer-muss*]
thermostat термостат [*tyirma-stat*]
these эти [*ettee*]; can I have these? дайте мне вот эти [*dı-tye mnye vot ettee*]
they они [*anee*]; are they coming? они идут? [*anee eedōōt*]; *see page 112*
thick (*dense*) густой [*goostoy*]; (*fat*) толстый [*tolstee*]; (*stupid*) глупый [*glōōpee*]
thief вор [*vor*]
thigh бедро [*byidro*]
thin тонкий [*tonkee*]; (*soup*) жидкий [*zheetkee*]
thing вещь (*f*) [*vyeshch*]; have you seen my things? вы видели мои вещи? [*vee vee-dyelee ma-yee vyesh-chee*]; first thing in the morning рано утром [*rahnuh ōōtrum*]
think думать/подумать [*dōōmat/pa-dōōmat*]; what do you think? что вы думаете? [*shto vee dōōma-yet-ye*]; I think so думаю, что да [*dōōma-yōō shto da*]; I don't think so я не думаю [*ya nye dōōma-yōō*]; I'll think about it я подумаю [*ya pa-dōōma-yōō*]
third party insurance обязательный страховой полис [*a-byazah-tyilnee strakha-voy poliss*]
thirsty: I'm thirsty мне хочется пить [*mnye khochitsa peet*]
this: this house этот дом [*ettut dom*]; this street эта улица [*etta ōōlitsa*]; this coat это пальто [*ettuh palto*]; this one этот/эта/это [*ettut/etta/ettuh*]; this is my wife это моя жена [*ettuh ma-ya zhena*]; this is my favo(u)rite café это моё любимое кафе [*ettuh ma-yo lyoobeemuh-ye kaff-e*]; is this yours? это ваше? [*ettuh vash-e*]
those те [*tye*]; not these, those не эти, а те [*nye ettee a tye*]
thread (*noun*) нитка [*neetka*]
throat горло [*gorluh*]
throat lozenges таблетки для горла [*tablyetkee dlya gorluh*]
throttle дроссель (*m*) [*dros-syil*]
through через [*che-ryiz*]; does this train go through Kiev? этот поезд идёт через Киев? [*ettut po-yezd ee-dyot che-ryiz kee-yeff*]; Monday through Friday от понедельника до пятницы [*at pa-nyi-dyelnika da pyatnitsee*]; straight through the city centre прямо через центр города [*pryamuh che-ryiz tsentr goruda*]
through train прямой поезд [*pryamoy po-yezd*]
throw бросать/бросить [*brassat/ bro-seet*]; don't throw it away не выбросьте это [*nye veebross-tye ettuh*]; I'm going to throw up меня сейчас вырвет [*minya syichass veer-vyet*]
thumb большой палец [*balshoy pah-lyets*]
thumbtack чертёжная кнопка [*chir-tyozhna-ya k-nopka*]
thunder (*noun*) гром [*grom*]
thunderstorm гроза [*graza*]
Thursday четверг [*chit-vyerk*]
ticket билет [*bi-lyet*]
ticket office билетная касса [*bi-lyetna-ya kassa*]
tie галстук [*gal-stook*]
tight (*clothes*) узкий [*ōōzkee*]; (*shoes*) тесный [*tyessnee*]; the waist is too tight слишком узко в талии [*sleeshkum ōōzkuh ftahlee*]
tights колготки [*kalgotkee*]
time время [*vrye-mya*]; what's the time? который час? [*katoree chass*]; at what time do you close? в котором часу вы закрываете? [*fkatorum chassōō vee zakriva-yet-ye*]; there's not much time осталось совсем немного времени [*astahluss sav-syem nyem-noguh vrye-myenee*]; for the time being пока [*paka*]; from time to time время от времени [*vrye-mya at vrye-myenee*]; right on time вовремя [*vo-vrye-mya*]; this time на этот

раз [*na ettut rass*]; last time в прошлый раз [*fproshlee rass*]; next time в следующий раз [*fslyedoo-yoosh-chee rass*]; four times четыре раза [*chiteer-ye rahza*]; have a good time! желаю хорошо провести время! [*zhila-yōō khara-sho pra-vyistee vrye-mya*]; *see page 119*

timetable расписание [*raspi-sahni-ye*]

tin (*can*) консервная банка [*kan-servna-ya banka*]

tinfoil фольга [*folga*]

tin-opener консервный нож [*kan-servnee nozh*]

tiny крошечный [*kroshech-nee*]

tip чаевые [*cha-yivee-ye*]; does that include the tip? это уже включает чаевые? [*ettuh oozh-e fklyoo-chayet cha-yivee-ye*]

tire (*car*) шина [*sheena*]

tired усталый [*ōōstahlee*]; I'm tired (*man*) я устал [*ya ōōstahl*]

tiring утомительный [*ōōtamee-tyilnee*]

tissues бумажные носовые платки [*boomahzh-nee-ye nassavee-ye platkee*]

to: to Moscow/England/London в Москву/ в Англию/в Лондон [*vmaskvōō/vang-glee-yōō/vlon-don*]; to the airport в аэропорт [*va-erraport*]; to the station/post office на вокзал/почту [*na vagzal/pochtōō*]; here's to you! (*toast*) за ваше здоровье! [*za vash-e zdarov-ye*]; *see page 107*

toast (*bread*) гренок [*gryinok*]; (*drinking*) тост [*tost*]

tobacco табак [*tabak*]

tobacconist, tobacco store табачная лавка [*tabachna-ya lafka*]

today сегодня [*syivo-dnya*]; today week ровно через неделю [*rovnuh che-ryiz nyidye-lyōō*]

toe палец ноги [*pah-lyets nagee*]

toffee ириска [*ireeska*]

together вместе [*vmyest-ye*]; we're together мы вместе [*mee vmyest-ye*]; can we pay together? я заплачу за оба счёта [*ya za-plachōō za oba s-chota*]

toilet туалет [*too-a-lyet*]; where's the toilet? где туалет? [*gdye too-a-lyet*]; I have to go to the toilet мне нужно в туалет [*mnye nōōzh-nuh ftoo-a-lyet*]; she's in the toilet она в туалете [*ana ftoo-a-lyet-ye*]

toilet paper туалетная бумага [*tōō-a-lyetna-ya boomahga*]

toilet water туалетная вода [*tōō-a-lyetna-ya vada*]

toll сбор [*zbor*]

tomato помидор [*pameedor*]

tomato juice томатный сок [*tamahtnee sok*]

tomato ketchup томатный соус [*tamahtnee so-ōōss*]

tomorrow завтра [*zahftra*]; tomorrow morning завтра утром [*zahftra ōōtrum*]; tomorrow afternoon завтра пополудни [*zahftra papa-lōōdnee*]; tomorrow evening завтра вечером [*zahftra vyecherum*]; the day after tomorrow послезавтра [*poss-lye-zahftra*]; see you tomorrow до завтра [*da zahftra*]

ton тонна [*tonna*]

tongue язык [*yazik*]

tonic (**water**) тоник [*tonik*]

tonight вечером [*vyecherum*]; not tonight не сегодня вечером [*nye syivo-dnya vyecherum*]

tonsillitis тонзиллит [*tanzileet*]

tonsils миндалины [*minda-leenee*]

too (*excessively*) слишком [*sleesh-kum*]; (*also*) тоже [*tozh-e*]; too much слишком много [*sleesh-kum mnoguh*]; me too я тоже [*ya tozh-e*]; I'm not feeling too good я неважно себя чувствую [*ya nyi-vahzh-nuh sibya chōōst-vōō-yōō*]

tooth зуб [*zōōp*]

toothache зубная боль [*zoobna-ya bol*]

toothbrush зубная щётка [*zoobna-ya shchotka*]

toothpaste зубная паста [*zoobna-ya pasta*]

top: on top of ... на ... [*na*]; on top of the car на крыше машины [*na kreesh-e masheenee*]; on the top floor на верхнем этаже [*na vyerkh-nyem ettazh-e*]; at the top наверху [*na-vyirkhōō*]; at the top of the hill на вершине горы [*na vyirsheen-ye garee*]; top quality самого высокого качества [*sahmuvuh vee-sokuvuh kah-chistva*]; bikini top лифчик купальника [*leefchik koopalnika*]

torch фонарик [*fanarik*]

total итог [*eetok*]

touch трогать/тронуть [*trogat/tronōōt*]; let's keep in touch давайте поддерживать связь [*davi-tye pad-dyerzhivat svyaz*]

tough (*meat*) жёсткий [*zhostkee*]; tough luck! не повезло! [*nye pa-vyizlo*]

tour (*noun*) экскурсия [*ekskōōrsi-ya*]; **is there a tour of ...?** можно совершить экскурсию по ...? [*mozh-nuh sa-vyirsheet ekskōōrsi-yōō pa*]

tour guide экскурсовод [*ekskōōrsa-vot*]

tourist турист [*tōōreest*]

tourist information office справочное бюро [*sprahvuch-nuh-ye byooro*]

touristy туристический [*tōōristee-chiskee*]; **somewhere not so touristy** место, где не так много туристов [*myestuh gdye nye tak mnoguh tōōreestuff*]

tour operator организующий поездку [*arganizōō-yōōsh-chee pa-yezd-kōō*]

tow: can you give me a tow? можете меня взять на буксир? [*mozhit-ye minya vzyat na book-seer*]

toward(s) к [*k*]; **toward(s) Moscow** к Москве [*kmask-vye*]

towel полотенце [*pala-tyen-tse*]

town город [*gorut*]; **in town** в городе [*vgorud-ye*]; **which bus goes into town?** каким автобусом можно попасть в город? [*kakeem avto-boossum mozh-nuh pa-past vgorut*]; **we're staying just out of town** мы остановились за городом [*mee astanavee-leess za-gorudum*]

town hall ратуша [*rahtoosha*]; (*in Soviet Union*) городской совет [*garatskoy sa-vyet*]

tow rope буксир [*book-seer*]

toy игрушка [*eegrōōshka*]

track suit тренировочный костюм [*tryeneero-vuchnee kas-tyōōm*]

trade union профсоюз [*prof-sa-yōōss*]

traditional традиционный [*traditsi-onnee*]; **a traditional Russian meal** традиционное русское блюдо [*traditsi-onnuh-ye rooskuh-ye blyōōduh*]

traffic движение [*dvizheni-ye*]

traffic circle движение автотранспорта по кругу [*dvizheni-ye avta-transporta pa krōōgōō*]

traffic jam пробка [*propka*]

traffic light(s) светофор [*svyita-for*]

traffic police (*in USSR*) ГАИ [*ga-ee*]

trailer (*for carrying tent etc*) прицеп [*pritsep*]; (*caravan*) жилой автоприцеп [*zhiloy avta-pritsep*]

train поезд [*po-yezd*]; **when's the next train to ...?** когда отходит следующий поезд в ...? [*kagda atkhodit slyedoo-yōōsh-chee po-yezd v*]; **by train** поездом [*po-yezdum*]

trainers (*shoes*) кеды [*kyedee*]

train station (*main line*) вокзал [*vagzal*]; (*metro*) станция [*stantsi-ya*]

tram трамвай [*tramvı*]

tramp бродяга [*bra-dyaga*]

tranquillizers успокаивающее средство [*ōōspaka-eeva-yōōsh-che-ye sryed-stvuh*]

transatlantic трансатлантический [*trans-atlanteechiskee*]

transfer desk транзитное бюро [*tranzeet-nuh-ye byooro*]

transformer трансформатор [*trans-far-mahtur*]

transit lounge (*at airport*) зал ожидания для транзитных пассажиров [*zahl azhidani-ya dlya tranzeetnikh passazheeruff*]

translate переводить/перевести [*pyiri-vadeet/pyiri-vyistee*]; **could you translate that?** пожалуйста, переведите это [*pazhahlsta pyiri-videet-ye ettuh*]

translation перевод [*pyiri-vot*]

translator (*man*) переводчик [*pyiri-vodchik*]; (*woman*) переводчица [*pyiri-vodchitsa*]

transmission (*of car*) трансмиссионный вал [*trans-missi-onnee vahl*]

Trans-Siberian Express транссибирский экспресс [*trans-sibeerskee ekspress*]

travel (*verb*) путешествовать [*poo-tyishest-vuvat*]; **we're travel(l)ing around the country** мы путешествуем по стране [*mee poo-tyishestvoo-yem pa stran-ye*]

travel agent бюро путешествий [*byooro poo-tyishestvee*]

travel(l)er путешественник [*poo-tyishest-vyennik*]

traveller's cheque, traveler's check туристский чек [*tōōreest-skee chek*]

tray поднос [*padnoss*]

tree дерево [*dye-ryivuh*]

tremendous огромный [*agromnee*]

trendy ультрасовременный [*ōōltra-sav-ryi-myennee*]

tricky (*difficult*) сложный [*slozhnee*]

trim: just a trim please только немного подровняйте волосы [*tol-kuh nyim-noguh padrav-nyı-tye volussee*]

trip (*journey*) поездка [*pa-yezdka*]; **I'd like to go on a trip to ...** я хочу совершить поездку в ... [*ya khachōō sa-vyirsheet pa-yezdkōō v*]; **have a good trip** счастливого пути [*s-chast-leevu-vuh pootee*]

tripod тренога [*tryinoga*]
troika тройка [*troyka*]
trolleybus троллейбус [*tra-lyay-booss*]
tropical тропический [*trapeechiskee*]
trouble (*noun*) неприятность (*f*) [*nyi-pree-yahtnust*]; I'm having trouble with . . . у меня неприятности с . . . [*oo minya nyi-pree-yahtnustee s*]; sorry to trouble you извините за беспокойство [*izvineet-ye za byis-pakoystvuh*]
trousers брюки [*bryookee*]
trouser suit брючный костюм [*bryooch-nee kas-tyoom*]
trout форель (*f*) [*fa-ryel*]
truck грузовик [*groozaveek*]
truck driver водитель грузовика [*vadee-tyil grooza-veeka*]
true верный [*vyernee*]; that's not true это неправда [*ettuh nyi-pravda*]
trunk багажник [*bagahzh-nik*]; (*case*) дорожный сундук [*darozhnee soondook*]
trunks (*swimming*) плавки [*plahfkee*]
truth правда [*pravda*]; it's the truth сущая правда [*soosh-cha-ya pravda*]
try: please try (*food*) пожалуйста, попробуйте [*pa-zhahlsta pa-proboo-i-tye*]; will you try to do it for me? постарайтесь это сделать для меня [*pa-stari-tyiss ettuh zdyelat dlya minya*]; I'll try я постараюсь [*ya pastara-yooss*]; I've never tried it before (*food*) я никогда раньше не пробовал это [*ya nee-kagda rahn-she nye probuval ettuh*]; can I have a try? можно мне попробовать? [*mozh-nuh mnye pa-probuvat*]; may I try it on? (*clothes*) можно примерить? [*mozh-nuh pree-myereet*]
tsar царь (*m*) [*tsar*]
T-shirt футболка [*foot-bolka*]
tube (*for tyre*) камера [*ka-myira*]
Tuesday вторник [*ftornik*]
tuition: I'd like tuition я хочу брать уроки [*ya khachoo braht oorokee*]

tulip тюльпан [*tyoolpan*]
tuna fish голубой тунец [*galoo-boy toonyets*]
tune мелодия [*myilodi-ya*]
tunnel тоннель (*f*) [*ton-nyil*]
Turkey Турция [*toortsi-ya*]
Turkmenistan Туркмения [*toork-myeni-ya*]
turn: it's my turn now моя очередь [*ma-ya ochir-yet*]; turn left сверните налево [*svyerneet-ye na-lyevuh*]; where do we turn off? где нам надо свернуть? [*gdye nam nahduh svyirnoot*]; can you turn the light on? можете включить свет? [*mozhit-ye fklyoo-cheet svyet*]; can you turn the light off? можете выключить свет? [*mozhit-ye vee-klyoo-cheet svyet*]; he didn't turn up он так и не появился [*on tak ee nye pa-yaveelsa*]
turning (*in road*) поворот [*pavarot*]
TV телевидение [*tyili-vee-dyini-ye*]; (*set*) телевизор [*tyili-veezur*]
tweezers пинцет [*pin-tset*]
twice дважды [*dvazht-dee*]; twice as much в два раза больше [*vdva raza bolsh-e*]
twin beds две односпальные кровати [*dvye adna-spalnuh-ye kravatee*]
twin room номер с двумя односпальными кроватями [*no-myir zdvoo-mya adna-spalnimee krava-tyamee*]
twins близнецы [*bleez-nyitsee*]
twist: I've twisted my ankle я вывихнул ногу [*ya vee-vikhnool nogoo*]
type тип [*teep*]; a different type of . . . совершенно другой тип . . . [*sa-vyirshennuh droogoy teep*]
typewriter пишущая машинка [*peeshoosh-cha-ya masheenka*]
typhoid брюшной тиф [*bryoosh-noy teef*]
typical типичный [*tipeech-nee*]; that's typical! это типично! [*ettuh tipeech-nuh*]
tyre шина [*sheena*]

U

Ukraine Украина [*ookra-yeena*]
ulcer язва [*yazva*]
Ulster Ольстер [*ol-styer*]
umbrella зонтик [*zontik*]
uncle: my uncle мой дядя [*moy dya-dya*]

uncomfortable неудобный [*nyi-oodobnee*]
unconscious потерявший сознание [*pa-tyir-yavshee saz-nahni-ye*]
under (*underneath*) под [*pot*]; (*less than*) меньше чем [*myensh-e chem*]

underdone (*meat*) недожаренный [*nyi-dazha-ryinnee*]

underground (*rail*) метро [*myitro*]

underpants трусы [*troo-see*]

undershirt майка [*mıka*]

understand: I don't understand я не понимаю [*ya nye panima-yōō*]; I understand я понимаю [*ya panima-yōō*]; do you understand? вы понимаете? [*vee panima-yit-ye*]

underwear нижнее бельё [*neezh-nye-ye byi-lyo*]

undo (*clothes*) расстёгивать/расстегнуть [*rass-tyogivat/rass-tyignōōt*]

uneatable: it's uneatable это несъедобно [*ettuh nyi-syidobnuh*]

unemployed безработный [*byiz-rabotnee*]

unfair: that's unfair это несправедливо [*ettuh nyispra-vyidleevuh*]

unfortunately к сожалению [*ksazha-lyeni-yōō*]

unfriendly недружелюбный [*nyi-drōōzhe-lyōōbnee*]

unhappy несчастный [*nyis-chastnee*]

unhealthy нездоровый [*nyi-zdarovee*]

Union of Soviet Socialist Republics Союз Советских Социалистических Республик [*sa-yōōss sa-vyets-kikh satsia-listee-chiskikh ryiss-pooblik*]

United States Соединённые Штаты Америки [*sa-yidin-yonni-ye shtahtee a-myerikee*]

university университет [*ōōni-vyirsi-tyet*]

unlimited mileage (*on hire car*) неограниченное расстояние [*nyi-agranee-chinnuh-ye rasta-yani-ye*]

unlock открывать/открыть [*at-krivaht/atkreet*]

unpack распаковывать/распаковать [*rasspako-vivat/rass-pakavat*]

unpleasant неприятный [*nyi-pree-yahtnee*]

unpronounceable непроизносимый [*nyipra-izna-seemee*]

untie развязывать/развязать [*raz-vyahzivat/raz-vyazat*]

until до [*do*]; until we meet again до скорой встречи [*da skoroy fstryechee*]; not until Wednesday не раньше среды [*nye rahnsh-e sryidee*]

unusual необыкновенный [*nyi-abikna-vyennee*]

up вверх [*v-vyerkh*]; up there там наверху [*tam na-vyirkhōō*]; further up the road дальше по этой улице [*dalsh-e pa ettoy ōōlits-e*]; he's not up yet он ещё спит [*on yish-cho speet*]; what's up? в чём дело? [*fchom dyeluh*]

upmarket шикарный [*shikarnee*]

upset stomach расстройство желудка [*ras-stroyst-vuh zhilōōtka*]

upside down вверх дном [*v-vyerkh dnom*]

upstairs наверху [*na-vyirkhōō*]; to go upstairs идти наверх [*eedtee na-vyerkh*]

Urals Урал [*oorahl*]

urgent срочный [*srochnee*]; it's very urgent это очень срочно [*ettuh ochin srochnuh*]

urinary tract infection воспаление мочевых путей [*vaspa-lyeni-ye macheveekh poo-tyay*]

us мы [*mee*]; with us с нами [*snahmee*]; for us для нас [*dlya nass*]; see page 112

use пользоваться/воспользоваться [*polzuvatsa/vass-polzuvatsa*]; may I use ...? можно мне воспользоваться ...? [*mozh-nuh mnye vass-polzuvatsa*]

used: I used to swim a lot я раньше много плавал [*ya rahnsh-e mnoguh plahval*]; when I get used to the cold когда я привыкну к холоду [*kagda ya priveek-nōō k-kholudōō*]

useful полезный [*pa-lyeznee*]

USSR СССР [*ess-ess-ess-er*]

usual обыкновенный [*abeekna-vyennee*]; as usual как обычно [*kak abeechnuh*]

usually обычно [*abeechnuh*]

U-turn разворот [*razvarot*]

Uzbekistan Узбекистан [*ooz-byikistan*]

V

vacancy: do you have any vacancies? (*hotel*) у вас есть свободные номера? [*ōō vass yist svabodni-ye no-myira*]

vacation отпуск [*otpōōsk*]; we're here on vacation мы здесь проводим свой отпуск [*mee zdyiss pravodim svoy otpōōsk*]

vaccination прививка [*priveefka*]

vacuum cleaner пылесос [*pi-lyisoss*]

vacuum flask термос [*tyermus*]

vagina влагалище [*vlagalish-che*]

valid (*ticket etc*) действительный [*dyayst-vee-tyilnee*]; how long is it valid for? каков срок действительности? [*kakoff srok dyayst-vee-tyilnustee*]

valley долина [*daleena*]

valuable (*adjective*) ценный [*tsennee*]; can I leave my valuables here? можно здесь оставить драгоценности? [*mozh-nuh zdyiss astahveet draga-tsennustee*]

value (*noun*) ценность (*f*) [*tsennust*]

van фургон [*foorgon*]

vanilla ваниль (*f*) [*vaneel*]

varicose veins расширение вен [*ras-shee-ryeni-ye vyen*]

variety show эстрадный концерт [*estradnee kantsert*]

vary: it varies бывает по-разному [*biva-yet pa rahznumoo*]

vase ваза [*vahza*]

vaudeville эстрадный концерт [*estradnee kantsert*]

VD венерическая болезнь [*vyi-nyireechiska-ya ba-lyezn*]

veal телятина [*tyi-lyatina*]

vegetables овощи [*ovush-chee*]

vegetarian (*man*) вегетарианец [*vyigitari-ahn-yits*]; (*woman*) вегетарианка [*vyigitari-ahnka*]

velvet бархат [*barkhat*]

vending machine торговый автомат [*targovee avtamaht*]

ventilator вентилятор [*vyinti-lyahtur*]

very очень [*ochin*]; I like it very much мне это очень нравится [*mnye ettuh ochin nrahvitsa*]; I speak just a very little Russian я говорю по-русски только немножко [*ya gava-ryoo pa-rooskee tol-kuh nyem-nozhkuh*]; just a very little for me только немножко для меня [*tol-kuh nyem-nozhkuh dlya minya*]

vest (*under shirt*) майка [*mıka*]; (*waistcoat*) жилет [*zhi-lyet*]

via через [*che-ryiz*]; *see page 106*

video (*film*) видео [*video*]; (*recorder*) видеомагнитофон [*video-magneetafon*]

view вид [*veet*]; what a superb view! какой замечательный вид! [*kakoy za-myicha-tyilnee veet*]

viewfinder (*of camera*) видоискатель (*m*) [*veeda-iskah-tyil*]

villa особняк [*asab-nyak*]

village деревня [*dyi-ryev-nya*]

vine виноградная лоза [*veena-grahdna-ya laza*]

vinegar уксус [*ook-sooss*]

vine-growing area виноградарство [*veena-gradarst-vuh*]

vineyard виноградник [*veena-gradnik*]

vintage wine марочное вино [*maruchnuh-ye veeno*]

visa виза [*veeza*]

visibility видимость (*f*) [*veedimust*]

visit посещать/посетить [*pa-syish-chaht*/*pa-syiteet*]; I'd like to visit . . . мне хочется посетить . . . [*mnye khochitsa pa-syiteet*]; come and visit us заходите к нам [*zakhadeet-ye k-nam*]

vital: it's vital that . . . необходимо, чтобы . . . [*nyi-abkhadeemuh shto-bee*]

vitamins витамины [*vitameenee*]

vodka водка [*votka*]

voice голос [*goluss*]

Volga Волга [*volga*]

voltage напряжение [*na-pryazheni-ye*]

vomit рвать/вырвать [*rvat*/*veer-vat*]

W

wafer (*with ice cream*) вафля [*vaf-lya*]

waist талия [*tali-ya*]

waistcoat жилет [*zhi-lyet*]

wait ждать/подождать [*zhdaht*/*pada-zh-daht*]; wait for me! подождите меня! [*pada-zhdeet-ye minya*]; don't wait for me не ждите меня [*nye zhdeet-ye minya*]; it was worth waiting for стоило ждать [*sto-eeluh zhdaht*]; I'll wait until my wife comes я подожду пока придёт моя жена [*ya pada-zhdoo paka pree-dyot ma-ya zhena*]; I'll wait a little longer я подожду ещё немного [*ya pada-zhdoo yish-cho nyem-noguh*]; can you do it while I wait? можете это сделать пока я жду? [*mozhit-ye ettuh zdyelat paka ya zhdoo*]

waiter официант [*afitsi-ant*]; **waiter!** товарищ официант! [*tavarishch afitsi-ant*]

waiting room (*stations etc*) зал ожидания [*zahl azhidani-ya*]; (*doctor's*) приёмная [*pree-yomna-ya*]

waitress официантка [*afisti-antka*]; **waitress!** девушка! [*dyevooshka*]

wake: will you wake me up at 7 o'clock? пожалуйста, разбудите меня в 7 часов [*pa-zhahlsta raz-boodeet-ye minya fsyem chassoff*]

Wales Уэльс ['*wales*']

walk: let's walk there давайте пойдём туда пешком [*davı-tye pı-dyom tooda pyishkom*]; **is it possible to walk there?** пешком туда далеко? [*pyishkom tooda da-lyiko*]; **I'll walk back** я вернусь пешком [*ya vyirnōōss pyishkom*]; **it's only a short walk** это совсем недалеко пешком [*ettuh sa-fsyem nyida-lyiko pyish-kom*]; **I'm going out for a walk** я пойду погуляю [*ya pıdōō pagoo-lya-yōō*]; **let's take a walk around town** давайте пройдёмся по городу [*davı-tye prı-dyomsa pa gorudōō*]

walking: I want to do some walking я хочу немного походить пешком [*ya khachōō nyim-noguh pa-khadeet pyish-kom*]

walking boots обувь для ходьбы [*obooff dlya khadbee*]

walking stick трость (*f*) [*trost*]

walkman (*tm*) плейер [*plye-yer*]

wall стена [*styina*]

wallet бумажник [*boo-mahzhnik*]

wander: I like just wandering around я люблю просто побродить [*ya lyoo-blyōō prostuh pa-bradeet*]

want: I want a . . . я хочу . . . [*ya khachōō*]; **I don't want any . . .** я не хочу . . . [*ya nye khachōō*]; **I want to go home** я хочу поехать домой [*ya khachōō pa-yekhat damoy*]; **I don't want to** я не хочу [*ya nye khachōō*]; **he wants to . . .** он хочет . . . [*on khochit*]; **what do you want?** что вы хотите? [*shto vee khateet-ye*]

war война [*vına*]

ward (*in hospital*) палата [*palahta*]

warm тёплый [*tyoplee*]; **it's warm today** сегодня тепло [*syivo-dnya tyiplo*]; **I'm warm** мне жарко [*mnye zharkuh*]

warning предупреждение [*pryidoo-pryizh-dyeni-ye*]

was: it was . . . было . . . [*beeluh*]; *see page 116*

wash мыть/помыть [*meet/pameet*]; **I need a wash** мне надо помыться [*mnye nahduh pameetsa*]; **can you wash the car?** можете помыть машину? [*mozhit-ye pameet masheenōō*]; **can you wash these?** можете это постирать? [*mozhit-ye ettuh pasteerat*]; **it'll wash off** это отмоется [*ettuh atmo-yitsa*]

washcloth рукавичка для обтирания лица [*rooka-veechka dlya abteerani-ya leetsa*]

washer (*for bolt etc*) прокладка [*pra-klahtka*]

washhand basin умывальник [*ōōmi-valnik*]

washing (*clothes*) бельё [*byi-lyo*]; **where can I hang my washing?** где можно развесить бельё? [*gdye mozh-nuh raz-vyeseet byi-lyo*]; **can you do my washing for me?** можете постирать мои вещи? [*mozhit-ye pasteerat ma-yee vyesh-chee*]

washing machine стиральная машина [*steeralna-ya masheena*]

washing powder стиральный порошок [*steeralnee parashok*]

washing-up: I'll do the washing-up я помою посуду [*ya pamo-yōō pa-sōōdoo*]

washing-up liquid жидкость для мытья посуды [*zheetkust dlya mi-tya pa-sōōdee*]

wasp оса [*assa*]

wasteful: that's wasteful это расточительство [*ettuh rasta-chee-tyilst-vuh*]

wastepaper basket корзина для мусора [*karzeena dlya mōōssura*]

watch (*wrist-*) часы [*chassee*]; **will you watch my things for me?** присмотрите, пожалуйста, за моими вещами [*pree-smatreet-ye pa-zhahlsta za ma-yeemee vyish-chahmee*]; **I'll just watch** я хочу только смотреть [*ya khachōō tolkuh sma-tryet*]; **watch out!** осторожно! [*astarozh-nuh*]

watch strap ремешок [*ryi-myishok*]

water вода [*vada*]; **may I have some water?** дайте мне немного воды [*dı-tye mnye nyim-noguh vadee*]

watercolo(u)r акварель (*f*) [*akva-ryel*]

waterproof (*adjective*) непромокаемый [*nyi-pramaka-yimee*]

waterskiing воднолыжный спорт [*vadna-leezhnee sport*]

water sports водный спорт [*vodnee sport*]

water wings плавательные пузыри [*plahva-tyilnee-ye pooziree*]

wave волна [*valna*]

way: which way is it? в каком направлении это? [*fkakom naprav-lyeni-ee ettuh*]; **it's this way** в этом направлении [*vettum naprav-lyeni-ee*]; **it's that way** в том направлении [*ftom naprav-lyeni-ee*]; **could you tell me the way to…?** как пройти в…? [*kak pritee v*]; **is it on the way to Leningrad?** это по пути в Ленинград? [*ettuh pa pootee vlyiningraht*]; **you're blocking the way** вы не даёте мне пройти [*vee nye da-yot-ye mnye pritee*]; **is it a long way to…?** до… далеко? [*do… da-lyiko*]; **would you show me the way to do it?** можете мне показать, как это делается? [*mozhit-ye mnye pakazat kak ettuh dyela-yitsa*]; **do it this way** сделайте так [*zdyelt-tye tak*]; **no way!** никак нет! [*neekak nyet*]

we мы [*mee*]; *see page 111*

weak слабый [*slahbee*]

wealthy богатый [*bagahtee*]

weather погода [*pagoda*]; **what foul weather!** какая отвратительная погода! [*kaka-ya atvratee-tyilna-ya pagoda*]; **what beautiful weather!** какая чудесная погода! [*kaka-ya choo-dyessna-ya pagoda*]

weather forecast прогноз погоды [*pragnoz pagodee*]

wedding свадьба [*svahd-ba*]

wedding anniversary годовщина свадьбы [*gadafsh-cheena svahd-bee*]

wedding ring обручальное кольцо [*abroo-chalnuh-ye kaltso*]

Wednesday среда [*sryida*]

week неделя [*nyi-dyel-ya*]; **a week (from) today** ровно через неделю [*rovnuh cheryiz nyi-dyel-yōō*]; **a week (from) tomorrow** завтра через неделю [*zaftra che-ryiz nyi-dyel-yōō*]; **Monday week** в понедельник на той неделе [*fpa-nyi-dyelnik na toy nyi-dyel-ye*]

weekend уикенд [*weekend*]; **at/on the weekend** в уикенд [*vweekend*]

weight вес [*vyess*]; **I want to lose weight** я хочу похудеть [*ya khachōō pakhoo-dyet*]

weight limit (*for baggage, bridge*) весовой лимит [*vyissavoy limeet*]

weird странный [*strannee*]

welcome: welcome to… добро пожаловать в… [*dabro pa-zhahluvat v*]

you're welcome (*don't mention it*) не за что [*nye-za-shto*]

well: I don't feel well я неважно себя чувствую [*ya nyi-vahzh-nuh sibya chōōstvōō-yōō*]; **I haven't been very well** мне нездоровилось [*mnye nyi-zdaroviluss*]; **she's not well** ей нездоровится [*yay nyi-zdarovitsa*]; **how are you? – very well, thanks** как вы поживаете? – спасибо, хорошо [*kak vee pazhiva-yit-ye – spa-see-buh khara-sho*]; **you speak English very well** вы очень хорошо говорите по-английски [*vee ochin khara-sho gavareet-ye pa-ang-gleeskee*]; **me as well** я тоже [*ya tozh-e*]; **well done!** молодец! [*mala-dyets*]; **well well!** (*surprise*) вот это да! [*vot ettuh da*]

well-done (*food*) хорошо прожаренный [*khara-sho prazha-ryinnee*]

wellingtons резиновые сапоги [*ryi-zeenuvee-ye sapagee*]

Welsh уэльский [*oo-elskee*]

were *see page 116*

west запад [*zahpat*]; **in the west** на западе [*na zahpad-ye*]; **to the west of…** к западу от… [*kzahpadōō at*]

West Indian (*man*) уроженец Вест-Индии [*oorazhen-yits vest-indi-ee*]; (*woman*) уроженка Вест-Индии [*oora-zhenka vest-indi-ee*]; (*adjective*) вест-индийский [*vest-ind-yeskee*]

West Indies Вест-Индия [*vest india*]

wet мокрый [*mokree*]; **it's all wet** это всё мокрое [*ettuh fsyo mokruh-ye*]; **it's been wet all week** всю неделю была дождливая погода [*fsyōō nyi-dyel-yōō beela dazhd-leeva-ya pagoda*]

wet suit водолазный костюм [*vada-laznee kas-tyōōm*]

what? что? [*shto*]; **what's that?** что это? [*shto ettuh*]; **what did he say?** что он сказал? [*shto on skazal*]; **I don't know what to do** я не знаю, что делать [*ya nye zna-yōō shto dyelat*]; **what a view!** какой вид! [*kakoy veet*]

wheel колесо [*ka-lyisso*]

wheelchair кресло-каталка [*kryesslo katalka*]

when? когда? [*kagda*]; **when will we get back?** когда мы вернёмся? [*kagda mee vyir-nyomsa*]; **when we got back** когда мы вернулись [*kagda mee vyirnōō-less*]

where? где? [*gdye*]; **where is…?** где..? [*gdye*]; **I don't know where he is** я не знаю, где он [ya nye zna-yōō gdye on]; that's where I left it вот где я оставил это [vot gdye ya astahveel ettuh]

which: which bus? какой автобус? [kakoy avto-booss]; which one? который? [katoree]; which is yours? который из этих ваш? [katoree iz ettikh vash]; I forget which it was я забыл, который [ya zabeel katoree]; the one which ... тот, который ... [tot katoree]

while пока [paka]; while I'm here пока я здесь [paka ya zdyiss]

whipped cream взбитые сливки [vzbeeti-ye sleefkee]

whisky виски [viskee]

whisper шептать/шепнуть [sheptaht/ shepnōōt]

white белый [byelee]

white wine белое вино [byeluh-ye veeno]

Whitsun духов день [dōōkhuff dyin]

who? кто? [kto]; who was that? кто это был? [kto ettuh beel]; the man who ... человек, который ... [chila-vyek katoree]

whole: the whole week всю неделю [fsyōō nyi-dyel-yōō]; two whole days целых два дня [tselikh dva dnya]; the whole lot всё [fsyo]

whooping cough коклюш [ka-klyōōsh]

whose: whose is this? чьё это? [chyo ettuh]

why? почему? [pachimōō]; why not? а почему нет? [a pachimōō nyet]; that's why it's not working вот почему не работает [vot pachimōō nye rabota-yet]

wide широкий [shirokee]

wide-angle lens ширикоугольный объектив [shiraka-ōōgolnee ab-yikteef]

widow вдова [vdava]

widower вдовец [vda-vyets]

wife: my wife моя жена [ma-ya zhena]

wig парик [pareek]

will: will you ask him? пожалуйста, спросите его [pa-zhahlsta spra-seet-ye yivo]; see page 115

win выигрывать/выиграть [vee-eegrivat/vee-eegrat]; who won? кто выиграл? [kto vee-eegral]

wind ветер [vye-tyir]

window окно [akno]; near the window у окна [ōō akna]; in the window (of shop) в витрине [v-veetreen-ye]

window seat место у окна [myestuh ōō akna]

windscreen, windshield ветровое стекло [vyitravo-ye styiklo]

windscreen wipers, windshield wipers стеклоочистители [styikla-acheestee-tyilee]

windsurf: I'd like to windsurf я хочу заниматься серфингом [ya khachōō za-neemahtsa syerfing-gum]

windsurfing серфинг [syerfink]

windy ветреный [vyet-ryinee]; it's so windy today такой ветреный день [takoy vyet-ryinee dyin]

wine вино [veeno]; can we have some more wine? ещё немного вина, пожалуйста [yish-cho nyim-noguh veena pa-zhahlsta]

wine glass рюмка [ryoomka]

wine list список вин [spee-suk veen]

wine-tasting дегустация вин [dyigoo-stahtsi-ya veen]

wing крыло [krilo]

wing mirror боковое зеркальце [bakavo-ye zyirkahlts-e]

winter зима [zeema]; in the winter зимой [zeemoy]

winter holiday зимние каникулы [zeemni-ye ka-neekoolee]

Winter Palace Зимний дворец [zeem-nee dva-ryets]

wire проволока [provuluka]; (electric) провод [provut]

wireless радио [rahdio]

wiring электропроводка [e-lyiktra-pravotka]

wish: wish you were here было бы хорошо, если бы были здесь [beeluh bee khara-sho ye-slee bee beelee zdyiss]; best wishes с наилучшими пожеланиями [sna-eelōōchimee pa-zhelahni-yamee]

with с [s]; with sugar с сахаром [s-sahkharum]; we're staying with ... мы остановились у ... [mee astanavee-leess ōō]

without без [byez]; without sugar без сахара [byez sahkhara]; without stopping не останавливаясь [nye astanah-vleeva-yass]

witness (eye witness) очевидец [achivee-dyits]; (legal) свидетель (m) [svi-dye-tyil]; will you be a witness for me? можете быть моим свидетелем? [mozhit-ye beet ma-yeem svi-dye-tyil-yem]

witty остроумный [astra-ōōmnee]

wobble: it wobbles (wheel) шатается [shata-yitsa]

woman женщина [*zhensh-china*]

women женщины [*zhensh-chinee*]

wonderful замечательный [*za-myicha-tyilnee*]

won't: the engine won't start мотор не заводится [*mator nye zavoditsa*]; *see page 117*

wood (*material*) дерево [*dye-ryivuh*]

woods (*forest*) лес [*lyess*]

wool шерсть (*f*) [*sherst*]

word слово [*slovuh*]; you have my word честное слово [*chest-nuh-ye slovuh*]

work работать/поработать [*rabotat/pa-rabotat*]; (*noun*) работа [*rabota*]; how does it work? как это работает? [*kak ettuh rabota-yet*]; it's not working это не работает [*ettuh nye rabota-yet*]; do you have any work for me? у вас есть работа для меня? [*ōō vass yist rabota dlya minya*]; when do you finish work? когда вы кончаете работу? [*kagda vee kancha-yit-ye rabotōō*]

worker рабочий [*rabochee*]

work permit разрешение на работу [*raz-ryisheni-ye na rabotōō*]

world мир [*meer*]; all over the world во всём мире [*va fsyom meer-ye*]

worn-out (*person*) измотанный [*izmotan-nee*]; (*clothes*) поношенный [*panoshennee*]

worry: I'm worried about him я беспокоюсь о нём [*ya byi-spako-yōōss a nyom*]; don't worry не беспокойтесь! [*nye byi-spakoy-tyiss*]

worse: it's worse ещё хуже [*yish-cho khōōzh-e*]; it's getting worse это становится всё хуже [*ettuh stanovitsa fsyo khōōzh-e*]

worst самый плохой [*sahmee plakhoy*]

worth: it's not worth 500 roubles за это не стоит платить 500 рублей [*za ettuh nye sto-yit plateet pyat-sot roob-lyay*]; it's worth more than that это намного ценнее [*ettuh nam-noguh tsi-nye-ye*]; is it worth a visit? туда стоит поехать? [*tooda sto-yit pa-yekhat*]

would: would you give this to ...? передайте, пожалуйста ... [*pyiri-dıt-ye pa-zhahlsta*]; what would you do? что вы бы сделали? [*shto vee bee zdyela-lee*]

wrap: could you wrap it up? заверните, пожалуйста [*za-vyirneet-ye pa-zhahlsta*]

wrapping обёртка [*a-byortka*]

wrapping paper обёрточная бумага [*a-byortuchna-ya boomaga*]

wrench (*tool*) гаечный ключ [*ga-yechnee klyōōch*]

wrist запястье [*za-pyast-ye*]

write писать/написать [*pisaht/napisaht*]; could you write it down? запишите, пожалуйста [*zapi-sheet-ye pa-zhahlsta*]; how do you write it? как это пишется? [*kak ettuh peeshitsa*]; I'll write to you я буду писать вам [*ya bōōdōō pisaht vam*]; I wrote to you last week я написал вам на прошлой неделе [*ya napi-sahl vam na proshloy nyi-dyel-yōō*]

write-off: this car's a write-off эту машину можно списать [*ettōō masheenōō mozh-nuh spisaht*]

writer писатель (*m*) [*pissah-tyil*]

writing писание [*pissahni-ye*]; I can't read Russian writing я не могу читать по-русски [*ya nye magōō chitaht pa-rooskee*]

writing paper писчая бумага [*peess-cha-ya boomahga*]

wrong: you're wrong вы ошибаетесь [*vee ashiba-ye-tyiss*]; the bill's wrong вы сделали ошибку в подсчёте [*vee zdyelalee asheepkōō fpad-schot-ye*]; sorry, I've got the wrong number простите, я не туда попал [*pra-steet-ye ya nye tooda papahl*]; I'm on the wrong train я сел не на тот поезд [*ya syel nye na tot po-yezd*]; I went to the wrong room я попал не в ту комнату [*ya papahl nye ftōō komnatōō*]; that's the wrong key это не тот ключ [*ettuh nye tot klyōōch*]; there's something wrong with ... что-то не так с ... [*shto-tuh nye tak s*]; what's wrong? в чём дело? [*fchom dyel-uh*]; what's wrong with her? что с ней? [*shto snyay*]

X

X-ray рентгеновский снимок [*ryint-gyenuv-skee sneemuk*]

Y

yacht яхта [*yakhta*]

yard: in the yard на дворе [*na dva-rye*] *see page 120*

year год [*got*]

yellow жёлтый [*zholtee*]

yes да [*da*]

yesterday вчера [*fchira*]; yesterday morning вчера утром [*fchira ōōtrum*]; yesterday evening вчера вечером [*fchira vyecherum*]; the day before yesterday позавчера [*pazaf-chira*]

yet: has the post arrived yet? почта уже пришла? [*pochta ōōzh-e preeshla*]; not yet ещё нет [*yish-cho nyet*]

yog(h)urt йогурт [*yogōōrt*]; (*Russian style*) творог [*tvarok*]

you (*familiar singular*) ты [*tee*]; (*polite singular and plural, familiar plural*) вы [*vee*]; this is for you это для тебя/вас [*ettuh dlya tibya/vass*]; with you с тобой/с вами [*staboy/svahmee*]; *see page 112*

young молодой [*maladoy*]

young people молодые люди [*maladee-ye lyōōdee*]

your, yours (*with single objects*) (*familiar singular*) твой [*tvoy*]; (*polite singular and plural, familiar plural*) ваш [*vash*]; (*with more than one object*) (*familiar singular*) твои [*tva-ee*]; (*polite singular and plural, familiar plural*) ваши [*vashee*]; *see page 112*

youth hostel молодёжная турбаза [*mala-dyozhna-ya toor-baza*]

Yugoslavia Югославия [*yooga-slavia*]

Z

zero нуль (*m*) [*nōōl*]; below zero ниже нуля [*neezh-e nool-ya*]; does it ever get above zero? когда-нибудь бывает выше нуля? [*kagda-nibōōt bива-yet veesh-e nool-ya*]

zip, zipper застёжка-молния [*za-styozhka molni-ya*]; could you put a new zip on? пришейте, пожалуйста, новую молнию [*prishay-tye pa-zhahlsta novōō-yōō molni-yōō*]

zoo зоопарк [*za-apark*]

zoom lens объектив с переменным фокусным расстоянием [*ab-yikteef spyiri-myennim fokoosnim rasta-yahni-yem*]

Russian-English

LIST OF SUBJECT AREAS

Abbreviations
Airport and plane
Banks
Buses and coaches, trams
Cinemas, movie theatres
Clothing labels
Countries and nationalities
Cultural interest
Customs
Days
Do not ...
Drinks
Eating and drinking places
Emergencies
Food
Food labels
Forms
Garages
Geographical
Hairdresser
Historical interest
Hotels

Lifts, elevators
Medical
Medicine labels
Months
Notices in restaurants and bars
Notices in shops
Notices on doors
Place names
Post offices
Public buildings
Replies
Shopping
Street and road signs
Streets
Swearwords
Taxis
Telephone
Theatres, theaters
Timetables, schedules
Toilets, rest rooms
Trains and stations
Underground, subway

ABBREVIATIONS

А bus stop
АС coach station
АТС garage, filling station
бульв. boulevard
в. volt
ВДНХ permanent exhibition of economic achievements in Moscow
Вс. Sunday
Вт. Tuesday
г. town
г gram(me)
ГАИ traffic police
ГУМ State Department Store
д. house
Ж ladies, ladies' rest room
ж.д. railway, railroad
им. named
кв. flat, apartment
км kilometre, kilometer
коп. kopeck (100 kopecks = 1 rouble)
л litre, liter
м metre, meter
М underground, subway; gents, men's rest room
мин. minutes
МГУ Moscow State University
МХАТ Moscow Arts Theatre/Theater
пер. lane, street
пл. square
Пн. Monday
пр. avenue
Пт. Friday
р., руб. rouble
Сб. Saturday
Ср. Wednesday
СССР USSR
ст. station
Т taxi rank; tram stop; trolleybus stop
ТАСС Telegraph Agency of the Soviet Union, TASS
тв., тов. comrade
ул. street
Ф.И.О. surname, name, patronymic
ЦК КПСС Central Committee of the Communist Party of the Soviet Union
ЦУМ Central Department Store
ц. price
ч. hour

Чт. Thursday
шт. per item, each

AIRPORT AND PLANE

аэровокзал city air terminal
аэропорт airport
время отправления departure time
время регистрации latest check-in time
вход entrance
выдача багажа baggage claim
выход exit
**выход № gate no.
выход на лётное поле запрещён no admittance to tarmac
выход на посадку gate
для курящих smokers
для некурящих non-smokers
запрещено к перевозке restricted articles
застегните привязные ремни fasten seat belts
касса Аэрофлота "Aeroflot" booking office
камера хранения left luggage, baggage checkroom
не курить no smoking
отлёт departures
паспортный контроль passport control
пассажиров просят на посадку, выход № X [*passazheeruf pro-syat prītee na pasatkōō, veekhut no-myir*] passengers are requested to proceed to gate no. X
посадка boarding; landing
посадочный талон boarding card
посторонним вход воспрещён no admittance to unauthorized persons
прибытие arrivals
приём вещей на хранение left luggage, baggage checkroom
регистрация билетов и багажа check-in
рейс № flight no.
ручная кладь hand baggage
справочное бюро information
таможня customs
туалет toilet, rest room

BANKS

аккредитив letter of credit
банк bank

а б в г д е ё ж з и й к л м н о п р с т у ф х ц ч ш щ ъ ы ь э ю я
А Б В Г Д Е Ё Ж З И Й К Л М Н О П Р С Т У Ф Х Ц Ч Ш Щ Ъ Ы Ь Э Ю Я
a b v g d ye yo zh z ee i k l m n o p r s t oo f kh ts ch sh shch - ee - e yoo ya

бланк form

валютные   ограничения   exchange restrictions

виза visa

выходной день ... closed on ...

дата date

доллары dollars

дорожные чеки traveller's cheques, traveler's checks

касса cash desk

касса работает до 16.30 ч. cash desk closes at 16.30

квитанция receipt

копейка kopeck (100 kopecks = 1 rouble)

кредитная карточка credit card

курс дня exchange rate

курс иностранной валюты foreign exchange rate

паспорт № passport no.

перерыв на обед closed for lunch

платёжные   документы   payment documents

подпись signature

рубль rouble

фунты стерлингов pounds sterling

чек cheque, check

часы работы business hours

BUSES AND COACHES, TRAMS

автобус bus, coach

автомат ticket vending machine

без пересадки direct bus/trolley bus/tram

билет ticket

время отправления departure time

годен 2 месяца со дня выдачи valid 2 months from date of issue

дата выдачи date of issue

дата отправления date of departure

до to

единый билет season ticket

касса ticket office

компостер machine for stamping tickets

маршрут route

маршрутное такси minibus running regular service, 15 kopecks a ticket

места для пассажиров с детьми и инвалидов seats for invalids and passengers with children

остановка автобуса bus stop

от from

пять копеек five kopecks

пересадка change

продажа билетов и талонов tickets and season tickets

проездной билет season ticket

с пересадкой involves at least one change

сохранить до конца поездки retain for duration of journey

справочное бюро information

схема route map

талоны tickets (bought at a kiosk and stamped on boarding the bus)

через via

Т остановка трамвая tram stop; остановка троллейбуса trolleybus stop

трамвай tram

троллейбус trolleybus

CINEMAS, MOVIE THEATERS

балкон balcony

билет ticket

в главных ролях ... starring ...

вечерний сеанс evening performance

все билеты проданы all tickets sold

вход в зрительный зал entrance to the cinema/movie theater

двухсерийный   фильм   two-part film/movie

документальный фильм documentary

касса booking office

кинотеатр cinema, movie theater

кинохроника newsreel

комедия comedy

левая сторона left side

место seat

мультипликационный фильм cartoon

на завтра for tomorrow

на сегодня for today

партер stalls

правая сторона right side

предварительная продажа билетов advance booking office

продажа билетов на сегодня sale of tickets for today's performances

режиссёр director

сеанс performance

фильм film, movie

широкоэкранный фильм wide screen film/movie

CLOTHING LABELS

замша suede

искусственный шёлк rayon

качество quality

кожа leather
махровая ткань towelling
нейлон nylon
поплин poplin
размер size
резина rubber
рост height
сорт: 1 сорт highest quality; 2 сорт good quality
шёлк silk
шерсть wool
хлопок cotton

COUNTRIES AND NATIONALITIES

Австралия Australia
Азия Asia
Америка America
американский American
английский English
Англия England
Армения Armenia
Африка Africa
Великобритания Great Britain
Германия Germany
Грузия Georgia
Европа Europe
Канада Canada
Китай China
Россия Russia
русский Russian
Советский Союз Soviet Union
советский Soviet
США USA
Украина Ukraine
Франция France
Япония Japan

CULTURAL INTEREST

балет ballet
Большой театр Bolshoi Theatre/Theater
гид guide
Дворцовая площадь Palace Square (Leningrad)
Зимний дворец Winter Palace (Leningrad)
икона icon
Исаакиевский собор St Isaac's Cathedral (Leningrad)

Исторический музей Historical Museum (Moscow)
Казанский собор Kazan Cathedral (Leningrad)
кладбище cemetery
Красная площадь Red Square (Moscow)
Кремлёвский Дворец Съездов Congress Palace (Moscow)
Кремль Kremlin
крейсер "Аврора" Aurora (museum ship in Leningrad)
Библиотека имени Ленина Lenin Library (Moscow)
Мавзолей Ленина Lenin's Mausoleum (Moscow)
Медный Всадник Bronze Horseman (Leningrad)
могила tomb
монастырь monastery
музей museum
музей древнерусского искусства имени А. Рублева Museum of Old Russian Art (Moscow)
Музей революции Museum of the Revolution
Невский Проспект Nevsky Prospekt (main street in Leningrad)
Новодевичий монастырь Novodevichy Monastery (Moscow)
Оружейная палата Armoury (Moscow)
памятник memorial
памятник А.С. Пушкину Pushkin memorial
памятник Петру Первому memorial to Peter the Great (Leningrad)
Петропавловская крепость Peter and Paul Fortress (Leningrad)
Русский музей Russian Museum (Leningrad)
Спасская башня Spassky tower (main tower in the Moscow Kremlin)
Третьяковская галерея Tretiakov Gallery (Moscow)
Храм Василия Блаженного St. Basil's Cathedral (Moscow)
Эрмитаж Hermitage (Leningrad)

CUSTOMS

бланк form

а	б	в	г	д	е	ё	ж	з	и	й	к	л	м	н	о	п	р	с	т	у	ф	х	ц	ч	ш	щ	ъ	ы	ь	э	ю	я
А	Б	В	Г	Д	Е	Ё	Ж	З	И	Й	К	Л	М	Н	О	П	Р	С	Т	У	Ф	Х	Ц	Ч	Ш	Щ	Ъ	Ы	Ь	Э	Ю	Я
a	b	v	g	d	ye	yo	zh	z	ee	i	k	l	m	n	o	p	r	s	t	oo	f	kh	ts	ch	sh	shch	-	ee	-	e	yoo	ya

валюта foreign currency
документы documents
запрещено к перевозке restricted articles
золото gold
книги books
подарки gifts
пошлина tax
сигареты cigarettes
спиртные напитки alcoholic drinks
таможенная декларация customs declaration
таможня customs

DAYS

понедельник Monday
вторник Tuesday
среда Wednesday
четверг Thursday
пятница Friday
суббота Saturday
воскресенье Sunday

DO NOT ...

воспрещается forbidden
въезд запрещён no entry
запрещён/запрещена/запрещено prohibited
здесь не курят no smoking here
купаться воспрещается no bathing
курить воспрещается no smoking
не do not
не курить no smoking
не прислоняться do not lean against the door
нет no
нет входа no entry
нет выхода no exit
не фотографировать no photography
обгон запрещён no overtaking/passing
опасно для жизни! danger!
перехода нет do not cross the road here
по газонам не ходить do not walk on the grass
посторонним вход запрещён no unauthorized persons
просьба не курить please do not smoke
сквозного проезда нет no through road, dead end
стоянка запрещена no parking
фотографировать воспрещается no photography

DRINKS

абрикосовый сок apricot juice
апельсиновый сок orange juice
белое вино white wine
боржоми (tm) 'Borzhomi' mineral water
вермут vermouth
вишнёвый сок cherry juice
вода water
водка vodka
вино wine
виноградный сок grape juice
виски whisky
газированная вода soda water
газированная вода с сиропом soda water with syrup
горилка Ukrainian vodka
жигулёвское пиво (tm) Zhiguli beer
квас kvas (drink made of bread and water)
кефир kefir (sour drinking yog(h)urt)
коктейль cocktail
коньяк brandy
кофе coffee
кофе с молоком white coffee, coffee with milk
красное вино red wine
ликёр liqueur
лимонад lemonade
минеральная вода mineral water
молоко milk
Московская особая водка (tm) Moscow vodka
напитки drinks
нарзан (tm) 'Narzan' mineral water
перцовка pepper vodka
пиво beer
полусладкое вино medium-sweet wine
полусухое medium-dry
простокваша sour milk
ряженка soured baked milk
сладкое вино dessert wine
Советское шампанское (tm) Soviet champagne
соки-воды fruit juices and mineral water
Столичная водка (tm) Stolichnaya vodka
сухое dry
томатный сок tomato juice
Цинандали Georgian white wine
чай tea
чай с лимоном tea with lemon
чёрный кофе black coffee
шампанское champagne
яблочный сок apple juice

EATING AND DRINKING PLACES

бар bar
блинная café specializing in bliny (Russian pancakes)
булочная-кондитерская baker
буфет snack bar
закусочная snack bar
кафе cafeteria
кафе мороженое ice cream parlo(u)r
молочный буфет milk bar
пельменная café specializing in 'pelmeni' (Siberian meat dumplings)
пирожковая café specializing in 'pirozhki' (small pies with various fillings)
ресторан restaurant
соки-воды stand/kiosk selling fruit juices and soda water
столовая cafeteria-style restaurant
шашлычная café specializing in Caucasian 'shashlyk' (kebabs)

EMERGENCIES

авария accident
больница hospital
запасной выход emergency exit
милиция police
опасно! danger!
пожар fire
при пожаре звоните ... in case of fire phone ...
скорая помощь ambulance
стоп кран emergency brake

FOOD

Starters

блины с икрой [*bleenee sikroy*] pancakes with caviar
блины со сметаной [*bleenee sa smyitahnoy*] pancakes with sour cream
горячие закуски [*ga-ryachi-ye zakoo-skee*] hot hors d'oeuvres
грибы [*greebee*] mushrooms
грибы в сметане [*greebee fsmyitahn-ye*] mushrooms in sour cream
грибы маринованые [*greebee marinovanee-ye*] marinated mushrooms
грибы солёные [*greebee sa-lyonee-ye*] salted mushrooms

закуски [*zakoo-skee*] starters
икра [*ikra*] caviar
икра баклажанная [*ikra baklazhana-ya*] aubergines/eggplants with onions and tomatoes
икра зернистая [*ikra zyirneesta-ya*] fresh caviar
икра кетовая [*ikra kyetuva-ya*] red caviar
икра паюсная [*ikra pa-yoossna-ya*] pressed caviar
кильки [*keelkee*] Russian anchovies
красная икра [*kra-sna-ya ikra*] red caviar
лососина [*lassa-seena*] smoked salmon
маслины [*ma-sleenee*] olives
осетрина [*a-syitreena*] sturgeon
осетрина заливная [*a-syitreena zaleevna-ya*] sturgeon in aspic
осетрина с гарниром [*a-syitreena zgarneerum*] sturgeon with vegetables
сардины [*sardeenee*] sardines
сардины в масле [*sardeenee vmahss-lye*] sardines in butter
сёмга [*syomga*] smoked salmon
солёный помидор [*sa-lyonee pamidor*] pickled tomatoes
сыр [*seer*] cheese
фаршированные помидоры [*farshirovanee-ye pamidoree*] stuffed tomatoes
фирменные блюда [*feer-myenee-ye blyooda*] speciality dishes
холодные закуски [*khalodnee-ye zakoo-skee*] cold hors d'oeuvres

Soups

борщ [*borshch*] 'borshch', beef and beetroot/red beet soup
борщ украинский [*borshch ookra-eenskee*] Ukrainian 'borshch'
ботвинья [*batveen-ya*] cold fish and vegetable soup
бульон [*boo-lyon*] clear soup
бульон с пирожками [*boo-lyon spirazh-kahmee*] clear soup with small meat pies
бульон с фрикадельками [*boo-lyon sfrika-dyelkamee*] clear soup with meat balls
бульон с яйцом [*boo-lyon syitsom*] clear soup with egg
вегетарианский борщ [*vyigitarian-skee borshch*] vegetarian 'borshch'

а б в г д е ё ж з и й к л м н о п р с т у ф х ц ч ш щ ъ ы ь э ю я
А Б В Г Д Е Ё Ж З И Й К Л М Н О П Р С Т У Ф Х Ц Ч Ш Щ Ъ Ы Ь Э Ю Я
a b v g d ye yo zh z ee i k l m n o p r s t oo f kh ts ch sh shch - ee - e yoo ya

мясной бульон [*mya-snoy boo-lyon*] meat stock

овощной суп [*avashnoy soōp*] vegetable soup

окрошка [*akroshka*] cold summer soup based on 'kvas' (a slightly sour drink made of fermented bread or berries and water)

рассольник [*ras-solnik*] chicken giblets, vegetables and sour cream

свекольник [*svyikolnik*] vegetable soup made mainly of beetroots/red beet

солянка [*sa-lyanka*] Georgian hot soup made from fish or meat, onions, parsnip, mushroom, pickles and spices

суп [*soōp*] soup

суп из свежих грибов [*soōp iz svyezhikh gribov*] fresh mushroom soup

суп из телятины с зелёным горошком [*soōp iz tyi-lyatinee z-zi-lyonim garoshkam*] veal soup with green peas

суп картофельный [*soōp karto-fyilnee*] potato soup

суп-крем [*soōp kryem*] cream soup

суп-лапша с курицей [*soōp lapsha skoōri-tsay*] chicken noodle soup

суп мясной [*soōp mya-snoy*] meat soup

суп рагу из курицы [*soōp ragoō iz koōritsee*] chicken ragout soup

суп с грибами [*soōp zgreebah-mee*] mushroom soup

суп с кукурузой [*soōp skookoo-roōzoy*] soup with corn

суп с лапшой [*soop slapshoy*] noodle soup

суп томатный [*soōp tamahtnee*] tomato soup

уха [*ōokha*] fish soup

харчо [*kharcho*] thick, hot and spicy mutton soup from Georgia

щи [*shchee*] cabbage soup

Egg Dishes

омлет натуральный [*am-lyet natoorahlnee*] plain omelet(te)

омлет с ветчиной [*am-lyet svyit-chinoy*] ham omelet(te)

омлет фаршированный [*am-lyet far-shirovannee*] filled omelet(te)

омлет с зелёным горошком [*am-lyet z-zi-lyonim garoshkam*] omelet(te) with peas

салат зелёный с яйцами [*salaht zi-lyonee syaıt-sahmee*] green salad with eggs

фаршированные яйца [*far-shirovanee-ye yaıtsa*] stuffed eggs

яичница глазунья [*ya-eechnitsa glazoōn-ya*] fried eggs

яичница [*ya-eechnitsa*] scrambled eggs

яйца вкрутую [*aıtsa fkrootoō-yoō*] hard-boiled eggs

яйца всмятку [*yaıtsa fsmyatkoō*] soft-boiled eggs

яйцо [*yıtso*] egg

яйцо под майонезом [*yıtso pod mıa-nyezum*] egg mayonnaise

Fish

ассорти рыбное [*assortee ribnoy-ye*] assorted fish

жареная рыба [*zha-ryina-ya riba*] fried fish

жареное филе рыбы [*zha-ryinuh-ye filay ribee*] fried fillet of fish

заливная осетрина с хреном [*zaleevna-ya a-syitreena s-khryenum*] sturgeon in aspic with horseradish

заливная рыба [*zaleevna-ya riba*] fish in aspic

камбала [*kambala*] plaice

карп [*karp*] carp

карп жареный [*karp zha-ryinee*] fried carp

карп с грибами [*karp zgribahmee*] carp with mushrooms

кета [*kyeta*] Siberian salmon

копчёная сёмга [*kapchona-ya syomga*] smoked salmon

креветки [*kryi-vyetkee*] shrimps

налим [*naleem*] burbot

осетрина жареная [*a-syitreena zha-ryina-ya*] fried sturgeon

осетрина паровая [*a-syitreena parava-ya*] steamed sturgeon

осетрина под белым соусом [*a-syitreena pad byelim so-oōssum*] sturgeon in white sauce

осетрина под майонезом [*a-syitreena pod mıa-nyezum*] sturgeon in mayonnaise

осетрина с гарниром [*a-syitreena zgarneerum*] sturgeon with vegetables

осетрина с пикантным соусом [*a-syitreena spikantnim so-oōssum*] sturgeon in piquant sauce

осётр запечённый в сметане [*a-syotr za-pyichonnee fsmyitan-ye*] sturgeon baked in sour cream

отварная рыба [*atvarna-ya riba*] poached fish

палтус [*paltooss*] halibut

рак [*rak*] lobster

рыба с рисом [*riba sreessum*] fish with rice

рыбные блюда [*ribnee-ye blyooda*] fish dishes

салат из крабов [*salaht iz krabuff*] crab-meat salad

сельдь [*syeld*] herring

селёдка малосольная [*syi-lyodka malasolna-ya*] slightly salted herring

скумбрия запечённая [*skoombri-ya zapyichona-ya*] baked mackerel

сом [*som*] sheat-fish

судак [*soodak*] pike-perch

судак в белом вине [*soodak v-byelum veenye*] pike-perch in white wine

судак жареный в тесте [*soodak zha-ryinee ftyest-ye*] pike-perch fried in batter

судак по-русски [*soodak pa-rooskee*] pike-perch Russian style

судак с соусом тартар [*soodak s-so-oossum tartar*] pike-perch with tartar sauce

треска [*tryiska*] cod

тресковая печень в масле [*tryiskova-ya pyechen vmahss-lye*] cod liver in oil

тунец [*too-nyets*] tuna fish

устрицы [*oostritsee*] oysters

фаршированная рыба [*far-shirovana-ya riba*] stuffed fish

форель [*fa-ryel*] trout

шпроты [*shprotee*] sprats

щука [*shchooka*] pike

Meat

азу [*azoo*] small pieces of meat in a savo(u)ry sauce

ассорти мясное [*assortee mya-snoy-ye*] assorted meats

битки [*beetkee*] meat balls

голубцы [*galooptsee*] meat with rice wrapped in a cabbage leaf

дичь [*deech*] game

колбаса [*kalba-sa*] salami-type sausage

колбаса с грибами [*kalba-sa zgreebahmee*] salami-type sausage with mushrooms

копчёная колбаса [*kapchona-ya kalba-sa*] smoked sausage

кулебяка [*koo-lyi-byaka*] pie with meat, fish or cabbage filling

мясо [*mya-suh*] meat

плов [*ploff*] pilaf

плов по-узбекски [*ploff pa-ooz-byek-skee*] Uzbek pilaf

рулет [*roo-lyet*] meat roll

сосиски [*sa-seeskee*] frankfurters

студень [*stoo-dyin*] aspic

тефтели с рисом [*tyef-tyelee sreessum*] small meat balls with rice

филе [*filay*] fillet

шашлык [*shashlik*] kebab

эскалоп [*eskalop*] escalope

Pork

буженина с гарниром [*boozheneena zgarneerum*] cold boiled pork with vegetables

варёная нашпигованная свинина [*varyona-ya na-shpigovanna-ya svineena*] boiled pork with bacon fat

ветчина [*vyitchina*] ham

ветчина с гарниром [*vyitchina zgarneerum*] ham with vegetables

жареная свинина [*zha-ryina-ya svineena*] fried pork

заливное из жареной свинины [*zaleevno-ye iz zha-ryinoy svineenee*] fried pork in aspic

запеканка из свинины [*za-pyikanka iz svineenee*] casserole of pork

картофель с ветчиной и шпиком [*kartofyil zvyitchinoy ee shpeekum*] potatoes with ham and bacon fat

кебаб из свинины с рисом [*kyibap iz svineena sreessum*] pork kebab with rice

рагу из свинины [*ragoo iz svineenee*] pork ragoût

копчёные свиные рёбрышки с фасолью [*kapchonee-ye svinee-ye ryobreeshkee sfa-sol-yoo*] smoked pork ribs with beans

поросёнок с кашей [*para-syonuk skashay*] roast sucking pig with kasha (buckwheat grains boiled or baked, like porridge)

окорок [*okuruk*] gammon

свиная корейка [*svina-ya ka-ryayka*] pork brisket

свинина [*svineena*] pork

а	б	в	г	д	е	ё	ж	з	и	й	к	л	м	н	о	п	р	с	т	у	ф	х	ц	ч	ш	щ	ъ	ы	ь	э	ю	я
А	Б	В	Г	Д	Е	Ё	Ж	З	И	Й	К	Л	М	Н	О	П	Р	С	Т	У	Ф	Х	Ц	Ч	Ш	Щ	Ъ	Ы	Ь	Э	Ю	Я
a	b	v	g	d	ye	yo	zh	z	ee	i	k	l	m	n	o	p	r	s	t	oo	f	kh	ts	ch	sh	shch	-	ee	-	e	yoo	ya

свинина жареная с гарниром [*svineena zha-ryina-ya zgarneerum*] fried pork with vegetables

свинина с квашеной капустой [*svineena skvashenoy kapōostoy*] pork with sauerkraut

свинина тушёная [*svineena tooshona-ya*] stewed pork

свиные отбивные [*svinee-ye atbivnee-ye*] pork chops

свиные отбивные с яичницей глазуньей [*svinee-ye atbivnee-ye syı-eechnitsay glazōon-yay*] pork chops with eggs

суфле с ветчиной [*sooflay zvyitchinoy*] ham soufflé

украинский студень из свинины [*ōokra-eenskee stōo-dyin iz svineenee*] Ukrainian pork in aspic

Lamb

баранина [*baranina*] mutton, lamb

баранина отварная [*baranina atvarna-ya*] boiled lamb

бараньи котлеты [*baranee kat-lyetee*] lamb chops

баранина на вертеле [*baranina na vyer-tyil-ye*] spit-roasted mutton

баранья ножка заливная [*baran-ya nozhka zaleevna-ya*] leg of lamb in aspic

битки из баранины [*beetkee iz baraninee*] lamb meat balls

запеканка из молодой баранины [*za-pyikanka iz maladoy baraninee*] spring lamb casserole

кебаб из молодой баранины [*kyibap iz maladoy baraninee*] lamb kebab

молодая баранина с картофелем [*malada-ya baranina skarto-fyi-lyem*] spring lamb with potatoes

рагу из баранины [*ragōo iz baraninee*] lamb ragoût

Beef

антрекот [*antrekot*] entrecote steak

беф-строганов [*byef stroganuff*] beef Stroganoff

бифштекс [*bif-shtyeks*] beefsteak

бифштекс натуральный [*bif-shtyeks natoorahlnee*] plain, fried or grilled beefsteak

говядина [*ga-vyadina*] beef

говядина отварная [*ga-vyadina atvarna-ya*] boiled beef

говядина отварная с хреном [*ga-vyadina atvarna-ya s-khryenum*] boiled beef with horseradish

говядина с мясным фаршем [*ga-vyadina smya-snim farshem*] beef stuffed with meat

говядина тушёная [*ga-vyadina tooshona-ya*] stewed beef

говяжье филе с начинкой [*ga-vyazh-e filay snachinkoy*] stuffed fillet of beef

гуляш из говядины [*goo-lyash iz ga-vyadinee*] beef goulash

зразы из говядины [*zrazee iz ga-vyadinee*] beef cutlets with filling

котлеты с грибами [*kat-lyetee zgreebahmee*] steak with mushrooms

рагу из говядины [*ragōo iz ga-vyadinee*] beef ragoût

ромштекс с луком [*romshteks slōokum*] minced/ground steak with onion

ростбиф [*rostbif*] roast beef

ростбиф с гарниром [*rostbif zgarneerum*] cold roast beef with vegetables

Veal

битки [*beetkee*] meatballs

запеканка из телятины с картофелем [*za-pyikanka iz tyi-lyatinee skarto-fyi-lyem*] veal casserole with potatoes

рагу из телятины [*ragōo iz tyi-lyatinee*] veal ragout

рулет из рубленой телятины [*roo-lyet iz rōob-lyinoy tyi-lyatinee*] minced/ground veal roll

телятина [*tyi-lyatina*] veal

телятина со свежими грибами [*tyi-lyatina sa svyezhimee greebahmee*] veal with fresh mushrooms

телятина тушёная [*tyi-lyatina tooshona-ya*] stewed veal

телячьи отбивные [*tyi-lyachee atbeevnee-ye*] veal chops

телячий язык отварной [*tyi-lyachee yazik atvarnoy*] boiled calf tongue

фрикадели из телятины в соусе [*frika-dyelee iz tyi-lyatinee vso-ōoss-ye*] veal meat balls in gravy

шницель с яичницей глазуньей [*shnitsel sya-eechnitsay glazōon-yay*] schnitzel with fried egg

Poultry and Game

блюда из птицы [*blyōoda iz pteetsee*] poultry dishes

голубь [*golup*] pigeon

гусь [*gōōss*] goose

гусь жареный с капустой или яблоками [*gōōss zha-ryinee skapōōstoy eelee yablukamee*] roast goose with cabbage or apples

дикая утка [*deeka-ya ōōtka*] wild duck

заяц [*za-yats*] hare

индейка [*in-dyayka*] turkey

котлеты по-киевски [*kat-lyetee pa-kee-yevskee*] chicken breast stuffed with garlic butter, chicken Kiev

котлеты по-пожарски [*kat-lyetee pa-pazharskee*] minced chicken

котлеты столичные [*kat-lyetee staleechnee-ye*] pieces of chicken with butter

кролик [*krolik*] rabbit

курица [*kōōritsa*] chicken

куропатка [*koora-patka*] partridge

панированный цыплёнок [*panirovanee tsip-lyonuk*] chicken in breadcrumbs

птица [*pteetsa*] poultry

рябчик жареный [*ryabchik zha-ryinee*] roast hazel-grouse

тушёная курица [*tooshona-ya kōōritsa*] stewed chicken

утка [*ōōtka*] duck

фазан [*fazan*] pheasant

цыплёнок [*tsip-lyonuk*] chicken

цыплёнок в тесте [*tsip-lyonuk ftyest-ye*] chicken in a pastry covering

цыплёнок по-охотничьи [*tsip-lyonuk pa-akhotnichee*] chicken chasseur

цыплёнок "табака" [*tsip-lyonuk tabaka*] Caucasian chicken with garlic sauce

цыплёнок фрикасе [*tsip-lyonuk frikassay*] chicken fricassé

чахохбили [*chakhokh-beelee*] chicken casserole

Other Types of Meat

жареные мозги с яйцами [*zha-ryinee-ye mazgee syaïtsahmee*] fried brains with eggs

жареный рубец [*zha-ryinee roo-byets*] fried tripe

кость [*kost*] bone

мозги [*mazgee*] brains

панированные мозги с картофелем [*panirovannee-ye mazgee skarto-fyi-lyem*]

brains in breadcrumbs with potatoes

панированный язык под соусом с хреном [*panirovanee yazik pod so-ōōssum skhryenum*] tongue in breadcrumbs with horseradish sauce

язык с гарниром [*yazik zgarneerum*] cold tongue with vegetables

печёнка [*pyichonka*] liver

почки [*pochkee*] kidneys

рубец [*roo-byets*] tripe

рубленое мясо [*rōōb-lyinuh-ye mya-suh*] mince meat, ground beef

рубленые котлеты [*rōōb-lyinee-ye kat-lyetee*] rissoles

Salads

винегрет [*vini-gryet*] vegetable salad

зелёный салат [*zi-lyonee salaht*] green salad, lettuce

огурцы со сметаной [*agoortsee sa smyitanoy*] cucumber in sour cream

салат "здоровье" [*salaht zdarov-ye*] 'health' salad, mixed vegetable salad

салат из жареного стручкового перца [*salaht iz zha-ryinuvuh strooch-kovuvuh pyertsa*] fried pepper salad

салат из капусты [*salaht iz kapōōstee*] cabbage salad

салат из картофеля [*salaht iz karto-fyi-lya*] potato salad

салат из лука [*salaht iz lōōka*] spring onion salad

салат из огурцов [*salaht iz agoortsoff*] cucumber salad

салат из печёного стручкового перца [*salaht iz pyichonuvuh strooch-kovuvuh pyertsa*] baked pepper salad

салат из помидоров [*salaht iz pamidoruff*] tomato salad

салат из помидоров с брынзой [*salaht iz pamidoruff zbrinzoy*] tomato salad with goat's cheese

салат из редиски [*salaht iz ryideeskee*] radish salad

салат московский [*salaht maskovskee*] Russian salad

салат мясной [*salaht mya-snoy*] meat salad

салат с крабами [*salaht skrabamee*] crab salad

а б в г д е ё ж з и й к л м н о п р с т у ф х ц ч ш щ ъ ы ь э ю я
А Б В Г Д Е Ё Ж З И Й К Л М Н О П Р С Т У Ф Х Ц Ч Ш Щ Ъ Ы Ь Э Ю Я
a b v g d ye yo zh zee i k l m n o p r s t o o f kh ts ch sh shch - ee - e yoo ya

Pasta and Rice

вермишель [*vyirmi-shel*] vermicelli
вермишель домашняя [*vyirmi-shel damahsh-nya-ya*] home-made vermicelli
лапша [*lapsha*] noodles
макароны [*makaronee*] macaroni
ризото [*rizotuh*] risotto
рис [*reess*] rice

Bread

баранки [*barankee*] ring-shaped rolls
батон [*baton*] long loaf
белый хлеб [*byelee khlyep*] white bread
бородинский хлеб [*baradeenskee khlyep*] sweet bread
булки [*boolkee*] rolls
бутерброд [*boo-tyerbrot*] slice of bread and butter, sandwich
бутерброд с мясом [*boo-tyerbrot smya-sum*] meat sandwich or roll
бутерброд с сыром [*boo-tyerbrot s-seerum*] cheese sandwich or roll
буханка [*bookhanka*] loaf
орловский хлеб [*arlovskee khlyep*] rye bread
ржаной хлеб [*rzhanoy khlyep*] rye bread
хлеб [*khlyep*] bread
хлеб с маслом [*khlyep smah-slum*] bread and butter
чёрный хлеб [*chornee khlyep*] black bread

Vegetables

баклажан [*baklazhan*] aubergine, eggplant
белокочанная капуста [*byila-kachanna-ya kapoosta*] white cabbage
гарнир [*garneer*] vegetables
горошек [*garoshek*] peas
жареные кабачки [*zha-ryinee-ye kabachkee*] fried zucchinis/courgettes
жареный картофель [*zha-ryinee karto-fyil*] fried potatoes
зелёный горошек [*zi-lyonee garoshek*] green peas
кабачки [*kabachkee*] zucchinis, courgettes
кабачки с сыром запечённые [*kabachkee s-seerum za-pyichonnee-ye*] baked zucchinis/courgettes with cheese
капуста [*kapoosta*] cabbage
картофель [*karto-fyil*] potatoes
картофельное пюре [*karto-fyilnuh-ye pyooray*] mashed potatoes

кислая капуста [*kee-sla-ya kapoosta*] sauerkraut
консервированный горошек [*kanser-veeruvannee garoshek*] tinned/canned peas
краснокочанная капуста [*krasna-kachanna-ya kapoosta*] red cabbage
красный перец [*krasnee pye-ryits*] red pepper
лук [*look*] onions
лук-порей [*look pa-ryay*] leeks
маринованные огурцы [*marinovanee-ye agoortsee*] pickled cucumbers
молодой картофель [*maladoy karto-fyil*] new potatoes
морковь [*markoff*] carrots
овощи [*ovushchee*] vegetables
огурец [*agoo-ryets*] cucumber
отварной картофель [*atvarnoy karto-fyil*] boiled potatoes
перец [*pye-ryits*] pepper
петрушка [*pyitrooshka*] parsley
помидоры [*pamidoree*] tomatoes
с гарниром [*zgarneerum*] with vegetables
свёкла [*svyokla*] beetroot, red beet
сельдерей [*syil-dyi-ryay*] celery
спаржа [*sparzha*] asparagus
солёные огурцы [*sa-lyonee-ye agoortsee*] salted cucumbers
стручковый перец [*strooch-kovee pye-ryits*] pepper, capsicum
укроп [*ookrop*] dill
фасоли [*fa-solee*] French, haricot or kidney beans
хрен [*khryen*] horseradish
цветная капуста [*tsvyitna-ya kapoosta*] cauliflower
чёрный перец [*chornee pye-ryits*] black pepper
чеснок [*chisnok*] garlic
чечевица [*chichi-veetsa*] lentils
шпинат [*shpinaht*] spinach

Fruit and Nuts

абрикосы [*abrikossee*] apricots
айва [*iva*] quince
апельсины [*a-pyil-seenee*] oranges
арбуз [*arbooz*] water melon
банан [*banan*] banana
виноград [*vinagrat*] grapes
вишня [*veesh-nya*] morello cherries
грецкий орех [*gryetskee a-ryekh*] walnut
груши [*grooshee*] pears
дыня [*deen-ya*] melon

ежевика [*yizhi-veeka*] blackberries
земляника [*zim-lyaneeka*] wild strawberries
инжир [*inzheer*] figs
клубника [*kloobneeka*] strawberries
клюква [*klyōokva*] cranberries
красная смородина [*krasna-ya smarodina*]
redcurrants
лимон [*limon*] lemon
малина [*maleena*] raspberries
мандарины [*mandareenee*] mandarins
миндали [*mindahlee*] almonds
орехи [*a-ryekhee*] nuts
персик [*pyer-sik*] peach
слива [*sleeva*] plums
смородина [*smarodina*] currant
финики [*feenikee*] dates
фрукты [*frooktee*] fruit
черешня [*che-ryesh-nya*] cherries
чёрная смородина [*chorna-ya smarodina*]
blackcurrant
черника [*cherneeka*] bilberries
яблоки [*yablukee*] apples

Pies, Pastry

изделия из теста [*iz-dyeli-ya iz tyesta*]
pastry dishes
пельмени [*pyil-myenee*] meat dumplings
пельмени сибирские [*pyil-myenee
sibeerski-ye*] Siberian meat dumplings
пирог [*pirok*] pie
пирожки [*pirazhkee*] pies
пирожки с капустой [*pirazhkee
skapōostoy*] pies filled with cabbage
пирожки с мясом [*pirazhkee smya-sum*]
pies filled with meat
пирожки с рисом [*pirazhkee sreessum*] pies
filled with rice
тесто [*tyestuh*] dough, pastry

Sweets, Desserts

бисквит [*biskveet*] sponge cake
блинчики с вареньем [*bleenchikee sva-
ryen-yem*] pancakes with jam
блины [*bleenee*] pancakes
блины со сметаной [*bleenee sa smyitanoy*]
pancakes with sour cream

вареник [*va-ryenik*] curd or fruit dumpling
ватрушка [*vatrōoshka*] cheesecake
галушка [*galōoshka*] dumpling
десерт [*dyi-sert*] dessert
желе [*zhilay*] jelly
желе варенье [*zhelay va-ryen-ye*]
fruit jelly
желе из вишен [*zhilay iz veeshen*] morello
cherry jelly
заварной хлеб [*zavarnoy khlyep*] parboiled
bread
запеканка [*za-pyikanka*] baked pudding
кекс [*kyeks*] fruit cake
кисель [*ki-syel*] thin fruit jelly/kisel (kind of
starchy jelly)
кисель из абрикосового компота [*ki-syel
iz abrikosuh-vuvuh kampota*] apricot
jelly/kisel
кисель из клубники [*ki-syel iz kloobneekee*]
strawberry jelly/kisel
кисель из чёрной смородины [*ki-syel iz
chornoy smarodinee*] blackcurrant jelly/kisel
компот [*kampot*] stewed fruit
компот из груш [*kampot iz grōosh*] stewed
pears
компот из смеси сушёных фруктов
[*kampot iz smyessee sōoshonikh frooktuff*]
stewed dried fruit mixture
конфета [*kan-fyeta*] sweet
коржики [*korzhikee*] flat dry shortbread
кофейный крем [*ka-fyaynee kryem*] coffee
cream filling
крем [*kryem*] butter cake filling
крем ванильный [*kryem vaneelnee*] vanilla
cream
крем желе [*kryem zhilay*] cream jelly
крем желе из апельсинов [*kryem zhilay iz
a-pyil-seenuff*] orange cream jelly
кулич [*kooleech*] Easter cake
лепёшка [*lyi-pyoshka*] flat type of cake
манная каша [*manna-ya kasha*] semolina
pudding
масляный крем [*mah-slyanee kryem*] cake
filling made with butter
молочный кисель [*malochnee ki-syel*] milk
jelly
мороженое [*marozhenuh-ye*] ice cream
мороженое клубничное [*marozhenuh-ye
kloobneech-nuh-ye*] strawberry ice cream

а б в г д е   ё ж з и й к л м н о п р с т у ф х ц ч ш   щ   ъ ы ь э ю я
А Б В Г Д Е   Ё Ж З И Й К Л М Н О П Р С Т У Ф Х Ц Ч Ш   Щ   Ъ Ы Ь Э Ю Я
a b v g d ye   yo zh zee i k l m n o p r s t oo f kh ts ch sh shch - ee - e yoo ya

мороженое малиновое [*marozhenuh-ye maleenuvuh-ye*] raspberry ice cream

мороженое молочное [*marozhenuh-ye malochnuh-ye*] dairy ice cream

мороженое молочное с ванилином [*marozhenuh-ye malochnuh-ye svaneelinum*] dairy ice cream with vanilla

мороженое "пломбир" [*marozhenuh-ye plambeer*] ice cream with candied fruit

мороженое шоколадное [*marozhenuh-ye shakaladnuh-ye*] chocolate ice cream

овсяный кисель [*av-syannee kee-syil*] oatmeal jelly

оладьи [*alahdee*] thick pancakes

ореховый торт [*a-ryekhuvee tort*] nut cake

печенье [*pyichen-ye*] biscuits

пирог с повидлом [*pirok spaveedlum*] pie with jam

пирог с яблоками [*pirok syablukamee*] apple pie

пирожное [*pirozhnuh-ye*] small cake

повидло [*paveed-luh*] thick jelly

пончики [*ponchikee*] doughnuts

пудинг [*poodink*] pudding

рисовая каша [*ree-suva-ya kasha*] rice pudding

ромовая баба [*romuva-ya baba*] rum baba

салат из яблок [*salaht iz yabluk*] apple salad

сдобное тесто [*zdobnuh-ye tyestuh*] sweet pastry

сладкое [*sladkuh-ye*] dessert, sweet course

слоёное тесто [*sla-yonuh-ye tyestuh*] puff-pastry

слоёный торт [*sla-yonee tort*] layered cake

сырники [*seernikee*] cheesecakes

торт [*tort*] cake, gâteau

фруктовое мороженое [*frooktovuh-ye marozhenuh-ye*] fruit ice cream

шоколад [*shakalat*] chocolate

шоколадная глазурь [*shakaladna-ya glazōōr*] chocolate icing

эскимо [*eskimo*] choc-ice

Cheese

брынза [*brinza*] sheep's cheese

плавленый сыр [*plah-vlyinee seer*] processed cheese

сыр [*seer*] cheese

творог [*tvarok*] cottage cheese

Basics

ванильный соус [*vaneelnee so-ōōss*] vanilla sauce

варенье [*va-ryen-ye*] preserves

горчица [*garcheetsa*] mustard

гренки [*gryinkee*] toast, croûtons

гречка [*gryechka*] buckwheat

гречневая каша [*gryech-nyiva-ya kasha*] buckwheat porridge

грибной соус [*gribnoy so-ōōss*] mushroom sauce

джем [*jem*] jam

жир [*zheer*] lard

изюм [*iz-yōōm*] sultanas

каша [*kasha*] kasha, cooked buckwheat

корица [*kareetsa*] cinnamon

лавровый лист [*lavrovee leest*] bay leaf

маргарин [*margareen*] margarine

масло [*mahss-luh*] butter, oil

мёд [*myod*] honey

медовый [*myidovee*] honey

молочная каша [*malochna-ya kasha*] milk porridge

панировочные сухари [*panirovuchnee-ye sookharee*] dried breadcrumbs

подсолнечное масло [*pad-sol-nyichnuh-ye mahss-luh*] sunflower seed oil

рассол [*rassol*] pickle

сало [*saluh*] fat, lard

сахар [*sakhar*] sugar

сливки [*sleefkee*] cream

с лимоном [*slimonum*] with lemon

сливочное масло [*sleevuchnuh-ye mahss-luh*] butter

сметана [*smyitana*] sour cream

сметанный соус [*smyitannee so-ōōss*] sour cream sauce

солёное печенье [*sa-lyonuh-ye pyichen-ye*] savo(u)ry biscuit, cracker

соль [*sol*] salt

соус винегрет [*so-ōōss vini-gryet*] vinaigrette

соус майонез [*so-ōōss mıa-nyez*] mayonnaise sauce

соус тартар [*so-ōōss tartar*] tartar sauce

соус хрен [*so-ōōss khryen*] horseradish sauce

сухарь [*sookhar*] dried crust

сухое печенье [*sōōkho-ye pyichen-ye*] dry biscuit/cookie

тмин [*tmeen*] thyme

томат-пюре [*tamat pyooray*] tomato purée

томатный соус [*tamatnee so-ōōss*] tomato sauce

уксус [*ооksооss*] vinegar

Methods of Preparation

домашний [*damashnee*] home-made
жареный [*zha-ryinee*] fried, grilled, roast
жареный на вертеле [*zha-ryinee na vyer-tyil-ye*] grilled on a skewer
копчёный [*kapchonee*] smoked
на вертеле [*na vyer-tyil-ye*] on a skewer
начинка [*nachinka*] filling, stuffing
отварной [*atvarnoy*] boiled, poached
печёный [*pyichonee*] baked
сырой [*siroy*] raw
тушёный [*tooshonee*] stewed
фаршированный [*far-shirovannee*] stuffed

Menu Terms

блюдо [*blyооduh*] dish, course
диетическое блюдо [*dee-eteechiskuh-ye blyооd-uh*] for special diets
завтрак [*zaftrak*] breakfast
меню [*myi-nyоо*] menu
национальные русские блюда [*natsianahlni-ye rooski-ye blyооda*] Russian national dishes
порция [*portsi-ya*] portion
русская кухня [*rooska-ya kооkh-nya*] Russian cuisine
обед [*a-byet*] lunch
ужин [*ооzhin*] dinner
шеф повар рекомендует сегодня [*shef povar ryika-myindoo-yit syivo-dnya*] the Chef recommends:

FOOD LABELS

высший сорт highest quality
годен до sell by
ГОСТ GOST Soviet Standard
нетто 140 г. net weight 140 gram(me)s
сорт второй second grade
сорт первый first grade
срок годности expiry date
хранить в сухом месте keep in a dry place
хранить при температуре минус 4 keep at minus 4 degrees
цена price

FORMS

адрес address
анкета form, questionnaire
в какую страну следует country of destination
выезд до . . . exit by . . .
гражданство citizenship
дата date
дата выдачи date of issue
дата рождения date of birth
доллары США US dollars
из какой страны прибыл country of departure
из страны country of departure
имя и отчество name and patronymic
иностранная валюта currency
кем выдан паспорт place of issue
количество quantity
куда, кому address and name
лица, внесенные в паспорт persons included in the passport
марки ФРГ German marks
место рождения place of birth
наименование description
национальность nationality
отметки notes, remarks
паспорт действителен до . . . this passport is valid until . . .
паспорт серия № passport no.
подпись signature
пол sex
прописью in words
служебные отметки for office use
совместно следуют accompanied by
срок настоящего паспорта продлен до . . . the validity of this passport is extended to . . .
таможенная декларация customs declaration
телеграмма telegram
фамилия surname
Ф.И.О. surname, name, patronymic
французские франки French francs
фунты стерлингов pounds sterling
цель поездки (деловая, туризм, личная и т.п.) purpose of travel (business, tourism, personal etc)
цифрами in numbers

а	б	в	г	д	е	ё	ж	з	и	й	к	л	м	н	о	п	р	с	т	у	ф	х	ц	ч	ш	щ	ъ	ы	ь	э	ю	я
А	Б	В	Г	Д	Е	Ё	Ж	З	И	Й	К	Л	М	Н	О	П	Р	С	Т	У	Ф	Х	Ц	Ч	Ш	Щ	Ъ	Ы	Ь	Э	Ю	Я
a	b	v	g	d	ye	yo	zh	z	ee	i	k	l	m	n	o	p	r	s	t	oo	f	kh	ts	ch	sh	shch	-	ee	-	e	yoo	ya

GARAGES

автозаправочная станция petrol/gas station
авторемонтная мастерская auto repairs
аккумулятор battery
бензин petrol, gas
бензин высшего качества high quality petrol/gas
бензозаправочная колонка petrol/gas station
бюро проката автомобилей car hire/rental
гараж garage
давление pressure
дистиллированная вода distilled water for batteries
масло oil
обыкновенный бензин ordinary petrol/gas (lower grade)
открыто в будни от 6 часов утра до 8 часов вечера open weekdays from 6 a.m. till 8 p.m.
открыто круглые сутки open 24 hours
пункт мойки автомобилей car wash
пункт технического обслуживания repairs and servicing
шины tyres, tires

GEOGRAPHICAL

автономная республика autonomous republic
гора mountain
город town
долина valley
залив bay
край territory, land
море sea
область district
озеро lake
океан ocean
остров island
район region
республика republic
столица capital
страна country

HAIRDRESSER

борода beard
бритва razor
брить shave

волосы hair
косметика beauty treatment
лак для волос hair lacquer
лак для ногтей nail varnish
маникюр manicure
модные причёски modern hairstyling
окрасить to dye
парик wig
парикмахер hairdresser, barber
парикмахерская hairdresser's shop/salon
педикюр pedicure
перманент permanent wave
причёска hair style
стрижка hair cut
холодная завивка shampoo and set

HISTORICAL INTEREST

Великая Октябрьская Социалистическая революция the Great October Socialist Revolution
Великая Отечественная война the Great Patriotic War, Second World War
Екатерина Великая Catherine the Great
Иван IV Васильевич (Иван Грозный) Ivan the Terrible
Пётр Великий Peter the Great

HOTELS

администратор manager
буфет snack bar
бюро обслуживания tourist service bureau
выход exit
гардероб cloakroom, checkroom
гостиница hotel
дежурная floor lady (attendant on each floor of hotels who looks after the floor and collects the keys for guests on that floor)
дежурная по этажу floor service
дежурный floor service
запасной выход emergency exit
к себе pull
листок для приезжающих for hotel guests
лифт lift, elevator
мест нет no vacancies
на какой срок duration of visit
номер room
номер на двоих room for two
номер на одного room for one
от себя push

первый этаж ground floor
прачечная laundry
ресторан restaurant
химчистка dry cleaning
чистка обуви shoe shine
этаж floor

LIFTS, ELEVATORS

1-ый этаж ground floor (UK), first floor (US)
аварийный сигнал emergency button
вверх up
вниз down
кнопка button
лифт lift, elevator
лифт не работает lift/elevator out of order
максимальная нагрузка maximum weight limit
подвал basement

MEDICAL

антибиотики antibiotics
больница hospital
зуб tooth
зубной врач dentist
кабинет surgery (room)
консультация consultation
медсестра nurse
палата скорой помощи casualty ward
поликлиника surgery
регистратура registration
талон на приём appointment card
укол injection

MEDICINE LABELS

20 таблеток покрытых оболочкой 20 coated tablets or dragées
50 таблеток по 0.02 г. 50 tablets at 0.02 gram(me)s each
аптека chemist
годен до … expires on …
доза dose
лекарство medicine
наружное for external use only
одну таблетку каждые четыре часа one tablet every four hours

перед едой before meals
по две капли two drops
по одному порошку три раза в день one powder three times a day
порошок powder
принимайте это лекарство take this medicine
растворите две таблетки в стакане тёплой воды dissolve two tablets in a glass of warm water
рецепт prescription
средство от насморка (от кашля, от гриппа) medicine for cold (cough, flu)
таблетка tablet
хранить в сухом, прохладном месте keep in dry, cold place
хранить в сухом, тёмном месте keep in dry, dark place

MONTHS

январь January
февраль February
март March
апрель April
май May
июнь June
июль July
август August
сентябрь September
октябрь October
ноябрь November
декабрь December

NOTICES IN RESTAURANTS/BARS

впуск посетителей прекращается в 23.00 no customers admitted after 11 p.m.
все места заняты all seats taken
гардероб cloakroom, checkroom
заказано reserved
здесь не курят no smoking here
книга жалоб и предложений complaints book
мест нет all seats taken
ресторан restaurant
ресторан закрыт restaurant closed
ресторан закрыт на ремонт (на учёт) restaurant closed for repairs (stocktaking)

а	б	в	г	д	е	ё	ж	з	и	й	к	л	м	н	о	п	р	с	т	у	ф	х	ц	ч	ш	щ	ъ	ы	ь	э	ю	я
А	Б	В	Г	Д	Е	Ё	Ж	З	И	Й	К	Л	М	Н	О	П	Р	С	Т	У	Ф	Х	Ц	Ч	Ш	Щ	Ъ	Ы	Ь	Э	Ю	Я
a	b	v	g	d	ye	yo	zh	z	ee	i	k	l	m	n	o	p	r	s	t	oo	f	kh	ts	ch	sh	shch	-	ee	-	e	yoo	ya

ресторан открыт с 11.00 до 24.00 the restaurant is open from 11 a.m. to midnight
стол заказан reserved

NOTICES IN SHOPS

бюро доставки deliveries
выдача покупок collection counter (for goods purchased)
выходной день ... closed on ...
касса cash desk
магазин открыт (закрыт) the shop is open (closed)
магазин работает с 8.00 часов до 19.00 the shop is open from 8 a.m. to 7 p.m.
новинка new!
перерыв на обед 13.00-14.00 ч. closed for lunch from 13.00 to 14.00
платите в кассу pay at the cash desk
просьба не курить please do not smoke
санитарный день cleaning day
сегодня в продаже on sale today
стол заказов orders
у нас не курят no smoking here

NOTICES ON DOORS

вход entrance
вход воспрещён no admittance
выход exit
директор manager
к себе pull
не входить no admittance
не прислоняться do not lean on the door
нет входа no entrance
нет выхода no exit
от себя push
посторонним вход запрещён no admittance
хода нет no admittance

PLACE NAMES

Алма-Ата Alma Ata
Архангельск Archangel
Баку Baku
Батуми Batumi
Бухара Bukhara
Вильнюс Vilnius
Владивосток Vladivostok
Волгоград Volgograd
Вологда Vologda
Воронеж Voronezh

Горький Gorky
Душанбе Dushanbe
Ереван Yerevan
Загорск Zagorsk
Запорожье Zaporozhe
Иркутск Irkutsk
Казань Kazan
Калининград Kaliningrad
Киев Kiev
Ленинград Leningrad
Львов Lvov
Минск Minsk
Москва Moscow
Мурманск Murmansk
Новосибирск Novosibirsk
Одесса Odessa
Рига Riga
Самарканд Samarkand
Сочи Sochi
Таллин Tallin
Ташкент Tashkent
Тбилиси Tbilisi
Ялта Yalta

POST OFFICES

авиаоткрытка airmail postcard
авиаписьмо airmail letter
адрес address
бандероль small packet
выдача корреспонденции "до востребования" poste restante, general delivery
заказное письмо registered letter
марки stamps
международная телеграмма international telegram
начальник отделения post office manager
номер почтового отделения post office no.
обратный адрес sender's address
письмо letter
посылка parcel
почта post office
почтовая открытка postcard
почтовое отделение sub post office
приём и выдача корреспонденции letters
приём и выдача переводов money orders
приём и выдача посылок parcels
продажа конвертов, марок, открыток envelopes, stamps, postcards
простая телеграмма ordinary telegram
срочная телеграмма urgent telegram

телеграф cable
телеграфный бланк cable form
телефон telephone

PUBLIC BUILDINGS

больница hospital
выставка exhibition
гостиница hotel
государственный ... state ...
дворец palace
дом house
дом культуры arts centre/center
завод factory
институт institute
картинная галерея art gallery
кино cinema, movie theater
консульский отдел consular department
концертный зал concert hall
министерство ministry
монастырь monastery
музей museum
поликлиника clinic
посольство embassy
собор cathedral
стадион stadium
театр theatre, theater
университет university
церковь church

REPLIES

да [da] yes
ладно [lahd-nuh] OK
не за что [nye-za-shtuh] you're welcome
нет [nyet] no
ничего [neechivo] it's nothing, it doesn't matter
пожалуйста [pa-zhahlsta] please, you're welcome
спасибо [spa-see-buh] thank you
хорошо [khara-sho] fine

SHOPPING

аптека chemist
бакалея grocer
Берёзка "Beriozka" foreign currency shop
бумага paper

бюро доставки deliveries
булочная baker
булочная-кондитерская cake shop
букинистический магазин second-hand books
вино wines and spirits
выдача покупок collection counter for goods bought
галантерея miscellaneous goods
гастроном foodstore, supermarket
головные уборы hats
грампластинки records
Детский Мир Children's World department store in Moscow
детская одежда children's clothes
Дом книги bookshop, bookstore
женская одежда ladies' clothes
игрушки toys
канцтовары stationery
комиссионный магазин second-hand shop
консервы tinned/preserved foods
книги books
культтовары musical instruments, games, sports goods
магазин shop, store
мелодия music shop/store
меха furs
молоко milk, dairy products
мужская одежда menswear
мясо meat
обувь footwear
овощи vegetables
овощи-фрукты fruit and vegetables
одежда clothes
оптика optical goods, optician
парикмахерская hairdresser
парфюмерия perfumes and toiletries
папиросы-сигареты tobacconist, tobacco store
посуда crockery, flatware
продовольственный магазин (продмаг) foodstore
радиотовары radio and TV
рыба fish
союзпечать newspaper kiosk
спорттовары sports goods
стол заказов orders
сувениры souvenirs

а	б	в	г	д	е	ё	ж	з	и	й	к	л	м	н	о	п	р	с	т	у	ф	х	ц	ч	ш	щ	ъ	ы	ь	э	ю	я
А	Б	В	Г	Д	Е	Ё	Ж	З	И	Й	К	Л	М	Н	О	П	Р	С	Т	У	Ф	Х	Ц	Ч	Ш	Щ	Ъ	Ы	Ь	Э	Ю	Я
a	b	v	g	d	ye	yo	zh	z	ee	i	k	l	m	n	o	p	r	s	t	oo	f	kh	ts	ch	sh	shch	-	ee	-	e	yoo	ya

табак tobacconist, tobacco store
ткани textiles, fabrics
универмаг department store
фарфор china
фото(товары) cameras, photography
хлеб bread
хрусталь glass
ювелирные изделия jewel(le)ry
электротовары electrical goods

STREETS

бульвар boulevard
кольцо ring road
линия line (in Leningrad = **1-ая линия** = line (street) no.1)
мост bridge
набережная embankment
переулок lane
площадь square
проезд lane
проспект avenue
улица street
шоссе road

STREET AND ROAD SIGNS

берегись автомобиля! beware of cars!
ГАИ traffic police
железнодорожный переезд level crossing
идите! go, cross
одностороннее движение one-way traffic
остановка запрещена no stopping
осторожно! caution
объезд diversion
переход pedestrian crossing
перехода нет do not cross here
пешеходный переход pedestrian crossing
пешеходы pedestrians
подземный переход subway, pedestrian underpass
стойте! stop, halt!
стоп stop
стоянка запрещена no parking

SWEARWORDS

говно! [*gavno*] shit!
дерьмо! [*dyirmo*] shit!
дура! [*dōora*] fool! (to a woman)
дурак! [*doorak*] fool! (to a man)
идиот! [*idiot*] idiot!

куда прёшься? [*kooda pryosh-sa*] where the hell are you going?
пошёл к чёрту! [*pashol kchortōo*] go to hell!
сволочь! [*svoluch*] scum!
сукин сын! [*sōokin seen*] son of a bitch!
чёрт возьми! [*chort vazmee*] damn!
чтоб тебя! [*shtob tibya*] damn you!

TAXIS

маршрутное такси 'route taxi' (shared taxi that runs like a bus only with fewer stops and charging a higher fare)
стоянка такси taxi rank
такси taxi

TELEPHONE

2-х копеечная монета 2 kopeck piece
международный international
междугородный intercity
наберите номер dial number
телефон telephone
телефон-автомат public phone box/booth
телефонный переговорный пункт trunk call office

THEATRES, THEATERS

(*See also* Cinemas, movie theaters)
администратор manager
амфитеатр circle
антракт interval, intermission
бельэтаж dress circle
Большой театр Bolshoi
вход в зрительный зал после третьего звонка воспрещён no admittance after third bell
все билеты проданы sold out
гардероб cloakroom, checkroom
консерватория conservatoire
Кремлёвский Дворец съездов The Kremlin Congress Palace
курительная комната smoking room
ложа box
не курить no smoking
программа program(me)
ряд row
середина middle
спектакль performance
театр theatre, theater
театральная касса box office
фойе foyer
ярус circle

TIMETABLES, SCHEDULES

без пересадки no changing, through train
время time
время отправления departure time
день day
до to
мин. minutes
№ поезда train no.
от from
по местному времени local time
прибытие arrival
пункт назначения (от Москвы) destination (from Moscow)
расписание timetable, schedule
с пересадкой with change
час hour
через via

TOILETS, REST ROOMS

женский (ж) ladies, ladies' rest room
мужской (м) gents, men's room
питьевая вода drinking water
туалет toilets, rest rooms
туалетная бумага toilet paper
уборная toilet, rest room

TRAINS AND STATIONS

билет ticket
билетная касса ticket office
буфет refreshments
вагон carriage, car
вагон-ресторан restaurant car
ваш билет, пожалуйста! [*vash bi-lyet pa-zhahlsta*] tickets please!
вокзал station
время отправления departure time
вход entry
входа нет no entry
выход exit
(выход) в город way out to street
выхода нет no exit
женский туалет ladies, ladies' rest room
зал ожидания waiting room
зал продажи билетов booking office hall

камера хранения left luggage, baggage checkroom
к перронам to the platforms/tracks
к поездам to the trains
мужской туалет gents, men's room
мягкий вагон first class sleeping car
на Москву to Moscow
начальник станции station manager
пассажирский поезд stopping train
платформа platform, track
плацкартное место reserved seat
поезд train
поезда дальнего следования long-distance trains
посадочный талон boarding card (for sleepers)
прибытие arrivals
пригородные поезда suburban trains
прямой поезд through train
расписание поездов timetable, schedule
скорый поезд express train
спальный вагон sleeping car
справки information
справочное бюро information
станция station
электричка electric suburban train
экпресс express

UNDERGROUND, SUBWAY

(*See also* Trains and stations)
держитесь левой (правой) стороны keep to the left (right)
M underground, subway
метро underground, subway
нет входа no entry
нет выхода no exit
не прислоняться do not lean against the door
осторожно, двери закрываются attention, the doors are closing
переход change (for a different line)
размен change (machine)
следующая станция ... the next stop is ...
схема plan

| а б в г д е ё ж з и й к л м н о п р с т у ф х ц ч ш щ ъ ы ь э ю я |
| А Б В Г Д Е Ё Ж З И Й К Л М Н О П Р С Т У Ф Х Ц Ч Ш Щ Ъ Ы Ь Э Ю Я |
| a b v g d ye yo zh z ee i k l m n o p r s t oo f kh ts ch sh shch - ee - e yoo ya |

REFERENCE GRAMMAR

ARTICLES

There are no articles in Russian, no words for 'a' or 'the'. So, for example:

> **книга**

can mean 'a book', 'the book' or simply 'book', depending on its context. Similarly the plural form:

> **книги**

can mean 'the books', 'some books' or 'books'.

NOUNS

GENDER

Nouns are either masculine, feminine or neuter.

As a general rule, nouns ending in a consonant or in **-й** are masculine:

дом	house
музей	museum

Those ending in **-a** or **-я** are feminine:

гостиница	hotel
тётя	aunt

Nouns ending in **-ь** are either masculine or feminine:

словарь	dictionary	(*masc*)
ночь	night	(*fem*)

Their gender must be learned separately. (The gender of nouns ending in **-ь** is indicated in the English-Russian section of this book).

Nouns ending in **-o**, **-e** or **-ё**, and all nouns ending in **-мя,** are neuter:

окно	window
поле	field
время	time

Men's names and a certain number of nouns ending in **-a** and **-я** denoting animate beings are masculine:

Никита	Nikita
мужчина	man
дядя	uncle

PLURALS

To form the plurals of nouns, follow the rules given below:

Masculine nouns ending in a consonant   `·`   **add -ы**

> **стол/столы**   table/tables

Masculine nouns ending in **-й**		change **-й** to **-и**
трамвай/трамваи	tram/trams	

Feminine nouns ending in **-а**		change **-а** to **-ы**
женщина/женщины	woman/women	

Feminine nouns ending in **-я**		change **-я** to **-и**
буря/бури	storm/storms	

Masculine and feminine nouns ending in **-ь**   change **-ь** to **-и**

кость/кости	(*fem*)	bone/bones
рояль/рояли	(*masc*)	piano/pianos

Neuter nouns ending in **-о**		change **-о** to **-а**
вино/вина	wine/wines	

Neuter nouns ending in **-е** or **-ё**   change **-е** (or **-ё**) to **-я**

здание/здания	building/buildings

Neuter nouns ending in **-мя**		change **-мя** to **-мена**
имя/имена	name/names	

Some common nouns have an irregular plural:

город/города	town/towns
брат/братья	brother/brothers
поезд/поезда	train/trains
друг/друзья	friend/friends
сын/сыновья	son/sons
мать/матери	mother/mothers
дочь/дочери	daughter/daughters
англичанин/англичане	Englishman/Englishmen

CASES

Russian is an 'inflected' language. This means that nouns and adjectives change their endings according to their function in a sentence. There are six different cases, singular and plural: nominative, accusative, genitive, dative, instrumental, prepositional

1. The nominative is used as the subject of a sentence, for example:

Иван живёт в Москве
Ivan lives in Moscow

The nominative is also used for addressing people:

Иван/Катя, здравствуйте!
hello, Ivan/Katya

2. The accusative is used as the object of most verbs (see page *117*):

я понимаю это слово
I understand this word

It is also used after certain prepositions when they convey the idea of motion or direction (**в** to, into, **на** to, onto, **через** across, via, **за** beyond, **сквозь** through):

она идёт в школу	мы едем через Москву
she is going to school	we are travelling via Moscow

3. The genitive indicates possession ('of'):

скрипка Дмитрия	стены Кремля
Dmitri's violin	the walls of the Kremlin

It is also used after certain prepositions (**без** without, **вместо** instead of, **для** for, **до** up to, till, **из** from, out of, **около** about, **от** from, **после** after, **у** at, by etc):

чай без сахара	это для меня?
tea without sugar	is this for me?

Masculine singular animate nouns and all animate nouns in the plural use the *genitive* case instead of the accusative case endings when functioning as the object of a sentence. For example:

мы не любим нашего учителя	я не вижу Ивана
we dislike our teacher	I can't see Ivan

4. The dative is used to denote direction (but not motion) towards someone or something. It is used for the indirect object with verbs of giving, sending etc, often preceded in English by the preposition 'to', for example:

я дал ключ начальнику
I gave the key to the manager

It is also used with certain prepositions (**к** towards, **по** along, according to):

к выходу
towards the exit

5. The instrumental is used to indicate the means by which an action is carried out, usually denoting "how", "what with", "by":

он писал карандашом	поездом
he wrote in pencil	by train

It is also used after certain prepositions (**за** behind, **между** between, **над** above, **перед** in front of, **под** under, **с** with):

чай с молоком	он стоит перед вами
tea with milk	he's standing in front of you

The instrumental is also used in certain expressions of time:

вечером	**весной**
in the evening	in spring

6. The prepositional is only used after certain prepositions:

в Ленинграде	in Leningrad
на почте	at the post-office
о тебе	about you

Here are declension tables showing the case endings of Russian nouns:

Singular

Masculine

	(table)	*(event)*	*(dictionary)*
nom	стол	случай	словарь
acc	стол	случай	словарь
gen	стола	случая	словаря
dat	столу	случаю	словарю
instr	столом	случаем	словарём
prep	столе	случае	словаре

Feminine

	(map)	*(earth/land)*	*(news)*	*(army)*
nom	карта	земля	новость	армия
acc	карту	землю	новость	армию
gen	карты	земли	новости	армии
dat	карте	земле	новости	армии
instr	картой	землёй	новостью	армией
prep	карте	земле	новости	армии

Neuter

	(window)	*(field)*	*(building)*
nom	окно	поле	здание
acc	окно	поле	здание
gen	окна	поля	здания
dat	окну	полю	зданию
instr	окном	полем	зданием
prep	окне	поле	здании

Plural

Masculine

nom	столы	случаи	словари
acc	столы	случаи	словари
gen	столов	случаев	словарей
dat	столам	случаям	словарям
instr	столами	случаями	словарями
prep	столах	случаях	словарях

Feminine

nom	карты	земли	новости	армии
acc	карты	земли	новости	армии
gen	карт	земель	новостей	армий
dat	картам	землям	новостям	армиям
instr	картами	землями	новостями	армиями
prep	картах	землях	новостях	армиях

Neuter

nom	окна	поля	здания
acc	окна	поля	здания
gen	окон	полей	зданий
dat	окнам	полям	зданиям
instr	окнами	полями	зданиями
prep	окнах	полях	зданиях

USE OF CASES WITH NUMERALS

After numbers ending in 1 the noun always appears in the nominative singular:

41 солдат
41 soldiers

After numbers ending in 2, 3 or 4, the noun appears in the genitive singular:

44 солдата
44 soldiers

After all other numbers, the genitive plural is used:

46 солдатов
46 soldiers

ADJECTIVES

Russian adjectives agree in number, gender and case with the nouns to which they refer. There are three basic types as shown below:

новый new

	Singular			Plural
	masc	*fem*	*neut*	
nom	новый	новая	новое	новые
acc	новый	новую	новое	новые
gen	нового	новой	нового	новых
dat	новому	новой	новому	новым
instr	новым	новой	новым	новыми
prep	новом	новой	новом	новых

синий blue

		Singular		Plural
	masc	*fem*	*neut*	
nom	синий	синяя	синее	синие
acc	синий	синюю	синее	синие
gen	синего	синей	синего	синих
dat	синему	синей	синему	синим
instr	синим	синей	синим	синими
prep	синем	синей	синем	синих

хороший good

		Singular		Plural
	masc	*fem*	*neut*	
nom	хороший	хорошая	хорошее	хорошие
acc	хороший	хорошую	хорошее	хорошие
gen	хорошего	хорошей	хорошего	хороших
dat	хорошему	хорошей	хорошему	хорошим
instr	хорошим	хорошей	хорошим	хорошими
prep	хорошем	хорошей	хорошем	хороших

Examples:

> **у меня новое пальто**
> I have a new coat

> **подарок от моей русской бабушки**
> the present is from my Russian grandmother

> **вы знаете эти английские слова?**
> do you know these English words?

Ordinal numbers are declined like adjectives.

COMPARATIVES

The comparative can be formed in two ways, either by using **более** (more) or **менее** (less) with the adjective:

> **более красивое здание**
> a more beautiful building

or by changing the adjective ending **-ый** to **-ее**:

> **эта книга интереснее**
> this book is more interesting

To express 'than' use either **чем** and the nominative, or the genitive case alone:

> **моя жена красивее вашей**
> **моя жена красивее, чем ваша**
> my wife is prettier than yours

Several common adjectives have irregular forms of the comparative, for example:

большой	больше	(big, bigger)
высокий	выше	(high, higher)
громкий	громче	(loud, louder)
далёкий	дальше	(far, further)
молодой	моложе	(young, younger)
старый	старше	(old, older)
тихий	тише	(quiet, quieter)
частый	чаще	(often, more often)

SUPERLATIVES

The superlative is most commonly formed by using the adjective preceded by the adjective **самый** (in the appropriate case and gender), or else by the invariable adverb **наиболее**:

> **это самая дорогая гостиница в городе**
> this is the most expensive hotel in town

> **это наиболее удобный поезд**
> this is the most convenient train

ADVERBS

Most adverbs are formed by replacing the adjective endings **-ый** and **-ий** with **-о** or **-e** respectively

быстрый	quick	быстро	quickly
медленный	slow	медленно	slowly
искренний	sincere	искренне	sincerely

Adjectives ending in **-ский** usually form an adverb in **-ски**:

> **психологически** psychologically

POSSESSIVE ADJECTIVES

They are:

мой	my
твой	your (*singular familiar*)
его	his, its
её	her, its
наш	our
ваш	your (*singular polite, plural familiar and polite*)
их	their
свой	a possessive adjective referring back to the subject of the sentence, and which can therefore mean any of the above

The declension of **мой, твой** and **свой**

	masc	*fem*	*neut*	*plural*
nom	мой	моя	моё	мои
acc	мой	мою	моё	мои
gen	моего	моей	моего	моих
dat	моему	моей	моему	моим
instr	моим	моей	моим	моими
prep	моём	моей	моём	моих

The declension of **наш** and **ваш**

	masc	*fem*	*neut*	*plural*
nom	наш	наша	наше	наши
acc	наш	нашу	наше	наши
gen	нашего	нашей	нашего	наших
dat	нашему	нашей	нашему	нашим
instr	нашим	нашей	нашим	нашими
prep	нашем	нашей	нашем	наших

Его, её and **их** are invariable.

мой дом
my house

я знаю вашего брата
I know your brother

он ищет мою книгу
he's looking for my book

я ищу свою книгу
I'm looking for my (own) book

она ищет свою книгу
she is looking for her (own) book

это их машина
it's their car

PRONOUNS

PERSONAL PRONOUNS

Singular: **я**   I
         ты   you (*singular familiar*)
         он   he
         она   she
         оно   it

Plural: **мы**   we
         вы   you (*singular polite, familiar plural*)
         они   they

Like nouns, Russian pronouns decline. Their endings are as follows:

Singular

nom	я	ты	он	она	оно
acc	меня	тебя	(н)его	(н)её	(н)его
gen	меня	тебя	(н)его	(н)её	(н)его
dat	мне	тебе	(н)ему	(н)ей	(н)ему
instr	мной	тобой	(н)им	(н)ей	(н)им
prep	мне	тебе	нём	ней	нём

Plural

nom	мы	вы	они
acc	нас	вас	(н)их
gen	нас	вас	(н)их
dat	нам	вам	(н)им
instr	нами	вами	(н)ими
prep	нас	вас	них

In the 3rd person singular and plural the forms preceded by the letter н are used only following a preposition, otherwise they appear without it, for example:

с ними
with them

я дал ему рубль
I gave him a rouble

Examples:

that's for me	**это для меня**
give that to me	**дайте мне это**
I gave them to her	**я дал ей их**

Russian often omits the personal pronoun when it is the subject of a sentence:

не знаю
I don't know

не можем
we can't

YOU

There are two ways of saying 'you' in Russian.

ты   is used for informal address to a relative, close friend or child
вы   is used for formal address to one person, or else for addressing several persons.

THE REFLEXIVE PRONOUN

One form is used for all persons singular and plural; according to context it can mean myself/ yourself/ himself/ itself/ herself/ ourselves/ yourselves/ themselves.

acc	**себя**
gen	**себя**
dat	**себе**
instr	**собой**
prep	**себе**

я говорил о себе
I was talking about myself

она говорит о себе
she is talking about herself

INTERROGATIVE PRONOUNS

The principal interrogative pronouns are **кто** (who) and **что** (what). They decline as follows:

nom	**кто**	**что**
acc	**кого**	**что**
gen	**кого**	**чего**
dat	**кому**	**чему**
instr	**кем**	**чем**
prep	**ком**	**чём**

Кто-то (someone), **что-то** (something), **кто-нибудь** (anyone), **что-нибудь** (anything), **никто** (nobody), **ничто** (nothing) decline in the same way.

DEMONSTRATIVE PRONOUNS

These are **этот, эта, это** (this) and **тот, та, то** (that). They decline as follows:

	Singular			Plural	Singular			Plural
nom	**этот**	**эта**	**это**	**эти**	**тот**	**та**	**то**	**те**
acc	**этот**	**эту**	**это**	**эти**	**тот**	**ту**	**то**	**те**
gen	**этого**	**этой**	**этого**	**этих**	**того**	**той**	**того**	**тех**
dat	**этому**	**этой**	**этому**	**этим**	**тому**	**той**	**тому**	**тем**
instr	**этим**	**этой**	**этим**	**этими**	**тем**	**той**	**тем**	**теми**
prep	**этом**	**этой**	**этом**	**этих**	**том**	**той**	**том**	**тех**

сколько стоит эта книга?
how much is this book?

он не живёт в этом доме
he doesn't live in this house

The invariant form **это** is also used in phrases like: 'this is/ these are . . .', 'it is/ they are . . .'

это моя новая шляпа и пальто
this is my new hat and coat

это все мои книги
these are all my books.

VERBS

CONJUGATION OF VERBS

Verbs usually follow one of two basic conjugation patterns (indicated by the figures 1 or 2 after the infinitive in the list of common verbs on pages *116–17*). Here are examples of the two conjugations:

	Conjugation 1	*Conjugation 2*
	работать (to work)	говорить (to speak/say)
я	работаю	говорю
ты	работаешь	говоришь
он	работает	говорит
мы	работаем	говорим
вы	работаете	говорите
они	работают	говорят

As a general rule, most verbs ending in **-ать** and **-ять** are first conjugation. (The commonest exceptions are **лежать** (to lie), **держать** (to hold), **молчать** (to be silent), **спать** (to sleep), **кричать** (to shout) and **слышать** (to hear).) Verbs ending in **-ить** tend to be second conjugation. (Notable exceptions which are irregular are: **пить** (to drink), **лить** (to pour), **бить** (to beat).)

Note these three common irregular verbs:

есть (to eat)	**дать** (to give)	**хотеть** (to want)
я ем	дам	хочу
ты ешь	дашь	хочешь
он ест	даст	хочет
мы едим	дадим	хотим
вы едите	дадите	хотите
они едят	дадут	хотят

ASPECTS OF THE VERB

Most Russian verbs have two *aspects*.

The *imperfective* aspect usually expresses the idea of duration, continuation or repetition of an action. It is used to form the present, past and future tenses.

It is used for the Russian equivalent of, for example, 'I work', 'I am working', 'I do work' etc. The past tense of the imperfective gives the equivalent of 'I was working', 'I used to work', 'I worked', 'I had been working' etc. Similarly, the future imperfective renders 'I will/shall be working' etc.

The *perfective* usually represents the idea of a completed action either in the past or in the future.

In the past tense it conveys the idea of 'I have worked', 'I had worked', 'I did/have done/had done some work' etc. The future perfective gives the equivalent of 'I will/shall have worked', 'I will do some work', 'I will/shall work' etc. Virtually all the many English tense variants are thus catered for. When translating from English into Russian it may at first need thought as to which aspect to use - 'I worked' may have the sense of 'I used to work' (i.e. imperfective), or it could mean 'I did some work' (i.e. perfective).

In the English-Russian part of the book the first translation of a verb is the imperfective aspect. A list of imperfective forms is also given on pages *116–17*. The perfective form is the second of the pair of verbs given in the English-Russian section of the book and is the form given in column 3 on pages *116–17*.

Both aspects can take the endings given in the conjugation tables (see page *114*).

PRESENT TENSE

The present tense is formed by using the imperfective aspect of the verb:

куда вы идёте?
where are you going?

он хорошо говорит по-русски
he speaks Russian well

PAST TENSE

In Russian the past tense endings refer to the gender and number of the subject. They are formed by replacing the infinitive ending **-ть** with the endings: **-л** for masculine subject

-ла for feminine subject
-ло for neuter subject
-ли for plural subject

Both the imperfective and perfective aspects of the verb can be used, depending on the meaning to be conveyed:

вчера она получила письмо
yesterday she received a letter

опа часто получала письма от брата
she often received letters from her brother

The following past tense forms are irregular:

	идти (to go)	**нести** (to carry)	**вести** (to lead)
masc	шёл	нёс	вёл
fem	шла	несла	вела
neut	шло	несло	вело
plural	шли	несли	вели

FUTURE TENSE

The future tense is expressed in two ways. The imperfective future is formed by the present tense of the verb 'to be' followed by the imperfective infinitive of the verb, (see page *116*):

я буду покупать газету каждый день
I will buy a newspaper every day

The perfective future is formed by using the present tense conjugations with a perfective verb:

завтра я куплю газету
I will buy a newspaper tomorrow

TO BE

The verb 'to be' (**быть**) is normally omitted in the present tense.

> **ключи на столе**
> the keys are on the table.

> **я англичанин**
> I'm English

The past tense of **быть** is formed in the usual way: **был, была, было, были.**
The conjugated form of **быть** provides a future tense: **буду, будешь, будет, будем, будете, будут.**

TO HAVE

The usual way to indicate possession in Russian is to use the verb 'to be' with the preposition **y** (at) plus genitive case of the possessor; the thing possessed is the subject of the sentence. Example:

> **у нас было много багажа**
> [at us was a lot of luggage]
> we had a lot of luggage

> **у моего брата есть велосипед**
> [at my brother there is a bicycle]
> my brother has a bicycle

> **у вас будет возможность отдохнуть**
> [at you there will be the chance to rest]
> you will have the chance to have a rest

FORMATION OF THE PERFECTIVE

Many imperfective verbs form perfectives by adding the prefix **по-**. But many others are formed in a variety of different ways. Some even take a different verb altogether as a perfective partner, e.g. **брать** (1)/**взять** (1) to take; **говорить** (2)/**сказать** (1) to say; **садиться** (2)/**сесть** (1) to sit down.

The following is a list of common pairings: (excluding those merely adding **по-**):

	Imperfective	Perfective
to awaken (someone)	**будить** (2)	**разбудить** (2)
to wake up	**просыпаться** (1)	**проснуться** (1)
to see	**видеть** (2)	**увидеть** (2)
to return	**возвращать(ся)** (1)	**вернуть(ся)** (1)
to forbid	**запрещать** (1)	**запретить** (2)
to get up	**вставать** (1)	**встать** (1)
to do, make	**делать** (1)	**сделать** (1)
to wait	**ждать** (1)	**подождать** (1)
to forget	**забывать** (1)	**забыть** (1)
to order	**заказывать** (1)	**заказать** (1)
to close	**закрывать** (1)	**закрыть** (1)
to open	**открывать** (1)	**открыть** (1)
to engage, occupy	**занимать** (1)	**занять** (1)

to receive	получать (1)	получить (2)
to know	знать (1)	узнать
to study (subject)	изучать (1)	изучить (2)
to start	начинать (1)	начать (1)
to end, finish	кончать (1)	кончить (2)
to buy	покупать (1)	купить (2)
to sell	продавать (1)	продать (1)
to lie down	ложиться (2)	лечь (1)
to be silent	молчать (2)	замолчать (2)
to shout	кричать (2)	закричать (2)
to explain	объяснять (1)	объяснить (2)
to ask (question)	спрашивать (1)	спросить (2)
to answer	отвечать (1)	ответить (2)
to dress	одевать(ся) (1)	одеть(ся) (1)
to become	становиться (2)	стать (1)
to stop	останавливать (ся) (1)	остановить(ся) (2)
to remain	оставаться (1)	остаться (2)
to read	читать (1)	прочитать (1)
to write	писать (1)	написать(1)
to drink	пить (1)	выпить (1)
to eat	есть	съесть
to give	давать (1)	дать
to understand	понимать (1)	понять (1)
to remember	помнить (2)	запомнить (2)
to help	помогать (1)	помочь (1)
to invite	приглашать (1)	пригласить (2)
to tell	рассказывать (1)	рассказать (1)
to decide	решать (1)	решить (2)
to happen	случаться (1)	случиться (2)
to laugh	смеяться (1)	засмеяться (1)
to pay	платить (2)	заплатить (2)
to kill	убивать (1)	убить (1)
to be able	мочь (1)	смочь (1)
to know how to	уметь (1)	суметь (1)
to teach	учить (2)	научить (2)
to learn	учить (2)	выучить (2)
to want	хотеть	захотеть
to wash	мыть (1)	вымыть (1)
to be/fall ill	болеть (1)	заболеть (1)
to meet	встречать (1)	встретить (2)
to fall	упадать (1)	упасть (1)
to break	ломать (1)	сломать (1)

NEGATION

Verbs are made negative in Russian by placing **не** before them:

> **я не пью кофе**
> I don't drink coffee.

'Did not have/had not', 'do not have/have not', 'shall/will not have' is rendered by **не было, нет, не будет** respectively, followed by the genitive of the object; the person who 'has not' goes in the genitive after the preposition **у**:

> **у нас не было друзей в Москве**
> [at us there were not of friends in Moscow]
> we had no friends in Moscow

не must appear before the verb even if other negative expressions appear in the sentence.

> **никто здесь не работает**
> nobody works here

The object of a negative verb may very often be in the genitive case.

> **я не понимаю этого**
> I don't understand this

QUESTIONS

A statement can be turned into a question merely by adding a question mark or (in speech) by using a 'questioning intonation'.

> **они продают хорошие приёмники**
> they sell good radios

> **они продают хорошие приёмники?**
> do they sell good radios?

A question word (**кто** who, **когда** when, **где** where, **почему** why, **что** what) may be used. There is no inversion of subject and verb in Russian:

> **когда ваша тётя приезжает?**
> when is your aunt arriving?

A question may also be formed by placing the particle **ли** as second element in the sentence.

> **продают ли здесь зубные щётки?**
> do they sell toothbrushes here?

REFLEXIVE VERBS

Reflexive verbs are formed by adding **-ся** to verbs ending in a consonant and **-сь** after a vowel. The same form is used for myself, yourself, himself, ourselves etc:

> **они одеваются**   **она мылась**
> they are getting dressed   she was washing herself

Some verbs are only used in the reflexive form: **надеяться** (to hope); **смеяться** (to laugh); **бояться** (to fear); **нравиться** (to please, appeal to).

IMPERATIVES

The imperative is formed from the second person singular of a verb (imperfective or perfective, depending on the meaning required) by removing the ending **-ишь** or **-ешь** and adding **-и** for the familiar and **-ите** for the polite forms. If the stem ends in a vowel, add **-й** or **-йте**. Examples:

> **идите!**   **работай!**   **говорите медленно!**
> come!   work!   speak slowly!

Note the irregular imperatives:

езжай, езжайте	go (from **ехать**)
ляг, лягте	lie down (from **лечь**)
ешь, ешьте	eat (from **есть**)

TELLING THE TIME

what time is it?	**который час?** [*katoree chass*]
one o'clock	**час** [*chass*]
two o'clock	**два часа** [*dva chassa*]
eight o'clock	**восемь часов** [*vo-syem chassoff*]
at five o'clock	**в пять часов** [*fpyat chassoff*]
four a.m.	**четыре часа утра** [*chiteer-ye chassa ootra*]
nine p.m.	**девять часов вечера** [*dye-vyat chassoff vyechera*]
midday	**полдень** [*pol-dyin*]
midnight	**полночь** [*polnuch*]
five past nine	**пять минут десятого** [*pyat minoot dyi-syatuv-uh*]
ten to five	**без десяти пять** [*byez dye-syatee pyat*]
quarter past two	**четверть третьего** [*chet-vyert trye-tyivuh*]
quarter to four	**без четверти четыре** [*byez chet-vyertee chiteer-ye*]
half past one	**половина второго** [*palaveena ftarovuh*]
at half past ten	**в половине одиннадцатого** [*v palaveen-ye adeen-nad-tsatuvuh*]

RUSSIAN HANDWRITING

Handwritten Russian differs in some respects from printed Russian.
The following tables will help you decipher Russian handwriting.

CONVERSION TABLES

1. LENGTH

centimetres, centimeters
1 cm = 0.39 inches

metres, meters
1 m = 100 cm = 1000 mm
1 m = 39.37 inches = 1.09 yards

1 km = 0.62 miles = 5/8 mile

km	1	2	3	4	5	10	20	30	40	50	100
miles	0.6	1.2	1.9	2.5	3.1	6.2	12.4	18.6	24.9	31.1	62.1

inches
1 inch = 2.54 cm

feet
1 foot = 30.48 cm

yards
1 yard = 0.91 m

miles
1 mile = 1.61 km = 8/5 km

miles	1	2	3	4	5	10	20	30	40	50	100
km	1.6	3.2	4.8	6.4	8.0	16.1	32.2	48.3	64.4	80.5	161

2. WEIGHT

gram(me)s
1 g = 0.035 oz

g	100	250	500	
oz	3.5	8.75	17.5	= 1.1 lb

kilos
1 kg = 1000 g
1 kg = 2.20 lb = 11/5 lb

kg	0.5	1	1.5	2	3	4	5	6	7	8	9	10
lb	1.1	2.2	3.3	4.4	6.6	8.8	11.0	13.2	15.4	17.6	19.8	22

kg	20	30	40	50	60	70	80	90	100
lb	44	66	88	110	132	154	176	198	220

tons
1 UK ton = 1018 kg
1 US ton = 909 kg

tonnes
1 tonne = 1000 kg
1 tonne = 0.98 UK tons = 1.10 US tons

ounces
1 oz = 28.35 g

pounds
1 pound = 0.45 kg = 5/11 kg

lb	1	1.5	2	3	4	5	6	7	8	9	10	20
kg	0.5	0.7	0.9	1.4	1.8	2.3	2.7	3.2	3.6	4.1	4.5	9.1

stones
1 stone = 6.35 kg

stones	1	2	3	7	8	9	10	11	12	13	14	15
kg	6.3	12.7	19	44	51	57	63	70	76	83	89	95

hundredweights
1 UK hundredweight = 50.8 kg
1 US hundredweight = 45.36 kg

3. CAPACITY

litres, liters
1l = 1.76 UK pints = 2.13 US pints
½l = 500 cl
¼l = 250 cl

pints
1 UK pint = 0.57 l
1 US pint = 0.47 l

quarts
1 UK quart = 1.141 l
1 US quart = 0.95 l

gallons
1 UK gallon = 4.55 l
1 US gallon = 3.79 l

4. TEMPERATURE

centrigrade/celsius
$C = (F - 32) \times 5/9$

C	−5	0	5	10	15	18	20	25	30	37	38
F	23	32	41	50	59	64	68	77	86	98.4	100.4

Fahrenheit
$F = (C \times 9/5) + 32$

F	23	32	40	50	60	65	70	80	85	98.4	101
C	−5	0	4	10	16	20	21	27	30	37	38.3

NUMBERS

0	нуль	[nōol]
1	один	[adeen]
2	два	[dva]
3	три	[tree]
4	четыре	[chiteer-ye]
5	пять	[pyat]
6	шесть	[shest]
7	семь	[syem]
8	восемь	[vo-syem]
9	девять	[dye-vyat]
10	десять	[dye-syat]
11	одиннадцать	[adeen-nadsat]
12	двенадцать	[dvyi-nahdsat]
13	тринадцать	[tree-nahdsat]
14	четырнадцать	[chiteer-nadsat]
15	пятнадцать	[pyat-nahdsat]
16	шестнадцать	[shest-nahdsat]
17	семнадцать	[syem-nahdsat]
18	восемнадцать	[va-syem-nahdsat]
19	девятнадцать	[dyi-vyat-nahdsat]
20	двадцать	[dvahd-sat]
21	двадцать один	[dvahd-sat adeen]
22	двадцать два	[dvahd-sat dva]
23	двадцать три	[dvahd-sat tree]
24	двадцать четыре	[dvahd-sat chiteer-ye]
25	двадцать пять	[dvahd-sat pyat]
30	тридцать	[treed-sat]
31	тридцать один	[treed-sat adeen]
40	сорок	[soruk]
50	пятьдесят	[pyat-dyi-syat]
60	шестьдесят	[shest-dyi-syat]
70	семьдесят	[syem-dyi-syat]
80	восемьдесят	[vo-syem-dyi-syat]
90	девяносто	[dyi-vyanost-uh]
100	сто	[sto]
101	сто один	[sto adeen]
200	двести	[dvye-stee]
300	триста	[tree-sta]
400	четыреста	[chiteer-ye-sta]
500	пятьсот	[pyat-sot]
600	шестьсот	[shest-sot]
700	семьсот	[syem-sot]
800	восемьсот	[va-syem-sot]
900	девятьсот	[dyi-vyat-sot]
1000	тысяча	[tee-syacha]
2000	две тысячи	[dvye tee-syachee]
3000	три тысячи	[tree tee-syachee]
5000	пять тысяч	[pyat tee-syach]

ORDINAL NUMBERS

1st	первый	[pyervee]
2nd	второй	[ftaroy]
3rd	третий	[tryetee]
4th	четвёртый	[chit-vyortee]
5th	пятый	[pyatee]
6th	шестой	[shestoy]
7th	седьмой	[syidmoy]
8th	восьмой	[vassmoy]
9th	девятый	[dyi-vyahtee]
10th	десятый	[dyi-syahtee]